American Material Culture

American Material Culture
The Shape of Things Around Us

Edith Mayo

Bowling Green State University Popular Press
Bowling Green, Ohio 43403

Copyright © 1984 by Bowling Green State University Popular Press

Library of Congress Catalogue Card No.: 84-71338

ISBN: 0-87972-303-3 Clothbound
      0-87972-304-1 Paperback

Cover photo: Harrison campaign handkerchief, Courtesy
of the State Historical Society of Wisconsin.

Contents

Introduction

Focus on Material Culture

Edith Mayo

Archival and written sources have been the traditional research tools of the history discipline. With the rise of the New History came an intense historical interest in the study of demography, the family, the lives of women, blacks, laboring classes and other common folk. The study of social and political movements brought new techniques of inquiry and, thus, new tools of the trade were needed to obtain information about those whose lives were less likely to have been preserved in traditional, written records. The use of oral history techniques and photographic sources is now coming into its own as legitimate tools for reconstruction of the past. Parish records, censuses, inventories, marriage, birth, divorce records, land transactions and other such storehouses of information are now being eagerly combed for clues to life cycles, the family and work. But the mining of rich deposits in material culture is still too often neglected. Most historians are aware of the museum's existence as a material repository, but all too few are cognizant of it as a research resource.

It is precisely the historical questions asked by the New History, and the new methodologies required by it, to which Cary Carson addressed himself in a recent paper: "Recognition for history's neglected majority follows inevitably from the new emphasis historians are giving to society as a working organism, a community of individuals and groups who are mutually dependent on one another. This integrated, all-aboard view of society is fundamental to the New History perspective." Carson sees the utility of object study created by these new historical questions. "By investigating the smallest, most intimate groups in society, historians are making a place in their ideas for the serious study of material culture.[1]

In the rediscovery of our past, we cannot afford to let any resource go untapped—especially when this source can further illuminate, enhance, modify or even contradict the traditional written sources.

John A. Kouwenhoven in his article "American Studies: Words or Things," explains how we mistake words for reality. Words are generalizations, of necessity, and only partially describe an historical fact. Most people, because of cultural education, assume that reality corresponds to words. Kouwenhoven says, "We consequently have a weakness for mistaking words for things. Verbal evidence is plainly not enough."[2] He explains that by examining actual objects one can gain a more complete understanding of history.

Objects, therefore, can be used not simply as "footnotes" to existing historical theses but are themselves a primary source material for

1

extracting historical information.

The importance of material culture as an historical medium was discussed by a group of noted curators, historians and historic preservationists at the 1975 Winterthur Conference. Dr. Brooke Hindle, former Director of the National Museum of History and Technology, defined history as "the collective memory" and stated that "society recalls from history whatever it needs to function in a given direction at a given moment. What is needed constantly changes.... History as the collective memory calls up interpretations of past events when they are needed to understand current problems.... This is the reason that each generation has to re-write history." Hindle also spoke of history as a written abstraction, removed by the use of language several steps from the "reality of people and events,"[3] and stressed the importance of going back to an original source, the object. Hindle continued, "As a source material, the objects of material culture as well as all available information about them must be preserved. They have to be regarded in the same light as archives or manuscript sources...."[4]

Marshall Fishwick in his introduction to *Icons of America*, reminds us that "Professor James Harvey Robinson whose 'New History' (now over fifty years old) insisted that we study 'not only the written records, but the remains of buildings, pictures, clothing, tools, and ornaments'." Fishwick continues, "A promising start was made in the mid-twenties in the twelve-volume *History of American Life* series edited by Arthur M. Schlesinger and Dixon Ryan Fox in which attention was paid to 'non-literary remains and physical survivals.' T.J. Wertenbaker's volumes on *The Middle Colonies and The Puritan Oligarchy* made use of material culture." But, Fishwick notes sadly, an absence of material culture approaches in historiography after that and concludes, "*Word*-people simply don't know how to handle *images* and *icons*. Historians, for better or worse, have decided to put all their bluechips on words."[5]

Examination of material culture as a scholarly source material, however, has been a recognized and accepted methodology in other academic disciplines. The best known scholarly field which makes use of objects is archaeology. In this field, artifacts are central to the interpretation of a past culture. Both Cary Carson and Ivor Noel Hume addressed this subject in their presentations at the Winterthur Conference.[6]

The material remains of American architecture were well catalogued during the period 1920-1950, but only more recently has it been used to extract cultural information.[7] An outstanding example of this type of work is Alan Gowan's book *Images of American Living,* in which the author uses architectural features to assess patterns and values of American culture. An archaeology-architectural project, which has become a treasure of cultural information as well, is Colonial Williamsburg. An outstanding example of the recovered artifact as cultural document from that project is Ivor Noel Hume's work *Here Lies Virginia.*

In technological history, American manufactured artifacts were the subjects of surveys and monographs on the development of technology beginning in the mid-19th century.[8] This particular academic discipline has been given legitimate scholarly recognition with the founding in 1958 of the

Society for the History of Technology (SHOT), with object studies playing a central role in their scholarly studies.

In the museum field, objects were first collected as curios in the Renaissance, later as collections of antiquarian interest. Around the turn of the 20th century, museums began to see themselves as important tools for public education about the past. The concept of the "period room" was developed at that time to recapture the "feeling" or milieu of the past for the American public.

Since that time, the general thrusts in material culture approaches have been: (1) a descriptive phrase, from the 1920s to the 1950s, where emphasis was placed on describing the objects in a collection; (2) the use of objects as supplementary to documentary evidence, that is, objects appearing as "footnotes" or corroborative evidence to an already-existing historical thesis derived from written sources (in the 1950s); (3) the use of objects as important documents in conveying historical information about the past (in the 1960s); (4) the perception of cultural values reflected in the objects (the 1970s).

McClung Fleming of Winterthur Museum has written of the role of the decorative arts in illuminating seven areas pertinent to understanding a culture: (1) craftmanship as seen by tools, skills and techniques; (2) trade patterns as seen through origins of raw materials and distribution of finished product; (3) technology of the period; (4) wealth of the users; (5) customs, social patterns and social usage; (6) images reflecting the popularity of a subject; (7) the feeling for form and mood.[9]

According to Richard Latham in his article "The Artifact as Cultural Cipher," "Artifacts are symbols and can explain much about society: religious beliefs, forms of government, manual dexterity, level of intelligence, artistic comprehension, available natural materials, structure of commerce, and scientific and emotional sophistication of the producing society."[10]

The use of objects as source materials for scholarship has been increasingly legitimatized by the growth of American Studies programs which are now in the forefront in their work with objects. The use of the museum as a primary resource is currently being given a position of increasing importance in American Studies scholarship.

The National American Studies Faculty, under a program funded by the National Endowment for the Humanities, has set up a Community Museum Program to encourage the use of museums as an educational community resource and to encourage the study of objects.[11] Material culture has provided a rich opportunity for multi-disciplinary methods which are basic to the American Studies approach, and could serve as an example for other history disciplines as well. The use of material culture, then, should become an important resource and tool, either as an adjunct to, or on a par with, more traditional history methodologies. The past, as seen through the written record, can be confirmed and enriched by artifactual evidence.

Among "object" historians, there has been a good deal of discussion concerning the methodologies and approaches to the study of material culture. This volume seeks to *DO* it—in a variety of approaches. These essays serve to illustrate the exciting historical insights which can result when the methodologies of written history and material culture merge to produce a historic synthesis between the object and the written word. These essays feature the actual examination of objects in conjunction with their use in photographs, advertising, prints, magazines, trade catalogs and hospital and organizational records. The study of the objects is always placed within the social and cultural context.

Objects can stimulate new modes of perceiving the past and understanding the present. We must strive to understand, "...not only surface data (identification, description, authentication) but interior qualities (evaluation, interpretation, significance) ... [involving] an intense reappraisal of the thingness of things ... [and perceive] that objects ... are the building blocks of reality."[12]

This volume begins with an essay by Ron Marchese detailing the importance of the classification methods to the study and interpretation of American culture. The scholarly approach of the thesis and its exposition stand in stark contrast to the mundane nature of his selected examples. The shock value, however, will be valuable in emphasizing the point of the importance of "things" to history. Marchese's section on the Barbie doll contains the correct (I believe) inference that the doll's explicitly sexual overtones denote not "liberation" or maturity for women but an even more constricted, narrowly-defined role as sex object.

The theme of "woman's proper sphere" in the nineteenth century, and objects and social methodologies to reinforce it, are explored by Kenneth Ames in his study of the parlor organ and its significance to nineteenth century home life. Martha Pike, in her study of Victorian mourning objects, raises a number of important questions relating to the role of women and change in society. The rigid codification of mourning rituals, which apply particularly to women, suggests an equally rigid means of social control for women. We might also note that among women's roles in the nineteenth century was the performance of what might loosely be called "clerical duties" within the home. While the subject matter is different, note the similarity in the role enforcement apparent in both Ames' and Pike's essays.

Virginia Drachman's study of obstetrical and gynecological instruments in the nineteenth century shows not simply the technological development of a class of objects, but the actuality of their use within the context of case histories and actual availability to the medical community. Drachman makes excellent use of the New History techniques by utilizing hospital records, case histories and inventories integrated with material culture. The juxtaposition of both the written and artifactual records reveals a more accurate picture than would be the case of either alone.

Darlene Roth examines the architectural evidence of women's "city-building"—a role not often attributed to women—by examining the architectural record of their historic preservation and club-house building activities in Atlanta, Georgia. Viewing the type, structure and location of women's architecture as a cultural statement on the American landscape, Roth sees the building patterns as both following the prescribed roles of women as "culture bearer, preserver, and nurturer," and enlarging women's sphere by taking the feminine nurturing values of the home into the larger world. Her fascinating conclusions concerning women's role in the architectural development of the urban scene have gone previously unnoticed.

The campaign artifact comes under close scrutiny in the essays of Otto Thieme, Roger Fischer and Edith Mayo for its ability to illuminate the political process in this country. These essays integrate existing historical theses and the written record with object study to arrive at a better understanding of each, and suggest that campaign materials offer a fertile, and as yet almost untouched, field of research for political historians.

Bernard Mergen's essay on toys and games places them in the broader context of the changes in the family, the economy and the uses of time and leisure. In the study of these themes, scrutiny of actual objects is usually excluded. Mergen's essay suggests that such inclusion may further contribute to these fields.

Liz Cohen's article on the material culture of working-class homes presents a rebuttal in objects of the conventionally-accepted wisdom concerning reformers' attempts to "Americanize" immigrants. By the 1890s, particularly in urban areas, domestic science classes in the public schools promoted ideal domestic environments. Similarly, settlement houses in workers' neighborhoods fostered middle-class home standards through "Housekeeping Centers." Examination of the furniture actually selected by working class people shows an emphatic rejection of the reformers' "suggested" furniture styles in an attempt to maintain traditional cultural values and yet satisfy their new expectations with products available on the mass market. Ms. Cohen's findings also suggest implications concerning the social and physical isolation of the American housewife in the patterns inculcated in new immigrants which stressed "privatization" and isolation of the nuclear family from the community.

Michael Shute's essay on American furniture, and particularly the Chippendale chair, describes how our furniture, especially in the early days of the nation, manifested colonial ideals; Shute describes how these ideals have faired since the early times.

Stephen Smith's amusing essay on Southern foodways outlines how they developed, what they signify to the Southerner and to citizens of the rest of the nation, especially in mythology and ritual.

And Mary Johnson gives an indispensble discussion of the role of women and their artifacts in American culture. Her essay is an eye-opener and a mind-stimulator, enriching everyone who reads it.

It has been the premise of these historians that each object is infused with, and expresses, the cultural assumptions, modes, beliefs and technologies of its creators and cannot be isolated from that context. It is for the historian of material culture to read the meanings of the objects and, by placing them in context, to decipher their message. The intelligent assembly of artifacts can make a vital contribution to the ordering of reality. We hope these essays are a beginning toward that contribution and a stimulus and invitation to further inquiry.

Notes

I would like to express my gratitude to Bob Schurk for his support and for sharing with me his paper on "Material Culture Approaches," and Ken Ames and Roger Fischer for their assistance and encouragement during the compilation of this volume of essays.

[1]Cary Carson, "Doing History with Material Culture," in Ian M. Quimby, ed., *Material Culture and the Study of American Life* (New York: Norton & Co., 1978), 48, 51.

[2]John A. Kouwenhoven, "American Studies: Words or Things," in Marshall Fishwick, ed., *American Studies in Transition* (Philadelphia: Univ. of Pennsylvania Press, 1964).

[3]Brooke Hindle, "How Much is a Piece of the True Cross Worth?" in Ian M. Quimby, ed., *Material Culture and the Study of American Life* (New York: Norton, 1978), 8-9.

[4]Hindle, in *Material Culture*, 17.

[5]Marshall Fishwick, "Introduction," in Ray B. Browne and Marshall Fishwick, eds., *Icons of America* (Bowling Green, Ohio: Popular Press, 1978), 9.

[6]See Carson in *Material Culture*; Ivor Noel Hume, "Material Culture with Dirt on It," in Ian M. Quimby, ed., *Material Culture and the Study of American Life* (New York: Norton, 1978), 21-40.

[7]Kenneth Hudson, "Current Trends in Industrial Archaeology," *Victorian Studies* (Sept. 1972).

[8]Brooke Hindle, *Technology in Early America: Needs and Opportunities* (Chapel Hill: Univ. of North Carolina Press, 1966), 6.

[9]E. McClung Fleming, "Early American Decorative Arts as Social Documents," *The Mississippi Valley Historical Review* (Sept. 1958), 276-284.

[10]Richard Latham, "The Artifact as Cultural Cipher," in Lawrence B. Holland, ed., *Who Designs America?* (New York: Doubleday, 1966), 257-280.

[11]Place, Zangrando, Lea and Lovell, "The Object as Subject: The Role of Museums and Material Culture Collections in American Studies," *American Quarterly* XXVI (August 1974), 282.

[12]Fishwick, "Introduction," *Icons of America*, 8. This article contains a brief sketch of the neglect by academic historians of the use of objects as important research tools.

Suggested Periodicals in Material Culture and Museum Studies

American Anthropologist
American Architect
American Heritage
American Historical Review
American Quarterly
Antiques
Architectural Forum
Architectural Record
Architecture and Building
Art in America
Connoisseur
Curator
Engineering Magazine
Engineering News
Engineering Record
Folklore Forum
Historic Preservation
History News

ISIS (Journal for History of Science Society)
Journal of American Culture
Journal of American Folklore
Journal of American History
Journal of American Institute of Architects
Journal of Cultural Geography
Journal of Popular Culture
Museum News
New York Folklore Quarterly
Prospects
Smithsonian Studies in History and Technology
Society of Industrial Archaeology (Journal & Newsletter)
Technology and Culture
The Museologist
Winterthur Portfolio: A Journal of American Material Culture

General Sources of Information on Material Culture and Museum Studies

For listing of Museums, Historical Agencies, Museum Practices, and Excellent Museum/Material Culture Bibliography:
Merrilyn Rogers O'Connell and Frederick L. Rath, Jr., eds. *Guides to Historic Preservation, Historical Agencies, and Museum Practices: A Selective Bibliography.* (Cooperstown, N.Y.: New York State Historical Association, 1970). Contains an excellent bibliography on a wide variety of museum and material culture-related topics, plus advice for historical societies, small museums, etc. This work is periodically updated.

For Listings of University and Other Museum Training Programs:
Write to:
        Office of Museum Programs
        Smithsonian Institution
        Washington, D.C. 20560
        Directory of Museum Training Programs in the
        United States and Abroad

Museum Reference Center:
The Museum Reference Center, in the Office of Museum Programs at the Smithsonian Institution, houses the largest known collection of bibliographic and documentary materials on all aspects of museum operations: resources for local museums, funding, museum philosophy and operation, conservation aids and audio-visual presentations, grant project reports, and other museum-related information.

See: Paula Degen, "Light Under a Bushel: The Smithsonian's Museum Reference Center Offers Aid to Local Museums," *History News* 35 (Feb. 1980), 5-8.
Write:

Museum Reference Center
Office of Museum Programs
Arts & Industries Building, Rm. 2235
Smithsonian Institution
Washington, D.C. 20560

The Museum Workshop Series:
  A series of workshops/seminars to introduce and improve professional skills for individuals employed in museums. The series deals with such topics as soliciting and administering grants, design and production of exhibits, horticulture in museums and historic houses and sites, conservation and preventive care, museum insurance and loan agreements, computerization for museum collections, archives, museum lighting, energy conservation, evaluation of museum programs, museum management, label writing, museum registration methods, museum budgeting and accounting, museum protection, museum shops, volunteer programs, developing and maintaining collections, programs for the disabled and museum outreach programs:
Write:

Workshop Series
Office of Museum Programs
Arts and Industries Building, R. 2235
Smithsonian Institution
Washington, D.C. 20540

Museum/Material Culture Books and Technical Leaflets:
  Both the American Association of Museums and the American Association for State and Local History publish and distribute books and technical leaflets relating to all aspects of museum work and historic preservation. For a listing of available works
Write: AAM Books and Reprints
American Association of Museums
1055 Thomas Jefferson Street, N.W.
Washington, D.C. 20007

AASLH Books and Technical Leaflets
American Association for State and Local History
1400 Eighth Avenue, South
Nashville, TN 37203

Museum Grants:
  The National Endowment for the Humanities publishes *Guidelines for Museums and Historical Organizations Program* containing information on grant eligibility and application processes. These grants cover exhibition, program development, personnel development, and research and interpretation.
Write:

Museums and Historical Organizations Program
Division of Public Programs
National Endowment for the Humanities
806 15th St. N.W.
Washington, D.C. 20506

The Institute of Museum Services (IMS), an independent agency within the Department of Health, Education and Welfare, serves as the Federal agency whose basic mission is to assist museums of all types with general operating support. IMS assistance is designed to encourage museums to maintain or improve their public services; meet increasing financial needs; support their endeavors as educators, conservators, and exhibitors of the nation's cultural heritage. For information concerning grants and programs
Write:

Institute of Museum Services
Hubert Humphrey Bldg. Rm. 325H
Department of Health, Education and Welfare
200 Independence Ave. S.W.
Washington, D.C. 20202

Guide to Museum-Related Organizations:
This informative brochure appeared as a special supplement in: *Museum News* 57 (Nov./Dec. 1978), S1-S20.
Write:

The American Association of Museums
1055 Thomas Jefferson Street, N.W.
Washington, D.C. 20007

The Official Museum Directory of the United States and Canada published by the American Association of Museums, may be obtained from:

The National Register Publishing Company
5201 Old Orchard Road
Skokie, Il 60605

$30. for AAM Members: $40. for non-members

Comprehensive Museum Information:

See: National Endowment for the Arts, *Museums USA* (Washington, D.C.: U.S. Government Printing Office, 1974)

Contains detailed information on purposes and functions of museums, programs, attendance, accessibility, admissions, collections, exhibitions, trustees, personnel, facilities and finances.

For Museum Procedure and Method:

Ralph H. Lewis, *Manual for Museums* (Washington, D.C.: National Park Service, 1976). $4.50 Stock No. 024-005-00543-5
Write:
> Superintendent of Documents
> U.S. Government Printing Office
> Washington, D.C. 20402

Major Museum Studies/Material Culture Training Programs:

Winterthur Program (Winterthur Museum and Univ. of Delaware)
> Programs in Museum Studies, Early American Culture and conservation, Newark, Delaware.

Eleutherian Mills-Hagley Foundation Program (with the Univ. of Delaware).
> Program oriented toward technology and economics. Wilmington, Delaware.

The George Washington University, Washington, D.C.
> American Studies/Material Culture orientation. Other programs for art museums, museology and museum education are given in conjunction with D.C. area museums.

Cooperstown Program, Cooperstown, N.Y. (with the New York State Historical Association and the State Univ. of New York).
> Program includes folk art, material culture, conservation training.

Boston University, Boston, Mass.
> American Studies Program with museum courses.

University of Michigan, Ann Arbor.
> Program in museum studies, administration and education

Texas Tech University, Lubbock.
> Program in museum studies, administration, education and curatorial expertise.

New York University, New York (with the Institute of Fine Arts and the Metropolitan Museum of Art).
> Program in museum studies, art orientation.

Case-Western Reserve University, Cleveland, Ohio.
> Programs in history and museum studies and in art history and art museum studies.

See also: *Museum News* 57 (Nov./Dec. 1978) for an in-depth report by the American Association of Museums on musuem studies and training for a museum career.

Material Culture and Artifact Classification[1]

Ronald T. Marchese

Mark Twain once said that "we should not be too particular. It is better to have old, second-hand diamonds, than none at all."[2] *Things* are our gemstones, the discarded diamonds of society. As products of contemporary life, they provide an accurate barometer for the social, political, economic and cultural conditions which motivate man. Material remains do not lie.[3] They reinforce or refute the exaggerations of written testimonia and lore.[4] Things, or more accurately artifacts, are the concrete physical expressions of any social system. Social factors such as economy, organization and ideology appear in objects and these objects exhibit change before the wholesale transformation of any society occurs. Thus, the study of things, as part of material culture, becomes a worthwhile pursuit.

Two fundamental assertions about things can be made. The first is that material culture reflects human behavior which can be interpreted through scientific classification schemes, methods and techniques. The second tenet is that the variation in the pattern of material remains must be described and explained. Both assertions are valid in light of the significant number of us who are no longer concerned with describing specific events or persons, but rather the broader trends and movements in society. This shift in goals, I believe, is due in part to the adaptation of new research models and, more importantly, a broader definition of relevant data. This is especially seen in the systematic analysis of material culture in an historical framework and the utilization of methods employed by the prehistorian. Unfortunately, most traditionalists have ignored artifactual data and have stood fast in their use of written testimonia and/or personal observations as the sole barometers of any society. A whole body of data has been ignored and, more importantly, those who have made the transition to the study of material remains as a worthwhile occupation have been condemned as *pop* culturists or dilettantes but not historians, anthropologists, sociologists or social scientists concerned with the behavioral patterns of present or past society.[5] It is the purpose of this paper to examine the interrelationship between archaeological classification and behavioral history as seen through the material record.

Archaeology and History

History, as only one element within the social sciences, is defined as the study of individuals, groups and movements reacting to events as they struggle for power. It is the interplay of human intellect recorded in documents, contracts and constitutions which detail political, social, cultural and, finally, economic events. In this view history had come to mean four interacting denotations which are grouped into two categories: *Actuality* and *Abstraction*.[6] Each has two distinct meanings as seen in the following:

Actuality

1. means the totality of *past actuality* without chronological implications;

and

2. considers the chronological sequence of the past from the oldest to the most recent;

while

Abstraction

3. centers around the explanation of what *actually happened, more precisely, contemporary thought* about the past expressed in writing or oral commentary; and finally
4. defines the discipline as the formal study of events and methods of historical interpretation.

Thus history is a record—oral and written—of human actions expressed in a series of events which are defined in sequential time. Meanings 1 and 2 are the *events themselves,* from which inferences, abstractions, and contemporary interpretations defined in meanings 3 and 4 are made. Technically, history is a descriptive discipline and past actuality. Sub-consciously *all* historians are behaviorists who explore the actual chain of events in order to understand and interpret human attitudes, values and views which define the abstract aspect of past societies.

With this in mind, a new historiography centered around the social and cultural phenomena of common people, everyday life, and the normal happenings of life, has arisen. The mundane is the cornerstone of cultural history. It is in the realm of cultural history that the history of things, as elements of material culture, belongs. I perceive material culture as a discipline which characterizes society through the written word and, more important, through things. The latter provides a wealth of information unrecorded in formal testimonia. An example will best illustrate this point. Man inscribes his mundane life in a spatial context. Given a room, each inhabitant will organize space around his/her mental pattern. Decorations will indicate taste, things pushed into corners or placed in the center of the room, and things placed along the wall will provide a concrete image of personal and group behavior.[7] Yet the image, type, quality and expense of things which indicate economic, social, cultural, political and sexual ideologies will be unrecorded by society.

Since things mirror society, archaeology, with its well-developed methods of artifact classification, is a valid and necessary discipline. In a social-cultural context, archaeology investigates human behavior as seen in the relationship between mental processes and artifacts. Thus, archaeology and material culture can compare at three separate levels: 1) both deal with past and present actuality; 2) both are interested in man and his things; and 3) both proceed from problems to data, chronology, inference, generalizations, integration and finally the synthesis of knowledge in a cultural context.

Culture

History and archaeology deal with culture, be it things in the strictest sense, or ideas. In this respect, they are sister disciplines with similar objectives. Such objectives are easily seen in a definition of culture. Basically, culture is a combination of historically created designs for living, explicit, implicit, rational, irrational and non-rational which exist at any given time. It is a unique, expressive and sophisticated communication system which conveys mental processes and issues in concrete items. Culture is also an expression of man's reaction to situations.[8] For the purpose of this paper, culture

...refers to the total way of life of any society, not simply to those parts of this way which the society regards as higher or more desirable. Culture, when applied to our own way of life has nothing to do with playing the piano or reading Browning. For the social scientist such activities are simply elements within the totality of our culture. This totality also includes such mundane activities as washing dishes or driving an automobile, and for the purposes of cultural studies these stand quite on a par with 'the finer things of life.' It follows that for the social scientist there are no uncultured societies or even individuals. Every society has a culture, no matter how simple this culture may be, and every human being is cultured, in the sense of participating in some culture or other.[9]

Culture incorporates all aspects of life; it encompasses behavior, beliefs, attitudes, values as well as the physical product of human activity. Thus, each human culture is distinctive and possesses specific features of behavior and therefore different artifacts of behavior. All cultures are made up of a myriad of tangible and intangible traits, some inherited from earlier generations, others unique to contemporary society. Artifacts, as the physical remains of culture, symbolize human behavior and the mental processes which motivate society. Therefore the material remains of any cultural system can be classified in order to determine change, the image of society, its issues, its definitions of beauty, honesty and finally equalilty. The latter can be seen in the material remains of nineteenth century America with its wooden Indians, little black-boy hitching posts, and political and ethnic cartoons directed against Irish and Italian immigrants. The ideologies of past society appear as attributes and the clustering of attributes create artifact categories which mirror contemporary society and its issues (Fig. 1).

Material culture can be defined as any monument, non-perishable physical object, or bio-degradable garbage man produces.[10] They are all artifacts. As objects, they are capable of yielding a considerable amount of information about present and past society. It is from these very limited kinds of evidence that history can be inferred. Perhaps two examples will suffice; the first a hypothetical question with regard to the total absence of historical documents, the second, only a marginal record of an historical event. In the absence of all written records, Napoleon's invasion of Russia could be inferred from the distribution of burnt villages recovered by excavations and dated to the same time. Weapons of western European

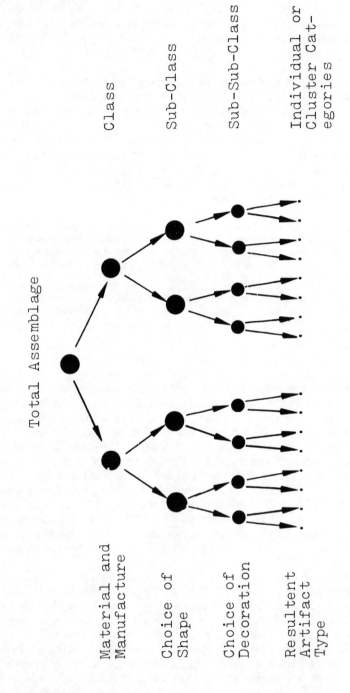

Total Assemblage

Class

Sub-Class

Sub-Sub-Class

Individual or
Cluster Cat-
egories

Material and
Manufacture

Choice of
Shape

Choice of
Decoration

Resultent
Artifact
Type

Fig. 1 Simplified Artifact Classification

manufacture would indicate that destruction came from the West. Also, it would be obvious from the artifacts that the native population soon regained control. The second example is based on the partial record of an historical event. We all know from written testimonia that Plymouth Colony was established in 1620 and that the ship bringing the colonists was the *Mayflower*, and that separate land grants were given the colonists in 1627.

This is the basic framework of the history of Plymouth Colony. Yet, no documents indicate what animals were used for food, when the first bricks were produced locally, or what type of nails were used in the construction of Plymouth houses. Only the archaeological record and the recovery of artifacts flesh out the bones of the historical events.[11]

Artifact Classification

Artifacts are identified as elements of human behavior and their identification serves to isolate phenomena amenable to the behavioral sciences, especially history and anthropology. Therefore, the role of classification is obvious. Classification is the means by which artifactual material is categorized and subject to manipulation.[12] It allows us to construct categories which can be explicitly defined and the means to identify *real* phenomena in the material world. Classification also produces definable units which are capable of evaluation. Once the field of classification is established, an analytic step is taken to determine the features to be used in the construction of units. In turn, each individual unit is evaluated according to the defining criteria which produces the classification scheme. Thus, classification is a self-contained technique for determining artifact categories and cultural processes.

Classifications must be valid and therefore consistent. If a classification is found to be inconsistent, it cannot serve as a classification because it does not provide any means of setting relationships between the classes. Four basic assumptions for the evaluation of classifications can now be stated. It must be remembered that the actual evaluation is one of choices made in (1) selecting a field; (2) selecting a particular scale from which classes are formed; (3) defining features for the creation of classes; and (4) selecting from the discriminating features those which are to be considered as definitive. To make such assumptions it is necessary that the classification have a specific, explicitly stated purpose.[13]

In turn each individual unit is evaluated according to the defining criteria. Thus classification is a self-contained technique for determiningg cultural processes in the material record. To construct a cultural process from the physical remains a society has left us, classification schemes are necessary. Since we infer knowledge from things, classification and therefore typology is important. All classifications are reflections of artifact categories which in turn reflect social organization. Artifact categories can also be labelled through typological considerations. We should draw an important distinction between classification and typology. Classification is any act of designating, and typology is a more ordered system of actions which obey certain laws and principles. Any group which is labelled a type must embrace material which can be shown to consist of individual variations in the execution of a definite idea. A typology establishes categories that conform to concrete human behavior and is the basic conceptual tool for cultural interpretation far beyond the level of mere classification. Thus, classification is defined as a broad term referring to the general process of ordering materials by placing them in similar groups while typology provides a more specific process whereby units and clusters are determined from larger groups.[14] Perhaps an example will suffice to clarify the difference between the two. Political events, as seen through material remains, provide a detailed understanding of election processes, visualized issues, beliefs, attitudes and remarks. In the broadest sense classification denotes categories and typology the sub-categories of attribute associations. Within the confines of one button, numerous attributes articulate information: date, issue at hand, logo, color, size, manufacture, embellishment, expense, personification of ethics and morality, regional affiliation, and ethnic appeal. All appear in one simple object or class of objects. At this level of explanation type categories appear (Fig. 1).

Much has been said about material culture. Everything man produces is part of his material culture, his artifact. Artifacts are defined as those objects that have been made, used or modified by human activity. We are surrounded by artifacts. Because so many different things are called artifacts, there are some commonly employed ways of categorizing them for the purpose of analysis, collection and publication. Any society can be treated as an artifact with specific modes of expression. To describe an artifact-laden society, we assemble into categories inventories of traits which embrace any artifact man employs at any given time (Fig. 2).

These in turn can be analyzed separately according to the criteria established in Table I.[15] Artifacts are social products and can be arranged according to type. The purpose of a type is to provide an organizational tool in order to group specimens into bodies which have shared cultural traits and thus historical meaning. In this respect, two broader typological categories exist: functional types and analytical types. Functional categories distinguish a variety of types current over a restricted area at a given time and are defined according to (inferred and real) function; while analytical categories indicate divergent social traditions which prescribe artifact ideology, preparation and use. Thus, artifact categories are constructed through attribute designations. It must be remembered that artifacts are concrete, types are conceptual designations defined by the classifier to represent abstract ideas in artifact classes.[16] Therefore, artifact types are created according to physical attributes which in turn are grouped into classes presumed to be of cultural and historical significance (Fig. 3).

Functional and analytical categories also can be defined according to objectivity and relativity. In our daily activities we build typologically-defined hierarchies in which we constantly place everything around us. These hierarchies are highly formalized in specific type designations. All are based on attribute definitions. Those classified as *objective types* consist of the actual variations in the observed material assemblage and appear in a single category according to cross-cultural and cross-social patterns. Those that form *relative* types include only those variations

Economic	Sociological	Ideological
1. Subsistence	Demographic	Scientific
2. Industry	Family	Religious
3. Transportation	Town Planning	Artistic
4. Commerce	Social Structure	Interpretation
5. War	Occupation	Political

Fig. 2 Institutional and Ideological Definitions of Society and Artifact Categories

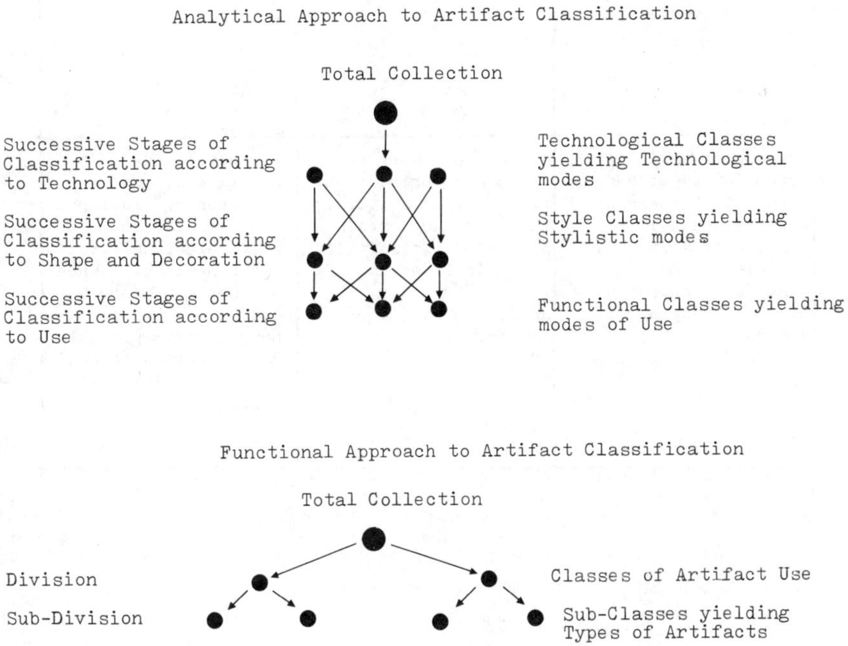

Analytical Approach to Artifact Classification

Total Collection

Successive Stages of
Classification according
to Technology

Technological Classes
yielding Technological
modes

Successive Stages of
Classification according
to Shape and Decoration

Style Classes yielding
Stylistic modes

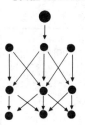

Successive Stages of
Classification according
to Use

Functional Classes yielding
modes of Use

Functional Approach to Artifact Classification

Total Collection

Division

Classes of Artifact Use

Sub-Division

Sub-Classes yielding
Types of Artifacts

Fig. 3 Classification Systems

	EMPIRICAL CATEGORIES (Observational)	CULTURAL CATEGORIES (Inferential)	CULTURE CATEGORIES (Inferential)
FORM	Individual manifestations, their empirical affinities and their constituent parts, "elements," "attributes," "designs," "specifications," "units," "items," etc.	The "use" and "function" and/or the technique of manufacture of an individual manifestation (or part thereof) as inferred from the empirical data.	The culture-idea, the culture-trait, objectified in the individual manifestations; also the "meaning" manifest in it. A "mode."
TYPE	A group of manifestations which possess certain specified similarities in their affinities and/or constituent parts, or an ideal abstracted therefrom, either mean, modal, or median.	A group of manifestations that possess certain specified similarities in their inferred "use," "function," and/or technique of manufacture.	The culture-idea objectified, and/or the "meaning" manifest, in a single type, either empirical or cultural. An "archetype."
CLASS	A group of empirical types (or types and forms) that possess certain specified similarities in their affinities and/or diagnostic criteria, i.e., a grouping of groups.	A group of types (or types and forms) either empirical or cultural, that possess certain specified similarities in their inferred "use," "function," and/or technique of manufacture.	The culture-idea objectified, and/or the "meaning" manifest in a class, either empirical or cultural. An "archeclass." When the classes under this heading are broad enough, it is probably best to designate the structuring idea as a "configuration."

Table I

which cluster around a common standard of *behavior*. Objective and relative types are formulated in material culture for different reasons: (1) *objective types* are useful in establishing the initial categories out of which relative types are to be isolated by a process of elimination; (2) for purely physical reasons; (3) for cross-cultural comparisons in areas where cultural considerations offer very little insight; while *relative types* (1) analyze and assemble structural models of social and cultural behavior within individual communities; and (2) provide a basis for intercommunity comparisons directed toward the determination of historical relationships. Typologies are thus formed and directed toward the production of units of meaning from the material record. Types are matters of qualification with numerous axioms: (1) an assumptive foundation; (2) a focus on units and not counts; and (3) a distinction between the real and the ideal.

Quantification follows qualification and plays a role in employing the classes and groups constructed from a given situation. Classifications are only preliminary steps to seriation.[18] Seriation attempts, through quantitative analysis, to determine the popularity of objects and their distribution. Thus, statistical clustering, which provides a clear record of the frequency with which attributes appear in the artifact record, is the final step in artifact classification from which inferential knowledge is gained (Fig. 4).

In the material record, artifacts are *real* data and classification our basic tool. Classification summarizes data and makes them manageable. It delineates unobserved facts and locates the physical and abstract boundaries of attributes in order to obtain categories that are comparable across cultural systems. Changes in social, political and economic organization are often reflected in the way people make things. By establishing attribute lists and type categories, it is possible to establish a relationship between the changes in manufacture and the changes in society. It is artifact types which indicate culture change.

A logical outcome of artifact types is artifact arrangement (Fig. 5).[19] All classes, groups and clusters are based on a constant definition of traits and features. This ordered set of contrasts amounts to a division in the field of classification into classes, sub-classes, and so on. Classification in this manner appears in four axioms: (1) classes are intentionally defined on the basis of features; (2) classes are units which exist independent of time and space and whose attributes can occur simultaneously at more than one location; (3) as a corollary, classes have distribution, groups location; and finally (4) classes are infinite in terms of their application.

The complexity of artifact classification can be simplified in two separate examples.[20] From each we can infer a change in human attitudes and, more importantly, general values in society.

The first example is toys. As a separate class of objects, toys incorporate an idea of human entertainment. Separate categories appear as sub-classes to the general collection: wheeled objects, battery powered, spring loaded, games with moveable parts, educational toys, and finally role-model toys. The latter can be sub-divided into further categories: for example, the category called dolls. These are types and are defined along sex lines; that is, male and female dolls form separate type categories based on observed

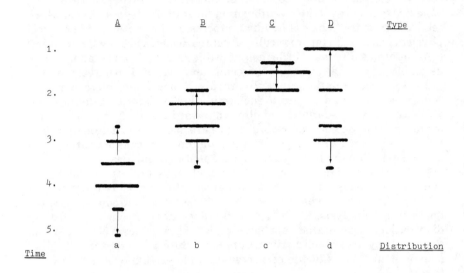

Fig. 4 Seriation Distribution of Artifact Frequencies

attributes. The female category is, perhaps, more interesting because the number of objects in the category can illuminate the separate roles women play or have played in society. For example, in the 1940s and 1950s the majority of dolls produced in the United States were babies, babies that closed their eyes when rocked, or wet their diapers. Such dolls reinforced the idea that women's roles were closely associated with the production and care of offspring and the maintenance of the family. The most popular "professional" doll was the nurse. In the 1960s and 1970s a transformation takes place. This is easily seen in the Mattel Barbie doll and the numerous imitations she fostered. The category of Barbie dolls forms a type which can be refined according to the evolution of the model. This is seen in the separate attributes which make up Barbie. From the combination of attributes we can infer the sexual revolution of the 1960s and 1970s in the following manner. The Barbie doll was initially introduced to provide an image of young maturity. As the 1960s progressed and a major break with the old morality occurred, Barbie's dress and physical attributes changed. In one attribute alone, Barbie's chest measurements show a remarkable change. The 1979 model is now a well-endowed female: blond, blue-eyed and tanned. She has an enviable lifestyle: her own place (actually three), her own sports car (actually four), her own beach accessories. As seen in the

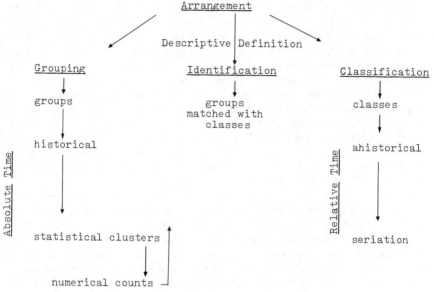

Fig. 5 Artifact Arrangement

evolution of dolls, and the Barbie doll in particular, we can infer the changing emphasis and role of the female in society from the producer of children and guardian of home life to a narrowly defined sex object.[21] The male doll also indicates a rather interesting image in society. Briefly, two types exist: the emasculated, body-beautiful, bronze, unisex Ken doll, and the dominating virile G.I. Joe, S.W.A.T. and Bionic models.

The second illustration, a mundane item, is the beer container. The evolution of the beer container from its class designation to the separate type categories provides an excellent example of things as the barometer of society. The initial class designation is broken down into separate categories: beer bottles, tin and aluminum cans.[22] The category of cans is further refined according to material and manufacturing techniques. As one attribute of the can, a further designation centered on openers and openings is possible; for example, the evolution from church-key openers, to pull tops, and finally push tops. The latter is extremely important since it solves a major environmental problem—what to do with the pull tab? From the logo of each brand we can gain further information. Brewing techniques, the purity of the water, the best hops, and emblazoned family names all form separate attributes of the same type. The creation of attribute categories based on physical qualifications and logo provide a body of knowledge which reflects society's concern for the environment and a natural, non-artificially created beverage.

Behavioral Categories and Material Culture
It is safe to assume that the social and cultural behavior of a community

is composed of a number of structures and sub-structures, and that each sub-structure is composed of a number of sub-sub-structures down to the minimal element of behavior, the individual artifact. From a behavioral point of view, the typing of material culture leads to broader issues of interpretation and generalization. Such generalizations can be stated in four axioms: (1) use material culture to answer specific descriptive and explanatory questions about the behavioral and organizational properties of past cultural systems; (2) pursue general questions in present material culture in order to acquire laws useful for the study of the past; (3) pursue general questions in the study of the past in order to derive behavioral laws of wide applicability for past as well as present human behavior; and (4) study present material objects in ongoing cultural systems in order to describe and explain human behavior in general.

Laws and axioms are necessary for the total use of material remains. We must seek to reconstruct cultural processes and systematically employ artifact analysis in order to determine the precise roles and functions of material items in society.[23] We seek to learn about society from fragmentary remains. Artifacts are such remains, the fossilized ideas of the past. Behavioral definitions in material culture after classification reflect mental processes since such processes are observable in the material remains of any social system (Fig. 6). Attributes are combined by individuals into patterns which permit inferences regarding behavioral patterns of individuals, so artifacts are combined into groups which reflect in their patterning the behavior of the group or individual responsible for their form.[24]

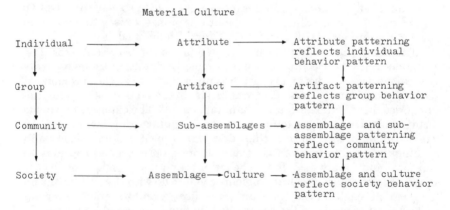

Fig. 6 Behavioral categories in material culture

Conclusion

The study of material culture can be stated through a systemic approach to society.[25] We infer from the material record generalizations, generalizations and interpretations which are valid in understanding past cultural sequences. In this respect, as students of material culture, we must arrange our evidence in all possible ways in order to produce useful information. We must not be satisfied with simple classifications since each artifact provides an infinite series of sense impressions, mental processes and attitudes. The function of artifact classification is to discover these processes.

Notes

[1]This paper was initially given as "Some Thoughts on Artifact Analysis" in *Things and Civilization* at the 9th Annual Joint Meeting of the Popular Culture—American Culture Assocation in Pittsburgh.

[2]Thomas R. Hester, Robert F. Heizer and John A Graham, *Field Methods in Archaeology* (Palo Alto, 1975), 207.

[3]For an example of this see Ivor Hume, "Material Culture with Dirt on It: A Virginia Perspective," in Ian M.G. Quimby, ed., *Material Culture and the Study of American Life* (New York, 1978), 26-31. If our methods of classification are correct, our inference about past society from the material remains will also be correct.

[4]See Cary Carson,"Doing History with Material Culture," in Ian M.G. Quimby, *Material Culture and the Study of American Life*, 42-64; and Roger A. Fischer, "1896 Campaign Artifacts: A Study in Inferential Reconstruction," in this volume.

[5]Glyn Daniel best summarizes this unfortunate attitude: "We are all historians, we are all studying the past of men whether we concentrate on Walpole, Beowulf, Stonehenge, or Lascaux. Manuscripts, microlighs, megaliths—it is all one. The past is the goal of the historian whether he is text aided or not.... There are historians, in the strict sense of the word, who are frightened when they see archaeologists advancing toward them with dirt on their boots and a brief case full of air photographs and Carbon 14 dates. Dugdale, Aubrey, Lhwyd, and Stukeley did not think they were other than historians, and, for that matter, historians who could be members of the Royal Society. We have taken the distinctions between history that is mainly derived from material resources and one that is derived from the aid of texts, too far." (Editorial in *Antiquity* 41: 169-173.).

[6]Walter W. Taylor, *A Study of Archaeology* (London: 1968), 28-30.

[7]An example of such a study appears in Bert Salwen, "Archaeology in Megalopolis," in Charles Redman, ed., *Research and Theory in Current Archaeology* (New York, 1973), 157ff.

[8]This *normative view* of culture treats culture as a body of shared ideas, values and beliefs. These are mental templates which are important in the creation of material culture. Thus, we study material remains in order to discover the ideas which governed the production of artifacts and in this way understand the cultural system in question. See Patty Jo Watson, Steven A LeBlanc and Charles Redman, *Explanation in Archaeology: An Explicitly Scientific Approach* (New York, 197 , 6 ff.

[9]Ralph Lindρn, *The Cultural Background of Personality* (New York, 1945), 30.

[10]Interesι in bio-degradable material has fostered a unique undergraduate course at the University of Arizona entitled Garbology 199. The student spends much of his time at the Tucson dump or searching through randomly sampled home garbage bins in order to understand what modern societies list as garbage. Not only can we learn much about modern families through their garbage; basically, we can reconstruct present society through material refuse. Hopefully, such a study will lead to laws and axioms about past societies.

[11]James Deetz, *Invitation to Archaeology* (New York, 1967), 4.

[12]Irving Rouse, "The Classification of Artifacts in Archaeology," in James Deetz, *Man's Imprint from the Past: Readings in the Methods of Archaeology* (Boston, 1971), 108-125.

[13]Robert C. Dunnell, *Systematics in Prehistory* (New York, 1971), 147ff.

[14]K.C.Chang, *Rethinking Archaeology* (New York, 1964), 9.

[15]Taylor, *A Study in Archaeology*, 114.

[16]Change, *Rethinking Archaeology*, 10; and James A. Ford, *"The Type Concept Revisited,"* in James Deetz, *Man's Imprint from the Past: Readings in the Methods of Archaeology*, 60ff.

[17]Rouse, "The Classification of Artifacts in Archeology," 111-113.

[18]For further information see James Deetz, "Seriation in Archaeology," in Ernestene L. Green, ed., *In Search of Man: Readings in Archaeology* (Boston, 1973), 134-140.

[19]Dunnell, *Systematics in Prehistory*, 44.

[20]Numerous examples appear in print. For further reference see Craig Gilborn, "Looking at the Coke Bottle," in *Museum News*, December 1968, 13-18; and James Deetz, *Invitation to*

Archaeology, 30ff.

[21]The evolution of the Barbie doll provides an excellent view of modern, middle-class America. Barbie has no profession but certainly enjoys all the material splendor of an affluent society. She is sold in a low-cut flaming red dress with high heels and has an assortment of "sexy" costumes. In many respects, the Barbie type epitomizes our conception of beauty: blond, blue-eyed, and tanned—the all-American girl! One final remark about the Barbie type appears in *North Liner,* April, 1979, 3: "And for the kids: 'Press the panel on her back and the new *Kissing Barbie* tilts her head, purses her lips, and plants an affectionate and audible 'smack' on her young owner's cheek, leaving a tiny 'lipstick' print! Dad, Mom, sisters and brothers—and even KEN—will be wearing a tiny lipstick mark whenever the *Kissing Barbie* is around...."

[22]The typical beer can collector merely gathers the different types of cans produced without regard to classification. A wall of cans can be a data bank of useful trivia. Type categories and attribute lists in a random sample of cans could easily provide information on the quality of the beverage, its alcoholic content, and brewing techniques.

[23]Frank Hole and Robert Heizer, *An Introduction to Prehistoric Archaeology* (New York, 1965), 360-364.

[24]James Deetz, "Human Behavior and Archaeological Remains," in Ernestene L. Green, ed., *In Search of Man: Readings in Archaeology,* 8-16.

[25]The use of "time capsules" in the late 1950s and early 1960s randomly collected objects and placed them in containers. No systematic approach was employed and no classification scheme applied to each object. Thus, real knowledge about the past has been lost since each object is divorced from its intitial context. They will only provide curios of our past without real intellectual substance.

Material Culture as Non Verbal Communication: A Historical Case Study

Kenneth L. Ames

Nonverbal communication involves far more than the exchange of new informaton or what is called body language; it includes an immense range of kinesic, natural and material culture signs, signals and symbols that play important roles in people's cognitive and affective lives. In this article, one form of material culture from the past, the parlor organ of Victorian America, provides a basis for a case study of some of the many ways artifacts may be said to communicate nonverbally. The emphasis here is on the object's role in certain human interactions as a device for maintaining the social order. Seen from this vantage point, objects like parlor organs are not passive cultural products but tools for social purposes; they become significant elements within what might be called social strategies.[1]

The objects discussed and illustrated in this article may appear quaint or old-fashioned but their social roles, their communicated content, will be familiar. While a people's societal needs remain relatively constant over time, the way these needs are met may vary considerably.[2] What differentiates Victorian Americans from us today is less a different set of needs than a distinctly different pattern of responses to those needs. Many of those responses, including parlor organs, survive today and constitute an accessible and reliable record of Victorian society. Thus the nonverbal communicative aspect of material culture continues beyond its original context; tools developed for a society to attain its own goals become for the historian of a later period a means to identify and analyze those goals.

One way to understand better how an object somewhat unfamiliar today, like the Victorian parlor organ, might have played communicative roles still familiar is to utilize, with both alterations and apologies, the archaeologists' polar concepts of tradition and horizon. While formulated from archaeological data and intended to facilitate work in that discipline, these concepts have considerable utility for other studies. As originally defined, traditional objects or behaviors were those that persisted with minimal change over considerable time in a limited geographical area. Horizonal objects or behaviors, on the other hand, were parts of short temporal sequences; produced or practiced only briefly before being eliminated or substantially altered, they were distributed over considerable areas. In adapting these ideas for studies of popular culture of the modern age, the temporal distinction between tradition and horizon remains important but because popular culture is widely distributed the space dimension becomes less significant.[3]

All objects incorporate elements of both tradition and horizon. The automobile, for example, may be described as a tradition in America and its changing styles viewed as a succession of horizons. Looking over a longer span of time, one might identify the automobile as a horizon within the tradition of wheeled vehicles. Tradition and horizon are relative terms rather than fixed measurements. The main justification for employing them is that they embody the dual historical forces of continuity and change and thereby work against any facile study of the human past or present that ignores either factor.

In the instance of the Victorian parlor organ, the object itself may be described as a horizon. The distinctive combination of musical and design traits that characterize the parlor organ flourished in America from about the time of the Civil War to World War I. Years of peak production can be pinpointed more narrowly between roughly 1870 and 1895.[4] Yet if the object, by being highly popular and widely distributed for only a generation or two, has the features of a horizon, some of its functions demonstrate considerably greater durability and, therefore, may be said to represent its tradition dimension. I will return later to this concept of the object as a horizonal embodiment of a traditional function but first several preliminary matters require discussion, including the form of evidence used for this study and the way the term function will be employed.

All objects, including parlor organs, may serve a variety of functions, some of them rather subtle. Sociologist Robert K. Merton made useful distinctions between what he called manifest and latent functions.[5] The manifest function of a parlor organ is the production of music. Its latent functions include providing a livelihood for organ manufacturers and dealers and encouraging the sale of sheet music, to mention only two. Another way of putting this is to say that music is not an end in itself but a means to a variety of other ends.

Lewis Binford identified three levels of function that help refine Merton's analysis.[6] What Binford calls technomic function refers to the utilitarian or physical use of an object and, in the instance of the parlor organ, is roughly equivalent to Merton's manifest function. Binford's other two classes of function are more relevant to this discussion. Ideotechnic function describes the use of objects in religious and psychological contexts; sociotechnic function involves their use in contexts of social interaction. While distinctions between these latter functions are arbitrary to a degree, the concept of function employed in this discussion of parlor organs is best described as sociotechnic. My focus will be on certain sociotechnic functions of the Victorian parlor organ as they constitute parts of behavior sequences or communicative interactions. Put another way, the parlor organ will be viewed as a sociotechnic tool, a nonverbal component of certain human interactions where it is understood to facilitate or enrich those interactions and convey information about attitudes, values, and affiliations.

It is difficult for the historian to recapture those sociotechnic functions. Clearly interactions long since over involving parlor organs cannot be re-enacted. Other forms of material culture, however, can provide important clues to the parlor organ's role as a nonverbal communicator. Because they constitute one of the most extensive, pervasive, and comprehensible of nonverbal communication systems, pictures are especially valuable, providing both illustrations of and models for behavior. The data used for this study are primarily pictorial and date from the late 19th and early 20th centuries. Some of the images, particularly the photographs, might be considered objective records. Others, like the advertising cards, are more obviously prescriptive. Yet because the latter are more explicit in their social purpose they are less difficult to interpret than the more ambiguous photographs.

Designed to sell a product, advertising images of the 19th century generally appealed to and endorsed the values of mainstream America. Advertising is sometimes accused of being a sinister scheme to create fraudulent needs in people and then offering products to meet those needs. This point of view gives advertisers more credit than they deserve, for they are hardly capable of altering the basic needs of humanity.[7] What distinguishes capitalist society is not the invention of new needs but the rapid succession of alternative solutions offered to meet persisting needs. What advertisers have done with great success within this system is to identify and appeal to certain of society's values and assumptions. It is the ability of advertisers to exploit people's ideals, hopes, values, and even fantasies that makes advertising useful to historians. The advertising images used here provide valuable clues about what Victorian Americans thought the parlor organ might feasibly communicate and, thereby, contribute to a fuller understanding of the popular mentality of the period.[8]

Because the parlor organ is in some ways similar to the piano it might seem arbitrary to concentrate on one and ignore the other. There are, however, significant enough differences between the two to justify studying the parlor organ alone. They differ in their musical quality and demands on the player, in their case design, spatial requirements, cost, class associations, and, in subtle ways, in the values they represented.

For example, while the parlor organ was well suited to playing chords and melodies, it lacked the rapid response and easy dynamics of the piano. The need to pump the foot pedals constantly to generate air for the reeds made playing the organ a different, and in some ways more awkward, experience than playing the piano. And the resulting sounds were not likely to be confused.

Neither would anyone normally confuse the appearance of the two. The parlor organ's case (Fig. 1) was more elaborate and intricate than that of the typical contemporary piano. The woodwork of the piano was conceived primarily as a protective enclosure for the works and, while elegant in design and finely finished, it remained subservient to and closely related to the internal workings of the instrument. This was only partially true for the parlor organ. While the lower portion of the case was primarily a protective enclosure for standardized mass-produced works and was consequently fairly consistent in configuration, the musically superfluous upper section was another matter. Often architectural in form, it frequently rose high on the wall, contributing to the verticality of the object and its ability to dominate a room.[9] This upper section included shelves, brackets, and niches for the display of a variety of objects. Thus, while the piano remained largely a musical instrument handsomely cased, the parlor organ was both

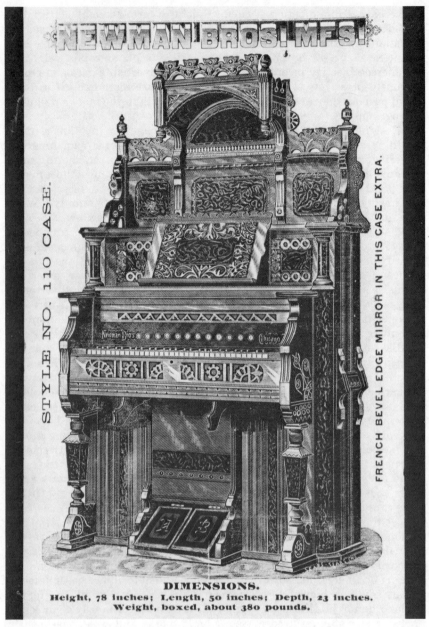

Fig. 1 Parlor organ manufactured by Newman Bros., Chicago, Illinois, © 1890. From a trade card in the Mendsen Collection, Winterthur Museum.

a musical instrument with an elaborate enclosure and a display piece. Its upper section incorporated technomic functions associated with the mantel, the etagere and the what-not.

Such synthesis of function was found not only in objects but also in whole rooms in 19th-century America and is largely an economic phenomenon. Middle- or working-class people often compressed into a single room, the parlor for instance, artifacts and activities for which the affluent created several specialized spaces. The wealthy installed tiers of paintings in clerestory-lit galleries in their mansions but people of moderate means hung a few pictures on their parlor walls and selected an image of special significance for display on a fabric-draped easel. While the affluent might place a Steinway or Chickering grand piano and a richly-carved etagere in the same spacious drawing room, those with limited means and small spaces synthesized musical and display functions in the more spatially efficient organ and installed it in the more humble parlor.[10] The organ occupied only about one-third of the floor space taken up by a conventional square piano and even a smaller portion of the greater area required for a grand. It is a historical irony that the parlor organ, in some ways the product of limited means, has become, because of its synthesis of functions, a richer object for today's historian to interpret than the once more prestigious piano.

Despite its fancy woodwork, its shelves and brackets, the parlor organ cost less than the piano. Organ works were so inexpensive that in the 1870s and 1880s the average parlor organ, even with extensive casework, sold for less than half the price of an average piano.[11] Yet while cheaper it was also more closely linked to changing styles and fashions. It is often difficult to date a piano by looking at its case. Square and grand pianos in the style of the 1850s were still in production in the 1870s and, in some cases, as late as the turn of the century. By resisting changing fashions, the piano conveyed a sense of stability, permanence and timeless good taste. The parlor organ, on the other hand, was a sensitive barometer of style in popular furnishings; its casework today aids rather than hinders attempts at dating. This emphasis on stylishness points up a second irony of the parlor organ. While the styles of organ cases were worldly, the object itself had obvious ecclesiastical associations. Thus the parlor organ combined the sacred and the profane. If the piano was largely an instrument for secular music in secular contexts, both by sound and history the organ was linked to the church.

The parlor organ then may be said to represent the intrusion of the church into the Victorian home, a point I shall return to later. Finally, the cost, size, religious associations, documented original ownership, and other factors indicate that the Victorian parlor organ was primarily a part of middle-class culture. Its study can contribute to a fuller picture of bourgeois America of the last century.

When people purchased a parlor organ they could not have foreseen all the ways it would subtly alter their lives nor could they guess all of its communicative possibilities (Fig. 2). They may have had a vague sense that it would articulate their lives by compartmentalizing and identifying time. Buying a prominent object like a parlor organ might initiate a new chapter

Fig. 2 Delivery of a parlor organ in the vicinity of Madison, Wisconsin, © 1873-1879. Andrew Dahl collection, State Historical Society of Wisconsin.

in a set of lives, not only by providing a new way to use time but also a new tool to measure time. In later years the object would serve to remind its owners of the day it first entered their home and of the time that had passed since then. It would not only structure their present but also their perceptions of their own past.

They also knew from experience that purchasing a major object could be a significant and momentous occasion in itself, a time of heightened positive emotions and feelings of well-being and importance. They knew, although we cannot say to what extent they expressed it, that a major purchase would transform them in their own eyes and in the eyes of others. They would become worth more, in Veblen's terms, and acquire greater status.[12] By so doing they would receive more respect and deference from others which would, in turn, make them feel better about themselves. Buying a parlor organ would make them something they were not before.

Without minimizing these very real feelings about purchases, I would like to shift attention to another series of results that people specifically expected to accompany the purchase of a parlor organ. For, in addition to the changes mentioned above, people had other hopes and expectations for this object; there were specific sociotechnic functions they expected the parlor organ to perform and certain statements about their positions in society, their attitudes and values they hoped to make through purchase of the object. Based on the evidence of pictorial documents and advertising in particular, there were four persisting or traditional sociotechnic functions they expected this horizonal object, the parlor organ, to perform. First, they expected it to help them engage in and extend conventionalized social roles. Second, they looked to it to help promote social and cultural continuity over time. Third, they hoped it would insure social bonding, whether it be marital, familial, or group over space. And, finally, they anticipated that the parlor organ would enhance their lives through the self-actualization and interaction with others it would make possible. All these expectations overlap; it might be more accurate to describe them as different sides of a multi faceted cluster of ways to maintain social order.

The parlor organ and conventionalized roles.
Like playing the piano in the home, playing the organ was considered an attribute of ladydom. It fit within that broader category of the cultivation of refined sensibilities seen as an appropriate part of the genteel female role. In most 19th-century pictorial materials showing someone playing an organ in a domestic context, and in all of those in this article, that person is female. Context is the significant variable. In the domestic sphere, conventionally seen as woman's domain, the musical instrument is typically played by a woman. In the outer world of the stage or the church, roles are reversed and a male is shown at the keyboard. The evidence of the images reinforces the arguments of historians who have maintained that the 19th century witnessed a heightened division of male and female realms: the outer masculine world of commerce and industry, the inner feminine world of domesticity and childrearing; the male world of energy and action, the female world of sentimentality and reflection.[13] In advertising images and photographs the parlor organ is represented as a

means for the display of feminine accomplishments, both in a narrow sense of learning an elegant skill and in the broader sense of successfully performing socially valued tasks.

Critics might maintain that the ability to play a parlor organ was a part of becoming an ornamental lady and a manifestation of what Veblen called conspicuous leisure.[14] Yet the matter is more complex. As Ann Douglas argued, "the lady's function in a capitalist society was to appropriate and preserve both the values and commodities which her competitive husband, father, and son had little time to honor or enjoy; she was to provide an antidote and a purpose to their labor."[15] Douglas maintains that the twin roles of consumer and saint were combined in the genteel 19th-century woman. Among woman's "saintly" traits was the performance of what might loosely be identified as clerical duties within the home. For if the parlor organ, as we argued before, represented the intrusion of the church into the household, woman presided over those churchly activities within the home. Both males and females made extensive use of material culture to help them perform their roles; the parlor organ was a significant tool both for the definition of certain aspects of the female role and for their aggrandisement. The parallel between the popularity of gospel music and the parlor organ is not just coincidental.[16] They represented different reflections of the same movement. Thus, while the parlor organ may be justifiably viewed as a tool for extending female influence over the family, that female power within the home was related to broader social movements outside the home. By influencing home life, woman also helped to preserve and promote socially functional values and behaviors. Thus the parlor organ was an element within an elaborate normative system that unified the home and the outside world. For many the possession of a parlor organ was a nonverbal statement of dedication to that system.[17]

The parlor organ and social and cultural continuity over time.

The parlor organ was a nonverbal statement of belief in the importance of perpetuating values, behaviors and social affiliations vertically, that is, over time. If the object's elaborately stylish case proclaimed the value of change, some of its sociotechnic functions endorsed continuity. Advertising and other images are rich in references to continuity. One Mason and Hamlin advertisement, for example, skillfully synthesizes words and images into a cohesive ideological package (Fig. 3). At the bottom of the image appear the words "Church, Chapel & Parlor Organs." On one level these words indicate the range of goods manufactured by the firm. On another level, the linking and the order of the words suggest both a logical association of the three places and a hierarchy, descending from church to parlor. Strung together in this way, these words confirm the ecclesiastical associations of the artifact and establish a parallel between the formal, institutionalized worship within a church, presided over by a male, and the informal socialization within the home, presided over by a woman.

As the young woman in the Mason and Hamlin illustration performs her sexually stereotyped role of playing the organ, other members of the family gather near her. The act of playing the organ provides an occasion for the assembling of three generations of a family. The meditative and

Fig. 3 Trade card for Mason & Hamlin, Boston, Massachusetts, © 1890. Mendsen Collection, Winterthur Museum.

reflective expressions on their faces suggest that their souls and spirits are uplifted by sharing the melody and its sentiments. Outside the window the sharp spire of a church points heavenward against the sunset sky, casting a sacred benediction over the assembled family group. This diminutive vignette is thus framed top and bottom by ecclesiastical references: the words church and chapel at the bottom; the church spire at the top.

This image also efficiently exploits the popular appeal of three clusters of associations, each designated by a single word: mother, home, and heaven (Fig. 4). In this picture and, presumably, in American society, mother, performing a sex-determined role within her home, her sphere of influence, instills Christian virtues and values in the family and prepares them for their eventual home in heaven. In this view of the family there is no male of working age present; he is presumably working to support the leisurely and spiritual activities of those within the image.

Specific reference to vertical continuity or continuity over time appears through the juxtaposition of people of widely different ages: the small child, the middle-aged mother, the grandparents. Yet the advertisement also includes a more succinct Victorian cliche for continuity, the very young and the very old side by side. This formula for continuity is common in 19th-century imagery and occurs in the canvases of high culture artists as well as in inexpensive prints for a mass audience. In an 1866 painting by Junius R. Sloan an old woman watches while a young girl practices her knitting (Fig. 5). The activity itself is ancient and has been performed by generations of women; the placement of the scene in an old interior indicates the traditional, perhaps even venerable, aspects of the task but the presence of the young girl indicates that the lore and learning of the past will be carried on by the future generations.

The frontierspiece of *The Royal Path of Life* is even more explicit (Fig. 6). In this image an old man holds a sleeping child in his arms. While the child slumbers the man stares emptily into the space before him, presumably meditating on the passage of time and his own mortality. The title beneath the engraving, "The Past and the Future," only repeats what was obvious to 19th-century viewers.

The designer of the Mason and Hamlin advertising card knew that contemporary viewers would understand the allusion to past and future and therefore continuity implicit in the close placement of the child and its grandmother. Victorian Americans did not find the idea that a parlor organ might perpetuate values from one generation to another ridiculous or offensive. Because the advertising image is wish-projection, there is no way to know whether this purpose was indeed fulfilled. What we do know is that Victorians were vulnerable to implicit promises of this sort; it seemed a reasonable sociotechnic expectation.

Victorian life was riddled with contradictions. If woman might be both consumer and saint, as Douglas claims, the parlor organ could be both a product of materialism and a producer of spirituality. The intense materialism and fervent revivalism of the last century, presumably antithetical, were both accommodated in the parlor organ. In acquiring the fashionably detailed object, woman's needs as consumer were satisfied. Yet once purchased, the object became a tool useful in fulfilling her saintly role.

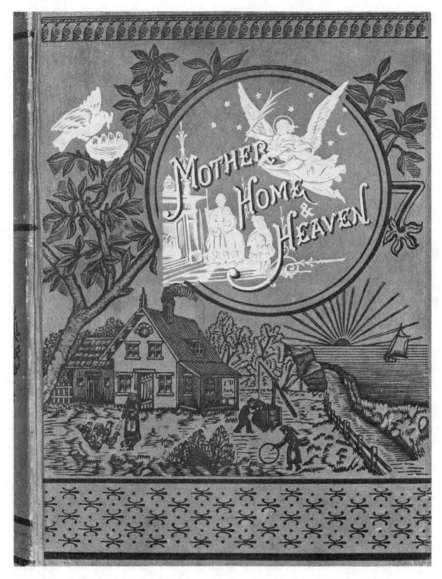

Fig. 4 Cover of Theo. L. Cuyler, *Golden Thoughts on Mother, Home, and Heaven* (Philadelphia: Garretson & Co., © 1882).

Fig. 5 "The Knitting Lesson," by Junius P. Sloan, 1866. Art Museum, Valparaiso University.

Fig. 6 "The Past and the Future," frontispiece to T.L. Haines and L. W. Yaggy, *The Royal Path of Life* (New York: Standard Publishing House, 1881).

Thus apparent opposites were reconciled, demonstrating not only society's ability to tolerate contradictions but also objects' capacity to perform widely varied and seemingly opposing functions.[18]

The parlor organ and social bonding over space.

If the parlor organ was perceived as a means to promote vertical or temporal continuity, it seems to have been even more important as a device for horizonal or geographic continuity or what might be termed social bonding. The goal of social bonding is to create or maintain amiable relations among people or groups of people, ranging from the intimate level of a couple to the more extended realm of an entire society or even several societies.[19]

At the level of the family, the parlor organ was advertised as a means to enhance and ensure the bonds of a marital pair or nuclear family. In an advertisement for the Packard Orchestral Organ the wife is shown at the instrument while her husband stands at her side; the organ and its music bring them together (Fig. 7). On the floor in the foreground a small child plays with blocks. The child in this context serves not only to testify to the drawing power of the organ but also to sanctify the relationship of the two adults and identify the setting as domestic. Any depiction of a man and woman in close proximity in a luxurious environment is not necessarily domestic; it could be a bordello scene. The child serves to signal that the situation is domestic and the close encounter of members of opposite sex is sanctified.[20] Put in a more positive way, the presence of the child, healthy and well dressed like its parents, implies that not only does the parlor organ belong in the home of cultivated, well-mannered, attractive and happily-married people but also is even a way of attaining these ends.

Photographs suggest that the parlor organ meant a lot to consumers for it figures prominently in scores of them. In one Van Schaick photograph, for example, a parlor organ serves as a backdrop for a double portrait of an elderly couple in their Wisconsin home (Fig. 8). It is impossible to know whether the setting was suggested by the photographer or the sitters themselves but in a sense it doesn't matter. What is important is that sitters and photographer agreed that the parlor organ provided a suitable and appropriate setting for a portrait. In fact, it is the largest and most prominent artifact in the photo, the dominant element within the constellation of artifacts drawn together for this memorial image.

In this Wisconsin home the organ is like a magnet, drawing to it not only the two sitters but also their extended families; three generations in portraits rest on the organ or hang on walls nearby. These images of relatives are augmented by attributes of learning and civilization, including books, music, an album, floral wallpaper with a frieze, a textile scarf on the table, doilies on the chair and lounge, a frilly glass vase on the organ, and a gold-framed print of photograph of some natural wonder in the corner.[21] The parlor organ dominates this accumulation of nonverbal communicators, becoming the focal point of this domestic shrine to learning, civilization and familial continuity over both time and space. In an uncanny way, distant and departed relatives and experiences are

Fig. 7 Trade card for the Packard Orchestral Organ, manufactured by the Fort Wayne Organ Co., Fort Wayne, Indiana, © 1885. Mendsen Collection, Winterthur Museum.

Fig. 8 Mr. and Mrs. Simon in the parlor of their home near Taylor, Wisconsin, © 1900. Van Schaick Collection, State Historical Society of Wisconsin.

reunited at the parlor organ. It becomes an element of stability in the face of aging and separation.

The parlor organ also expressed affiliation beyond the family. In the same way that it nonverbally suggested contact through music with other people for the couple in their Wisconsin home, it became a virtual symbol of civilization and community for other Americans at the edge of the frontier. The rich associations of the parlor organ as well as its synthesis of functions made it valued evidence of contact and affiliation with the larger world. Both written and nonverbal evidence are abundant. In Lady Mann's music school on the Idaho frontier, for example, the organ figures prominently as a technomic and sociotechnic device (Fig. 9). If it helps teach the children music, it also educates them to social roles; boys are present in the photograph but a girl plays the organ. If the music the children learn is for the benefit of their local community, it is not only a means to bond them together by providing occasions for interactions but also to affiliate them, still relatively isolated on the Idaho frontier, with the rest of Western civilization both present and past. The parlor organ then serves as a vehicle for expressing association with the larger society; by sharing its material culture affiliation and community are expressed. Yet the parlor organ is always multifunctional and in the Mann parlor it also performs the same shrine function it did for the old couple in their Wisconsin home, displaying an accumulation of ceramics, statuary, photographs, prints, flowers and other symbolic, communicative artifacts.

The parlor organ and the enhancement of life through self-actualization and social interaction.

Enhancing life by attaining a skill and sharing experience has been implicit in the three situations already discussed. In the case of the organist, achieving mastery or just competence in a contest with oneself or others can be immensely rewarding, allowing one to feel comfortably satisfied. Success may even bring prominence and flattering attention. For those who sing along or only listen there come the very real if indefinable delights of music, of being moved bodily and emotionally by the sounds and forming, if only for a short time, that powerful emotional bond that unites those who make music together or share it. Singing together is a ritual of bonding well understood within some religions. Like eating or drinking together it generates communion through identical activity and fosters powerful if senses that cannot be verbalized of affiliation and belonging. In this way the parlor organ played a part in one of humanity's most efficacious modes of generating feelings of positive identification with others, a mode possibly exceeded only by the act of love itself.

In discussing the parlor organ's sociotechnic functions the emphasis has been on the performance of established roles and the maintenance of bonds already formed. Yet the object's utility also reached back a step further to the initiation of roles and bonding. Put differently we can say that the parlor organ was a tool for change as well as for continuity. In an advertisement distributed by the Estey Organ Co., for example, the arrangement of the visual data suggests the formulation rather than maintenance of bonds (Fig. 10). The specifically religious, familial or

Fig. 9 Lady Mann's parlor in Boise, Idaho, © 1900. Idaho Historical Society.

Fig. 10 Trade card for the Estey Organ Co., Brattleboro, Vermont, © 1885. Mendsen Collection, Winterthur Museum.

marital associations of the previous images are absent from this interaction of elegantly dressed young people. While a pair of children gaze out the window at Estey's thriving industrial plant in Brattleboro and a chaperone sits in a lavishly upholstered chair at the left of the illustration, neither is the real focus of the picture. The larger area of the advertisement emphasizes the interaction of handsome, elegantly attired young people. The delights and excitement of the fashionable life are the real theme of this advertisement; with the Estey organ the world of high culture, of the Victorian "beautiful people" could be attained. The setting radiates richness through the luxurious rugs, window hangings, wallpapers, furniture, ceramics, a sculptured bust, plants and other trappings of the life of affluence and abundance.

The organ shown in this advertisement is one of the most expensive produced by the firm for domestic use, approaching the piano in price and perhaps in secular associations as well, for the context illustrated is fashionable and worldly, only slightly modified by the domesticating and sanctioning devices of children and chaperone. Thus the parlor organ may also have meant upward mobility through social interaction to some people. While in some contexts the instrument may have served to promote continuity, in others it initiated mobility and the breaking of some bonds for the establishment of others. It is not necessarily the object that varies, for objects are only receptacles for people's projected needs and desires.

Because the object is a receptacle, because it has no inherent meaning but only the meanings people make with it, there can be no real certainty in discussing its meaning or exactly what it communicated nonverbally to Americans of the last years of the 19th century and the early years of the 20th. While I have outlined some of the social functions of the parlor organ in Victorian America and thereby offer a few guidelines for interpretation, I want to conclude by stressing the uncertainties that remain. For it is one thing to analyze the sales pitch of an advertisement and another to determine which, if any, of the many and sometimes contradictory functions discussed were meaningful to any given individual or groups of individuals. Put another way, there may be considerable difference between the public meanings of objects as evident in advertising imagery and the personal or private meanings that these objects had for their owners and users. What can the historian say about the Van Schaick photograph of two girls at a parlor organ in a modest interior in the vicinity of Black River Falls, Wisconsin, in the early years of this century (Fig. 11)? With which of the previous images can it fairly be juxtaposed? Certainly it resembles all the advertisements in showing a woman again acting out a sexually determined role. Yet the humble surroundings, the inexpensive rocking chairs, the plant in the paper-wrapped tin can in the window, and the crazed window shade are in strong contrast to the elegant or at least prim settings of the prescriptive images. The discrepancy between those advertisements and this photograph reminds us not only how far dreams and hope may depart from reality but how difficult it is for historians to move beyond a generalized statement of meaning for some aspect of the past. The best they may be able to do is offer a series of meanings in the hope that at least one may prove applicable to a given instance.

Fig. 11 Two girls at a Newman Bros. parlor organ, vicinity of Black River Falls, Wisconsin, ©
1900. Van Schaick Collection, State Historical Society of Wisconsin.

The interactionists have shown us how people make meanings when they interact with objects.[22] People may receive and share generalized meanings current in society, yet they may also generate a realm of very private meaning which, if never recorded or shared, slips away without traces or clues. This distinction runs parallel to that between what Berger and Luckmann call objective facticity and subjective reality.[23] About objective facticity there is little question. In this Van Schaick photograph it is the demonstrable fact of two young women at a parlor organ in a room of describable artifacts. The reality of the moment, of the interaction for these two people, however, is locked inside their minds and inaccessible to us. To historians' frustration, while the available evidence can be combed for clues, the conclusions can never be more than tentative. This is one of the major shortcomings of historical studies.

In this article I have tried to widen the range of possible interpretations that might be offered for a prosaic artifact like the Victorian parlor organ. I have also tried to suggest the value of advertising images as historical tools. Despite their problems and hyperbole, these pictures are useful reminders of some of the many subtle ways people use objects in their social lives. And, as noted before, it is remarkable how familiar some of those uses are. Advertising today still appeals to the same values and needs but offers different products to affirm and fulfill them. Thus, we can see how these needs or functions might be described as traditions, and short-lived solutions like the parlor organ as horizons. By invoking this tradition/horizon dichotomy it is possible to sense more fully some of the ways we are still very much like the Victorians yet how very different, particularly in physical terms, our world of today is from theirs of a century ago.

Notes

A shorter version of this paper was delivered at the meeting of the Popular Culture Association in Cincinnati, April 21, 1978. For comments, suggestions and help in obtaining photographs I am indebted to Don Hibbard and George Talbot.

[1] Albert E. Scheflen, *Body Language and Social Order* (Englewood Cliffs, N.J.: Prentice-Hall, 1972). The treatment of nonverbal communication in this brief article is hardly exhaustive. One could, for example, analyze each of the figures in the ilustrations in terms of gesture, posture, facial expression, and other communicative elements.

[2] Amos Rapoport, *House Form and Culture* (Englewood Cliffs, N.J.: Prentice-Hall, 1969).

[3] Horizon and tradition are discussed in Gordon R. Willey and Philip Phillips, *Method and Theory in American Archaeology* (Chicago: University of Chicago Press, 1958), 11-43; James Deetz, *Invitation to Archaeology* (Garden City, N.Y.: Natural History Press, 1967), and *In Small Things Forgotten* (Garden City, N.Y.: Anchor Press/Doubleday, 1977).

[4] Robert F. Gellerman, *The American Reed Organ* (Vestal, N.Y.: The Vestal Press, 1973), 1-18. The electrified organs of the twentieth century might be described as another, distinct horizon.

[5] Robert K. Merton, *Social Theory and Social Structure* (London: The Free Press of Glencoe, 1957), 19-84.

[6] Discussed in James J.F. Deetz, "Ceramics from Plymouth, 1620-1835: The Archaeological Evidence," in Ian M.G. Quimby, ed., *Ceramics in America* (Charlottesville, Va.: The University Press of Virginia, 1973), 19-20.

[7] On advertising, see David M. Potter, *People of Plenty* (Chicago: University of Chicago Press, 1954), 166-188.

[8] All advertising images are from the Thelma Mendsen Collection, housed in the Winterthur libraries.

[9] On verticality, see Carroll L.V. Meeks, *The Railroad Station* (New Haven: Yale University

Press, 1962), 1-25.

[10]For more illustrations of parlor organs in 19th-century interiors, see William Seale, *The Tasteful Interlude* (New York: Praeger, 1975), and George Talbot, *At Home: Domestic Life in the Post-Centennial Era* (Madison: State Historical Society of Wisconsin, 1977).

[11]Comparative retail prices of parlor organs and pianos for the 1870s and 1880s, based on prices advertised in trade catalogues.

Organs	Estey & Co., 1874	*Pianos*	Decker Bros., 1973
	$160 to $400		$400 to $1500
	Packard, 1884		J. & C. Fischer, 1878
	$200 to $400		$350 to $1200
	Mason & Hamlin, 1886		J. & C. Fischer, 1883
	$100 to $400		$450 to $1200
	New England, 1880		Weber, 1880
	$150 to $300 (average)		$650 to $1600

Organ prices are for domestic models only. Church or lecture hall organs are more expensive. Fischer's $350 piano is an upright; square pianos start at about $500. The highest figures are for grand pianos.

[12]Thorstein Veblen, *Theory of the Leisure Class* (New York: Macmillan, 1912).

[13]This sexual division of life is well documented in popular images like those sold by Currier & Ives. The 19th century, however, did not invent sexually stereotyped roles. A tradition of representing a woman at the keyboard dates back to the 17th century, when it was an established image in Dutch painting.

[14]Abba Goold Woolson, *Woman in American Society* (Boston: Roberts Bros., 1873), 35-45; Veblen, *Theory of the Leisure Class.*

[15]Ann Douglas, *The Feminization of American Culture* (New York: Knopf, 1977), 60.

[16]Methodist and Baptist preachers reportedly sold reed organs; see Gellerman, *American Reed Organ*, 14. On gospel hymns, see Sandra Sizer, *Gospel Hymns and Social Religion* (Philadelphia: Temple University Press, 1978).

[17]On the home see Clifford E. Clark, Jr., "Domestic Architecture as an Index to Social History: The Romantic Revival and the Cult of Domesticity in America, 1840-1870," *The Journal of Interdisciplinary History,* VII (1976), 33-56; Kirk Jeffrey, "The Family as Utopian Retreat from the City," *Soundings,* LV (1972), 21-41; Paul Boyer, *Urban Masses and Moral Order in America, 1820-1920* (Cambridge, Harvard University Press, 1978), and Douglas, *Feminization of American Culture.*

[18]Douglas, *Feminization of American Culture,* 60, 74.

[19]Scheflen, *Body Language and Social Order.*

[20]The child as sanctioning agent also appears on the illustrated covers of sentimental Civil War music.

[21]Examples of what might be called shrine making appear in Talbot, *At Home.*

[22]Lars Lerup, *Building the Unfinished: Architecture and Human Action* (Beverly Hills, Ca.: Sage Publications, 1977).

[23]Peter L. Berger and Thomas Luckmann, *The Social Construction of Reality* (Garden City, Doubleday, 1966).

In Memory Of:
Artifacts Relating to Mourning in Nineteenth Century America

Martha Pike

'I have always thought,' he said reflectively, 'the system of mourning, of immuring women in crepe for the rest of their lives and forbidding them normal enjoyment is just as barbarous as the Hindu suttee.'[1]

Rhett Butler's comment to Scarlett O'Hara about mourning is probably the twentieth-century's best-known and most succinct damnation of nineteenth century mourning practices. But mourning customs of the nineteenth century, although they may appear bizarre, even morbid, to people of the twentieth century, served both societal and personal needs. Modern readers should be encouraged to view with some sympathy the ways in which the nineteenth century dealt with the universal incomprehensibility of death, and tried to make it meaningful.

Many objects related to these mourning customs are now in museum collections: clothing, costume accessories, jewelry, embroideries, paper ephemera, coffins and coffin plates, hearses, paintings, drawings and prints. Study of these artifacts in conjunction with the literature of the period shows that these mourning customs accurately reflected the society of the period, and provided a socially functional workable mechanism for dealing with the inevitable grief of death.

Artifacts of mourning in the nineteenth century may be grouped into at least three main categories: memorial[2] (items which perpetuate the memory of the loved one); ritualistic (objects prescribed for use in the ritualized etiquette of mourning); and funereal (artifacts actually used in the funeral services).

Memorial Mourning Pieces

The memorial aspect of mourning is seen in a plethora of objects which still exist today. One of the most fascinating of these objects is the memorial picture, painted or embroidered, usually on silk, or painted with watercolors on paper. This was a form of schoolgirl art which flourished in the first decades of the nineteenth century. Most studies of this type of art have focused on the art historically.[3] A fine example of this combination of painting and embroidery is seen in Fig. 1.

Such embroidered and/or painted memorial pictures were done primarily by an educated elite, young women whose families could afford to send them to select seminaries where such genteel arts as painting and needlework* were taught. In the late 1830s or early 1840s, however,

*Editor's Note: Most women learned utilitarian needlework at home or at school.

Fig. 1. Memorial Picture, silk and watercolor on silk, made by Lucretia Carew, Norwich, Connecticut. Dated 1800 on the glass, but probably made a decade later. Collection of The Museums at Stony Brook, Stony Brook, New York.

Nathaniel Currier and other print-makers began to publish low-priced prints of similar subjects. It is difficult to determine exactly when these began to be published, as the earlier prints are undated, but the dress styles in these prints are generally of the period 1838-1842. The earliest dated print located so far was entered in the Clerk's Office of a New York District Court in 1845. This print, similar to that in Fig. 2, is a mourning scene set in New York's St. Paul's churchyard. Nathaniel Currier published this particular print in several variations, possibly to afford the purchaser the appropriate selection of mourners for his or her personal situation. Almost all of these memorial prints have a blank space on the side of the tombstone with a printed inscription, usually "In Memory Of"; The purchaser filled in the blank with the name of the deceased, and frequently the date of his or her death. Memorial prints continued to be published throughout the 1840s and 1850s, though later less frequently, at least few new print designs were entered in the record according to act of Congress. During the Civil War, several prints were published for use as memorials to soldiers slain in the conflict.

Most of the mourning prints portrayed traditional churchyard burying places rather than rural cemeteries, which flourished in many urban centers in the United States during much of the nineteenth century. This raises a question as to the audience or purchasers of these prints: were they primarily rural people, and thus more used to the traditional churchyard than to the newer rural cemetery, or were they more sophisticated urbanites? Or did these prints reflect a nineteenth century mind steeped in nostalgia for the pre-industrial age, whose own art often selectively omitted the most modern and dynamic images—factories, mills, wars, strikes—in favor of a bucolic "nature" genre, and revealed a deep ambivalence toward change?

In addition to the popular taste for mourning prints, there was also a vogue for memorializing the dead in photographs and paintings taken after death. The taking of photographs of dead infants was particularly widespread; Fig. 3 is of a Rhode Island child. William Sidney Mount, one of the major American painters of the nineteenth century, did many portraits after death. Fortunately, he also kept copious journals, in which he made frequent references to the practice, which he found distasteful, of taking portraits of the dead. In an autobiographical sketch, Mount wrote: "I pass over several portraits, a few taken after death. I had rather paint the living but death is a patron to some painters."[4] Since most of Mount's portraits look perfectly lifelike, it is only by cross-referencing the paintings to the notes made by the artist that one is able to identify portraits of the dead. Fig. 4 is of young Jedediah Williamson, son of a neighbor of the Mounts: "I made a sketch of Col. Williamson's Son after he was killed by a loaded waggon passing over his body. A portrait. $15.00."[5]

William Sidney Mount's brother, Shepard Alonzo Mount, an able portraitist, left a poignant visual and written record of the death of his granddaughter Camille in 1868. The painting of the child is seen in Fig. 5; a letter to his son discusses Camille's death and his painting of her:

Telling you of Joshua and Edna—I am obliged to sadden your heart—They have lost their little

Fig. 2. Lithograph, Nathaniel Currier. No date. Courtesy of Greenfield Village and Henry Ford Museum.

Fig. 3. Photograph of Amos C. Barstow III, died June 29, 1879, aged 2 years and 22 days; Manchester Brothers; Providence, Rhode Island. Collection of The Museums at Stony Brook.

Fig. 4. William Sidney Mount, "Portrait of Jedediah Williamson," not dated, oil on panel. Collection of The Museums at Stony Brook; bequest of Ward Melville, 1977.

Fig. 5. Shepard Alonzo Mount, "Small Girl with Watch (Portrait of Camille)," not dated, oil on canvas. Collection of The Museums at Stony Brook; bequest of Dorothy DeBevoise Mount, 1959.

Camille—she is dead—the sweet beautiful babe is dead. She died from the effects of teathing [sic]. It so happened—providentially I thought—that I was at Glen Cove—and for two or three days before she died, I made several drawings of her, which enabled me, as soon as she was buried to commence a portrait of her and in 7 days I succeeded in finishing one of the best portraits of a child that I ever painted. All the family seem'd surprised, and delighted with it and to me it was real joy to have been the instrument of affording so much comfort to all—Joshua and Edna would sit before it for an hour together and Mr. and Mrs. Searing are in raptures with it. I have framed it and hung it up for all to see and love—for next to the dear babe herself—it is now the idol of the family. Alas! how everything fades from us—Joshua arrived home the day after she was buried. How sad the shock. She was laid out in a beautiful casket and she looked like an angel— Her eyes were bright and heavenly 'till the last. I painted her with Mr. Searings watch lying open in the foreground. the hands pointing to the hour of her birth. while she is seen moving up on a light cloud—the image of the lost Camille—[6]

In addition to prints, paintings, and photographs, memorial jewelry was quite common. Most historical collections include jewelry made of human hair. Although hair jewelry is commonly called mourning jewelry today, most pieces were mementoes of the living rather than of the dead: In Alcott's *Little Women* we see the common use of hair jewelry as a token of sentiment. " 'How can I be otherwise?' said Mrs. March gratefully, as her eyes went from her husband's letter to Beth's smiling face and her hand caressed the brooch made of gray and golden, chestnut and dark-brown hair, which the girls had just fastened on her breast."[7] Elaborate confections of hair, usually in the form of wreaths or floral arrangements, were also quite popular; these were ordinarily used for parlor ornaments. Instructions on how to make such jewelry or ornaments of hair appeared in many ladies' magazines. Unless there is a memorial inscription on a piece of hair jewelry or on an ornament, or there is an impeccable provenance as to its use as a memorial piece, such an item should be considered a sentimental piece rather than a mourning memorial.

Memorials to the dead often took more literal form than the personalized prints, paintings and jewelry. The burial place also began to take on a new configuration. The rural cemetery movement began in 1831 with the opening of Mount Auburn Cemetery in Cambridge, Massachusetts. Cities throughout the eastern and midwestern United States followed suit in the ensuing decades, for example, Laurel Hill, Philadelphia, in 1836; Green-Wood, Brooklyn, in 1838; Cave-Hill, Louisville, in 1848; and Oakland, Atlanta, in 1850.[8] These cemeteries can be considered artifacts in themselves. They reflect the hopeful, heavenward-looking religion of the nineteenth century, one markedly different from that more fearful and more starkly realistic religion evident in the crowded churchyard burying grounds of the seventeenth and eighteenth centuries. The rural cemeteries were consciously designed as new kinds of burying places:

A voice from 'the Green-Wood! A voice! and it said,
Ye have chosen me out as a home for your dead;
From the bustle of life ye have render'd me free;
My earth ye have hallowed; henceforth I shall be
A garden of graves, where your loved ones shall rest![9]

Guide books were published to some of the better-known cemeteries such as Mount Auburn and Green-Wood. These were often illustrated with engravings depicting the beauties of the cemeteries and demonstrating that mourners and sightseers were visiting the cemeteries. Individual prints of these cemeteries were published by print-makers, an example of which is the Nathaniel Currier print in Fig. 6. Many of these cemeteries were major sightseeing attractions during much of the nineteenth century.

The tombstones and tomb sculptures of these rural cemeteries reflect nineteenth century Christian beliefs—homeward bound was the major theme: angels transporting the dead toward heaven, children sleeping peacefully, angels pointing heavenward. All is confident expression of the hopeful belief in a happy afterlife. Curiously, the mourning family or individual is seldom portrayed in Victorian cemetery sculpture, although a few such monuments exist.

Ritualistic Mourning Objects

The second group of artifacts relates to the ritualistic practices of mourning, rather than to the memorializing of the dead. There were rigid guidelines for the behavior of the widow; the widower had much less restrictive guidelines to follow. Etiquette books and ladies' magazines are good sources of information about mourning rituals. The rigidity and complexity of mourning rituals described in etiquette books increased substantially during the latter half of the nineteenth century. Concurrently, however, there were increasingly frequent references to people's right to choose whether or not to go into mourning. Perhaps detailed guidelines of socially acceptable behavior only became necessary when there were increasing numbers of people wishing to do the proper thing, but not knowing the rules.

Etiquette books of the period 1830 to 1870 mentioned mourning in passing; perhaps it was assumed that appropriate behavior was known. A brief entry from *Godey's Lady's Magazine* (May 1844) editorializes:

We have always advocated the custom, old as the records of social life, of expressing by outward token the sorrow which every truly affectionate heart must endure under the bereavement of death. The custom of wearing mourning apparel will, we hope, never be discontinued.[10]

There are, however, no detailed descriptions of what was considered proper mourning apparel. Another brief mention of mourning appears in an etiquette book of the same year: "Do not wear *black* or colored gloves, lest your partners look sulky; even should you be in *mourning*, wear *white* gloves, *not black*. People in DEEP mourning have no business in a ballroom at all."[11]

Although etiquette books of the 1840s do not dwell on detailed descriptions of appropriate mourning behavior or dress, mourning prints of the period show women and children in deep black mourning. Comparison of the garments in such prints with descriptions and prints of mourning garb later in the century demonstrates that there was less rigid codification of proper dress in the earlier period. For example, lace and embroidery appear in some early garments, but they were frowned upon later in the century. An 1856 periodical included the following mention of mourning apparel:

At JACKSON'S we admired several long cashmere *bournous*, trimmed with crape, graceful yet

Fig. 6. Lithograph, Green-Wood Cemetery, Nathaniel Currier, 1855. Courtesy of Greenfield Village and Henry Ford Museum.

grave, from the deepest to the slightest mourning. Bugles and velvet are very much used, as are also embroideries on crape for collars and sleeves.[12]

Etiquette books of the last three decades of the nineteenth century frequently devoted at least a chapter to the etiquette of mourning, giving procedural details about how long mourning should be worn, how funeral invitations should be issued, how appropriate dress should be chosen and to what degree behavior should be restricted. Descriptions of acceptable fabrics, dress ornaments, and jewelry fill the pages of etiquette books, for example, in 1884:

The deepest mourning worn is that of a widow, which consists of crape and bombazine. The present fashion is to cover everything with crape. The widow's dress is made without ruffles or flounces, but heavily overlaid with crape. The veil reached to the feet, and is nearly wide enough to meet at the back. The hem is half a yard deep.

There is now in all large dry-goods stores a mourning department, where new goods for all grades of mourning are shown.[13]

Many of the objects mentioned in etiquette books and periodicals of the nineteenth century have survived, and are in private or museum collections. Full costumes of deep mourning are relatively rare, although some do exist in museum collections.[14] Some costumes of second or partial mourning also survive. Mourning dress was carefully graded: the deepest mourning was usually worn for at least a year by a widow, then it was gradually lightened, changing from solid black to black and white, gray, or lavender, before changing to colors. Mourning in its various states usually lasted a minimum of two years. Some widows, however, remained in heavy mourning until their own death. There appears to have been no general agreement on exactly how long each phase of mourning should last, although most writers on etiquette agreed on a total mourning period of at least two years.

Nineteenth century periodicals such as *Godey's Lady's Book, Peterson's,* and *Harper's Bazar* included not only hints on mourning etiquette, but also illustrations of proper and fashionable mourning dress; Figs. 7 and 8 are fashion plates from an 1895 *Harper's Bazar.*

Many black dresses covered with jet beads, usually from the 1880s, are sometimes called mourning dresses today simply because they are black. This is not necessarily true. The assumption that a dress was used as mourning apparel should be made only for those garments made of or trimmed with crape, or for those with reliable documentation of mourning use. These bead-decorated dresses *may* have been mourning, but it is not safe to assume that they were: "For lighter mourning jet is used on silk and there is no doubt that it makes a very handsome dress."[15]

The relative scarcity of full mourning costumes surviving today leads one to question whether or not the full panoply of mourning dress was often worn. Full mourning was undoubtedly expensive: "Mourning is very expensive, and often costs a family more than they can well afford."[16] This raises the question of artifact survival. Unlike wedding and christening dress, mourning dress was not symbolic of a happy event. This may explain why relatively few complete costumes have survived. On the other hand, more modest mourning accessories such as black crape veils and black-

Fig. 7. Mourning Costume with Cape, *Harper's Bazar*, New York, August 31, 1895, p. 708.

MOURNING BONNETS AND PARASOL.

Fig. 8. Mourning Bonnets and Parasol, *Harper's Bazar*, New York, August 31, 1895, p. 709.

bordered handkerchiefs have survived in large numbers. Because these items were small and did not go out of style quickly, they were probably saved for later use. Other small artifacts relating to mourning have survived. For example, to assure that no glint would relieve the sombreness of black, mourning pins, straight pins for fastening one's mourning veil, had black glass heads and shafts of blued steel. Stationery and calling cards were black-bordered, and many examples have survived:

Cards and notepaper are now put into mourning by those who desire to express conventionally their regret for the dead; but very broad borders of black look like ostentation, and are in undoubted bad taste. No doubt all these things are proper in their way, but a narrow border of black tells the story of loss as well as an inch of coal-black doom.[17]

Fig. 9 shows some of the accessories associated with mourning.

The large number of surviving mourning accessories leads one to suspect that mourning rituals were more widely practiced than one might

Fig. 9. Group of mourning artifacts including mourning stationery, crape veil, mourning pins, black bordered handkerchief and cuff. All late 19th century. Collection of The Museums at Stony Brook.

think from the number of garments that have survived. Women of limited means could have bought a widow's veil and bonnet and worn them with a dress dyed black to mourn, rather than going to the expense of full mourning. Additional research is yet to be done on the question of who carried out the mourning rituals dictated by etiquette books and ladies' magazines, and how widely spread in society these rituals were.

Jewelry considered appropriate for mourning was as strictly prescribed as the dress itself: jet or onyx were the preferred materials; occasionally pearls or brilliants were set into the jet or onyx. There was no consensus but some writers of etiquette books proscribed the wearing of any gold jewelry.

The question of men and how they mourned is little mentioned in the literature of the period. At most, the widower wore black or dark grey clothes, a crape band on his hat, black gloves and tie: "They knew of my affliction, they noticed the weed on my hat...."[18] Judging from surviving artifacts and from the literature, the burden of mourning fell primarily on women. Mourning was yet another sphere in which woman figured as the pillar of home and society. She was the one who came "from the *carbon* of *man's* flesh and bones, the pure diamond of purity and beauty, and light of moral perfectness, which he enshrined in the form of *woman*.[19] As late as 1888 Mrs. M.F. Armstrong, in an etiquette book originally written for the students of the Hampton Institute, wrote, "The principal power in general society undoubtedly lies in the hands of its female members—that is, it is to them that Society looks for a careful standard of refinement."[20] Women's lives, especially widows', were truly circumscribed.

Many of the mourning rituals in the United States derived from English customs.* Passages and even entire chapters of English etiquette books were published in American etiquette books, often without mention of the original source. But, as frequently occurred in America's borrowing of customs, mourning customs were somewhat changed to coincide with American tastes. Nineteenth century writings, especially etiquette books, show that there was considerable awareness of this: "We have shown the good taste of America in abolishing the hired mutes, the emblazement of the emblematic horrors of death, the skull and crossbones on the panels of the hearse, and all that 'luxury of woe' so remarkable in the English funeral.--[21]

Victorians of mainstream Protestant faiths professed belief in a blissful afterlife; evidenced in their grave sculptures, and in the optimism of their popular writings, and yet they, certainly the women, draped themselves in black.[22] Occasionally they noted the contradiction:

Therefore we have a difficulty to contend with in the wearing of black, which is in itself, to begin with, negatory of our professed belief in the resurrection. We confess the logic of despair when we drape ourselves in its gloomy folds.[23]

There are several possible explanations for this contradiction, none mutually exclusively: the drive for propriety was so strong that it overpowered the religious origin of behavior; the mourning rituals were symbolic of woman's place in the world, and became, possibly, a source of

*Editor's Note: Italians, Poles and others of Catholic background had different mourning customs, as did those of Jewish tradition.

her feminine power;[24] the bereaved were mourning for themselves rather than for the deceased, mourning because they were left behind while the loved one had gone on to a better world.

Funereal Items

The third category of artifacts is funereal, relating to the funeral itself. One of the most interesting artifacts in this category is the coffin, which underwent a curious change of both style and nomenclature during the nineteenth century. During the latter half of the century the "coffin," usually hexagonal and vaguely body-shaped, became the "casket," which was rectangular in shape. The use of the term "casket" was euphemistic:

> It is known, and some of you to whom I speak have had painful opportunity to know, that there has been, of late years, an improvement in the little depositories in which we convey the forms of infants and young children to their last resting-place.
>
> Their shape is not in seeming mockery of the rigid, swathed body; the broken lines and angles of the old coffin are drawn into continuous lines; they look like other things, and not like that which looks like nothing else, a coffin; you would be willing to have such a shape for the depository of any household article. Within, they are prepared with a pearly white lining; the inside of the lid is draped in the same way; the name is on the inside; and a lock and key supplant the remorseless screws and screw-driver.[25]

The change in the shape and name* of the repository for the body of the dead from coffin to casket paralleled the growing rigidification of mourning customs, and perhaps presaged the twentieth century avoidance of death, what Philippe Aries calls "forbidden death."[26] Concurrent with the change in the coffin was the gradual rise of the profession of funeral direction; the funeral director assumed the duties previously performed by a variety of people: providing the coffin (handmade by the local cabinet-maker in the first half of the nineteenth century, but often patented and mass-produced in the latter half of the century); preparing the deceased for burial (previously done by family members and friends); and counseling and consoling (previously done by friends and ministers). This intermediation of the funeral director between the immediate fact of death and the bereaved probably contributed to the avoidance of the concept of death which exists today.

The expression of private grief so acceptable, even required, in the nineteenth century, is forbidden today. As Aries wrote,

> Too evident sorrow does not inspire pity, but repugnance, it is the sign of mental instability or of bad manners: it is morbid.... One only has the right to cry if no one else can see or hear. Solitary and shameful mourning is the only recourse, like a sort of masturbation. (The comparison is Gorer's.)[27]

This standard of behavior leaves both the bereaved and his or her friends in anguished isolation. There are no guidelines for their behavior. Although nineteenth century attitudes and customs regarding death and mourning may appear to us to have been excessive, people of that time did have social

---

*Editor's Note: the change in linguistic meaning from "coffin" (the repository of a dead body) to "casket" (the repository of any treasured item to be preserved) signifies a perhaps subtle but powerful change from the connotation of death to that of "preservation" and treasuring.

mechanisms to deal with the inevitable grief of death.

Studies of past mourning customs may not only help us to evolve more useful patterns of behavior to cope with the grief of death, they should also lead to our greater understanding of earlier societies. The mourning customs of nineteenth century America, especially those of the period frequently called Victorian, accurately reflect that society; these customs comprehend the changes in religious thought, the uniquely idealized status of women, the relationship between the sexes and their relative positions in society, and the growing rigidification of social systems of the latter half of the nineteenth century.[28] That social entrenchment probably occurred in response to the increasing turbulence in society characterized by accelerated urbanization, industrialization and immigration.

The rigid guidelines for appropriate mourning behavior deteriorated toward the end of the nineteenth century; etiquette books mentioned ever more frequently the right of people to decide not to go into mourning. Rules for mourning procedures and dress appeared less and less often. By the turn of the century trade catalogues and periodicals devoted much less space to the accoutrements of mourning. The practice of mourning rituals continued, albeit less frequently, until the shattering cataclysm of World War I. Today, the remnants of Victorian mourning practices are seen in an abundance of collected nineteenth century artifacts, and in national public mourning for departed leaders.

Notes

[1]Margaret Mitchell, *Gone With The Wind* (New York: Macmillan, 1936), 122.

[2]See Phillippe Aries, *Western Attitudes Toward Death: From the Middle Ages to the Present* (Baltimore: Johns Hopkins Press, 1974), Chapter III, "Thy Death," 55-82.

[3]Anita Schorsch, *Mourning Becomes America: Mourning Art in the New Nation* (exhibition catalogue, William Penn Memorial Museum, Harrisburg, Pennsylvania, 1976); Betty Ring, "Memorial Embroideries by American Schoolgirls," *The Magazine Antiques* (October, 1971), 570-575; Beatrix T. Rumford, "Memorial Watercolors," *The Magazine Antiques* (October, 1973), 688-695.

[4]William Sidney Mount, autobiographical sketch (The Museums at Stony Brook, Stony Brook, New York).

[5]Mount, catalogue of portraits and paintings (The Museums at Stony Brook, Stony Brook, New York).

[6]Shepard Alonzo Mount, letter to his son William Shepard Mount, May 15, 1868 (The Museums at Stony Brook, Stony Brook, New York).

[7]Louisa May Alcott, *Little Women* (Boston: Little, Brown, 1968), 107.

[8]Stanley French, "The Cemetery as Cultural Institution: The Establishment of Mount Auburn and the 'Rural Cemetery' Movement," in David E. Stannard, ed., *Death In America* (Philadelphia: Univ. of Pennsylvania Press, 1974), 69-91.

[9]Nehemiah Cleaveland, *Green-Wood Illustrated* (New York: R. Martin, 1847), 10.

[10]*Godey's Lady's Magazine* (May, 1844), 244.

[11]Charles William Day, *Hints on Etiquette and the Usages of Society with a Glance at Bad Habits* (New York: A.V. Black, 1844), 76.

[12]*Frank Leslie's Gazette of Fashion and the Beau Monde* (December, 1856), 102.

[13]Mrs. M.S. Rayne, *Gems of Deportment and Hints of Etiquette* (Chicago: Tyler and Co., 1881), 410.

[14]See Barbara Dodd Hillerman, "The Evolution of American 'Widow's Weeds' 1865-1965, A Study in Social History," unpublished master's thesis (Univ. of Maryland, 1972).

[15]Mrs. John Sherwood, *Manners and Social Usage* (New York: Harper & Bros., 1884), 130.

[16]Sherwood, 128.

[17]Sherwood, 130.

[18]Nehemiah Adams, *Agnes and the Key to her Little Coffin* (Boston: S.K. Whipple & Co., 1857), 135.

[19]Sarah Josepha Hale, *Manners, or, Happy Homes and Good Society All the Year Round* (Boston: J.E. Tilton and Co., 1868), 19-20.

[20]Mrs. M.F. Armstrong, *On Habits and Manners* (Hampton, Va.: Normal School Press, 1888), 53.

[21]Robert Tomes, *The Bazar Book of Decorum* (New York: Harper & Bros., 1870), 268-269.

[22]See Ann Douglas, "Heaven Our Home: Consolation Literature in the Northern United States, 1830-1880," in David Stannard, ed. *Death in America* (Philadelphia: Univ. of Pennsylvania Press, 1974), 49-68.

[23]Sherwood, 125.

[24]See Ann Douglas, *The Feminization of American Culture* (New York: Knopf, 1977).

[25]Adams, 15.

[26]Aries, Chapter IV, "Forbidden Death," 85-107.

[27]Aries, 90.

[28]An exhibition, *"A TIME TO MOURN: Expressions of Grief in Nineteenth Century America"*, accompanied by a comprehensive catalogue, was held at The Museums at Stony Brook, Stony Brook, New York, May 24, 1980—November 16, 1980. The exhibition then travelled to the Brandywine River Museum of the Brandywine Conservancy, Chadds Ford, Pennsylvania, where it was exhibited January 17, 1981—May 17, 1981. This article was written when very preliminary research had been carried out on the subject of nineteenth century mourning practices. Exhibition and catalogue were made possible by a generous grant from the National Endowment for the Humanities. The catalogue is available from The Museum Store, The Museums at Stony Brook, Stony Brook, New York 11790.

Gynecological Instruments and Surgical Decisions at a Hospital in Late Nineteenth-Century America

Virginia G. Drachman*

The treatment of women's gynecological diseases changed dramatically in the nineteenth century. Throughout the first half of the century, doctors treating the gynecological problems of their female patients relied primarily on medical therapies such as douches and powders, and mechanical devices such as uterine belts and pessaries.[1] As the century progressed, the treatment of gynecological diseases lay with increasing frequency in the hands of surgeons who, by the last quarter of the century, could perform operations for previosuly incurable female maladies such as uterine tumors and vaginal tears. This rise of gynecological surgery went hand in hand with other developments in medical science. As doctors learned how to dimish pain, control bleeding and avoid infection, surgery became less dangerous and doctors grew less reluctant to attempt previously impossible operations.

The development of surgical technology also encouraged the growth of gynecological surgery.[2] Historians of nineteenth-century gynecology have paid particularly close attention to the role of instruments in the evolution of gynecology from a medical specialty into a surgical specialty. James Ricci, Harold Speert, and most recently Albert Lyons and Joseph Petruceli, for example, offer pictorial histories of gynecology which emphasize the development and use of gynecological instruments.[3] They point to such instruments as the trocars (Fig. 1) doctors employed to excise and remove tumors, the sounds (Fig. 2) they used to stretch the cervix and measure the size of the uterus, and the needles and sutures they used to repair vaginal tears. They use pictures to display the wide variation in knives, scissors, clamps, etc., which became available to nineteenth-century surgeons, and they rely on this visual presentation of the instruments to document the rise of what they see as the relatively steady progress in gynecological surgery throughout the century.

Of course it is important to use pictures so that we may see what the instruments looked like, but what is at issue here is not just their appearance, but their application by physicians who relied on them. To appreciate more fully the development of gynecological instruments, therefore, we must go beyond the context of technological development and look at what the new instruments meant to the doctors who used them. To do this, we need to examine the ways in which doctors actually practiced

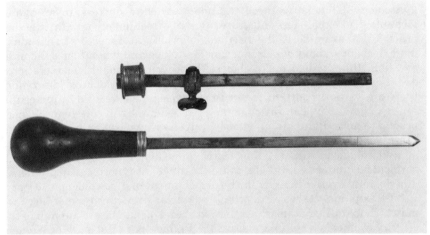

Fig. 1. Trocar

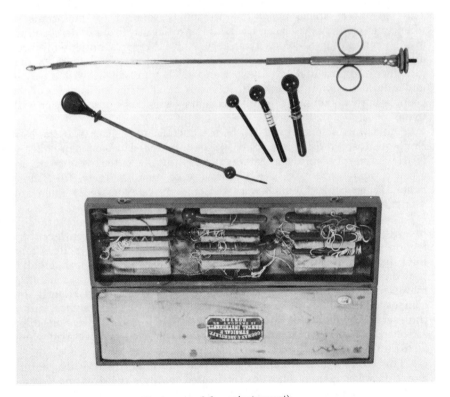

Fig. 2. Uterine sound (lower instrument);
Uterine dilators (center instruments).

gynecology. That is, we need to understand how doctors, in an age of technological expansion, integrated this new technology into their actual practice. For example, as the instruments proliferated, doctors had to make more decisions about which instruments to use and when to use them. In addition, they had to make choices, based on financial considerations, about which instruments to buy. The issue of physicians' discretion, therefore, is an important factor to consider when we study nineteenth-century gynecological instruments. An examination of gynecological practice sheds light on previously impenetrable issues in nineteenth-century medicine: the extent of doctors' reliance on the tools and techniques of gynecological surgery, the degree to which these instruments and surgical techniques were useful in the treatment of gynecological problems, and doctors' overall interest in the development of gynecological surgery.

To examine the ways in which physicians practiced gynecology we may turn to the hospitals where they worked. During the second half of the century, women's hospitals, such as the Philadelphia Hospital for Women, the Women's Hospital in New York City and the Women's Hospital in Chicago were founded to treat the special medical needs of female patients. The records of these hospitals, previously ignored by historians of nineteenth-century gynecology, can add significantly to our understanding of the growth of gynecological surgery. Annual reports, patient's records and physicians' private reports, for example, record doctors' actual practices and patients' actual experiences. They provide us with a way to understand the instruments within the context of the daily lives of the people—both doctors and female patients—who came into contact with them.

Our point of focus here will be the doctors and patients at the New England Hospital for Women and Children. Founded in Boston in 1862, the NEH was one of several contemporary hospitals dedicated to the treatment of sick women. Yet, the NEH was unique among nineteenth-century hospitals because its founders were women, its physicians were women, and its patients were women.

Because the NEH was staffed exclusively by women doctors, this investigation will provide a picture of the way a group of nineteenth-century female physicians practiced gynecology. Although their practices may have differed in some ways from their male colleagues', it is unlikely that they differed sharply, for the medical women at the NEH represented the mainstream of nineteenth-century medical thought. The NEH staff was composed exclusively of doctors who had been trained in regular, rather than sectarian medical schools. Furthermore, their medical decisions often reflected the wisdom of Boston's leading male physicians, several of whom were on the hospital's board of consulting physicians.[5]

The NEH is a particularly good place to study nineteenth-century gynecology because, as a hospital dedicated specifically to treating women, it attracted many patients with female diseases. A random sample of patients entering the hospital between 1872 and 1895 indicates that the majority (54%) of patients throughout the last quarter of the century entered the hospital with gynecological problems.[6] There were fluctuations in the percentages of women with gynecological problems from year to year. In

1875 and again in 1887, for example, almost two-thirds (65% and 62% respectively) of the patients had gynecological problems, while in 1888 and again in 1892 just over half (56% and 54% respectively) of the cases were gynecological.[7] Of course not all patients with gynecological problems were treated surgically. Yet, over time, increasing proportions of women admitted for gynecological problems received surgical treatment. Whereas in 1875 less than a third (29%) of the patients with female diseases were surgical cases, in 1887, 60% of the gynecological cases underwent operations, while only five years later 70% were treated surgically.[8]

The increase in the surgical treatment of patients with gyncological problems at the NEH was accompanied by an overall increase in surgery at the hospital between 1875 and 1900. In 1875 there were only 39 patients who were placed on the surgical ward, while 101 patients—two and half times as many—were treated on the medical ward. As the last quarter of the century progressed, the number and proportion of surgical patients at the NEH steadily increased. In 1879 there were 49 patients on the surgical ward and 109—just over twice as many—on the medical ward. In 1885 there were 125 surgical patients and 195—one and a half times as many—medical patients. Five years later the gap closed. There were 170 patients on the surgical ward and 176 on the medical ward. The numbers of surgical patients continued to keep pace with the numbers of medical patients throughout the last decade of the century.[9]

The increase in gynecological surgery as well as general surgery at the NEH fits the picture Ricci and others give us of the rise of gynecological surgery in the second half of the nineteenth century. At the same time, the types of operations doctors performed as the century drew to a close support their argument that there was significant progress in gynecological surgery during the second half of the century. While doctors at the NEH were operating more often, they were also performing difficult surgical operations more frequently. Abdominal sections, for example, were perhaps the most dangerous of all surgical procedures because of the high risk of infection and hemorrhage. One nineteenth-century physician expressed the sentiment of the medical profession when he declared that abdominal surgery was "an utterly unjustifable operation."[10] The doctors at the NEH performed abdominal sections infrequently until the 1890s. In 1885, for example, the surgeons did a total of three such procedures, one of which ended in the death of the patient. In the last decade of the century, however, they began to perform abdominal sections more frequently and with better results. In 1892, they performed 33 abdominal sections, four of which ended in death. In 1895 they performed 57 abdominal sections, almost twice as many as they had done three years before, but lost only five patients.[11]

While the surgeons at the NEH operated more frequently as the century drew to a close, the new instruments and techniques of gynecological surgery did not give them greater license to operate. Instead, the NEH doctors were always aware of the risks of surgery, and exercised great care and discretion in determining which patients would undergo surgery. They did not operate, for example, when they believed that surgery was unnecessary. In one case a forty-year old housewife from Maine entered the hospital complaining of "inflammation of the vagina." Examination disclosed a tumor in the uterus "the size of two fists or larger." Tumors which were high up in the uterus were extremely dangerous, perhaps impossible to operate on because they were inaccessible without abdominal surgery. This tumor, which was accessible through the vagina, was a surgical risk. Nevertheless, while the tumor was certainly an operable one, the doctors chose not to operate. Instead, they let the patient rest in the hospital for a week and then discharged her. According to the resident physician, this was sufficient treatment. "The rest here," she explained, "caused [the] patient to feel much less pain and discomfort than usual, and she went away feeling much better than before."[12]

In another case, the surgeons refused to operate because they believed that surgery was useless. A thirty-four year-old housewife from Massachusetts entered the NEH with a cancer in her breast which had spread thoughout her body. "The patient is very weak and suffers intensely," wrote the resident physician on the day of admission. The patient's condition deteriorated over the next few days, and when she became "too feeble to talk much," the doctors decided that she was too weak to survive an operation. "The patient begged very hard to be operated upon," wrote the resident physician, "even when told that she could not in all probability survive the operation." Despite the patient's pleadings for an operation and despite the technological advances at the doctors' fingertips, the doctors believed that surgery was useless and discharged the patient as "incurable." She died four days later at home.[13]

In difficult cases, the doctors operated only after seeking advice from the hospital's board of consulting physicians. The doctors who comprised this board were among Boston's most respected and powerful male physicians. They gave the NEH doctors crucial support at a time when women doctors were viewed with suspicion and hostility. The doctors at the hospital valued the opinions of their consulting physicians highly and turned to them when they felt in need of medical advice.

In 1874, for example, a thirty-nine year-old housewife from Massachusetts entered the hospital complaining of severe abdominal pain. Examination disclosed a large tumor in the abdomen. Since abdominal surgery was so dangerous, the doctors sought the advice of their consulting physicians, Drs. Samuel Cabot and Henry Bowditch, before deciding on a course of treatment. After several consultations, they decided to do a surgical procedure to remove fluid from the tumor. They inserted an aspirator (Fig. 3), an instrument which performed like a pump, through the vagina into the uterus and withdrew over 180 ounces of fluid from the tumor. The "patient bore the operation well," wrote the resident physician. Unfortunately the procedure was of little therapeutic value because the tumor was malignant. Realizing that they had exhausted the available technology and reached the limits of their ability to deliver safe surgical treatment the doctors discharged the patient as "incurable."[14]

The discretion the physicians used in deciding when to operate helps us to understand the low mortality among the patients who underwent surgery. The annual reports of the hospital reveal that the surgeons had a remarkably good record for gynecological surgery. In 1885, for example, of the fifty patients treated surgically for gynecological diseases, 64% (32) were

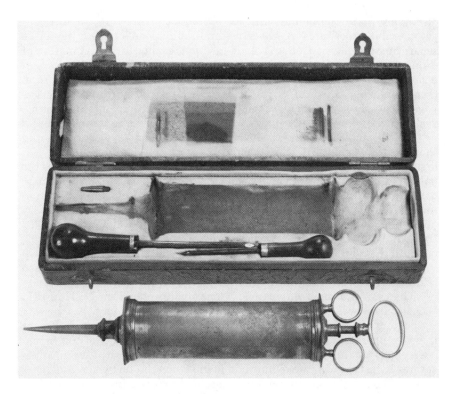

Fig. 3. Aspirator

discharged "well" and another 32% (16) went home "convalescent." The remaining 4% (2) went home "unimproved." There were no deaths—at least in the hospital.[15] This trend prevailed throughout the decade. In 1888, of the 101 gynecological patients on the surgical ward, over 82% had successful recoveries, while another 5% were "improved." Six percent (6) were unimproved, and 4% (4) died.[16] In 1892, 92% (159) of the patients undergoing surgery for gynecological problems were "cured," 1% (2) were "improved," 4% (7) were still recuperating in the hospital at the end of the year, and 3% (5) had died.[17] The sample of surgical patients revealed a similar trend. The overwhelming majority (64%) went home "well" or "improved" and another 28% went home "convalescent." Again, there were no hospital deaths. In general, when patients died as a result of gynecological surgery, it was usually because the doctors had made the choice to perform a particularly hazardous operation. In 1890, for example, nine of the ten patients who died in surgery had undergone abdominal hysterectomies or operations to remove uterine tumors.[18] Clearly, the low mortality in surgical cases at the NEH depended as much on doctors' diagnostic skills and ability to choose correctly when to use surgical instruments as it did on the availablilty of the instruments themselves.

Once the doctors made the decision to operate the surgical procedures seemed to go routinely. Two cases, one of a patient with a vesico-vaginal fistula and the other of a patient with a uterine tumor, illustrate the discretion, instruments and surgical techniques involved in two difficult, yet operable procedures. A vesico-vaginal fistula was a tear in the tissue separating the vagina from the bladder which resulted in a constant flow of urine through the vagina. They were a common result of long deliveries or of poor obstetrical care, and many nineteenth-century women suffered from them, enduring constant physical as well as social horrors. "A vesico-vaginal fistula is the greatest misfortune that can happen to a woman," declared one nineteenth-century physician. "The urine constantly flow[s] into the vagina,... runs down the labia, perineum, and over the nates and thighs," he explained, "producing a most intolerable stench. An insupportable itching and burning sensation," he continued, "tortures the patient. The comfort of a clean bed,... is not their lot, for it will soon be drenched with urine. The air of the room of the unfortunate woman nauseates the visitor, and drives him off. She sits," he concluded, "solitary and alone, in the cold, on a perforated chair. This is not fiction, but naked truth; and the cure for such an evil is the prize for which we labor."[19] In 1852, a South Carolina physician named James Marion Sims developed a surgical method of repairing vesico-vaginal fistulas. His success promised relief to many nineteenth-century women.[20]

The case of a nineteen year-old woman who entered the NEH in 1874 because urine was constantly escaping from her vagina describes the way the doctors repaired a vesico-vaginal fistula. The patient's record indicates that the operation was routine and successful. "The edges of the fistula [were] excised ... and the wound brought together with seven silver sutures," the type of sutures Sims had found so successful twenty five years earlier. Then "a flexible catheter with a rubber tube was introduced into the urethra so that urine could pass through it." The patient recovered easily from the surgery and slept comfortably, apparently without pain. She remained in the hospital for several weeks, making relatively steady improvement. A week after the operation, the sutures and catheter were removed and the fistula was found to be "entirely closed." Three weeks later she was discharged "well."[21]

Of course not all operations to repair vesico-vaginal fistulas were so successful. A twenty-nine year-old Irish domestic was a less fortunate patient. She endured two operations, neither of which fully repaired her fistula.[22] Unfortunately, it is difficult to determine either the total number of operations performed at the NEH from 1875 to 1900 for repair of vesico-vaginal fistulas or their outcomes. But of the six operations performed between 1887 and 1889, four were successful, and none ended in death.[23]

Surgical removal of uterine tumors occurred more frequently, but with less favorable results. Between 1882 and 1889, thirty-one such operations were performed. Of the fourteen operations performed between 1887 and 1889, seven were successful, and three ended in death.[24] The case record of a thirty-nine year-old dressmaker provides a description of one such operation. The patient entered the hospital complaining of a painful and offensive vaginal discharge which had been diagnosed by another physician as "catarrh of the womb," a non-specific inflammation of the uterus. Upon examination, the NEH doctor discovered a "fleshy, fibrous tumor" protruding from the uterus. The tumor, accessible through the vagina, was operable.

The patient record describes the instruments and procedures of the operation. First, the pedicle, or stem of the tumor "was partially severed by means of [an] ecraseur," an instrument consisting of a steel chain which was maneuvered around the tumor and then tightened forcefully to cut the growth (Fig. 5). The surgeon then carefully inserted a curved scissors into the vagina, using the "fingers of [her] left hand . . . to guard [the] points of [the] scissors," and cut the tumor completely (Fig. 4). Finally a forceps was introduced and "applied to [the] tumor [which was] removed by traction outwards and upwards (Fig. 4). During this final stage of the procedure, the patient suffered a "slight laceration of the perineum." She recovered from the surgery but was "very weak." She was discharged four weeks later "convalescent."[25]

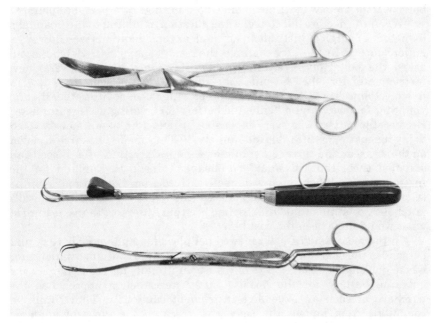

Fig. 4. Polyp forceps remover (top)   Remover (center)   Uterine pedicle scissors (lower)

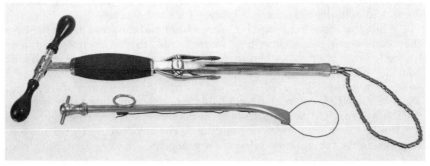

Fig. 5 Ecraseurs

As these two cases illustrate the NEH physicians used their surgical instruments with a strong mixture of discretion and skill. Indeed the history of surgical practice at the hospital supports the relationship Ricci and others have described between the developement of surgical instruments and the growth of gynecological surgery. But while Ricci and others argue that the proliferation and refinement of gynecological instruments were central to the rise of gynecological surgery, the situation seemed otherwise at the NEH. Despite the enormous increase in surgical practice at the hospital, the NEH physicians faced serious financial constraints which prevented them from acquiring the newest instruments as they became available. It was not until 1878, for example, that the board of physicians, which determined medical policy at the hospital, invested in a pair of forceps for the maternity ward. Until then, the doctors had been satisfied to borrow from the few staff members who had their own personal pairs.[26]

When the doctors did consider the question of adding to the hospital's inventory of surgical instruments, financial considerations were always a major concern. In 1887, for example, the resident physician, Helen Bissell, asked the board of physicians to allocate money to buy several new instruments for the hospital including an "ecraseur for use in hysterectomies", a "Clover Ether Inhaler which uses so little ether that no vomiting follows," and a "galvanic battery for treating uterine fibroids." Because the battery was "very expensive," the doctors "unanimously voted to lay the matter on the table indefinitely."[27] They made a positive decision on the ecraseur and clover ether inhaler a month later only after Bissell had satisfied them that "it would be cheaper to send to England for the instruments."[28] When the instruments arrived from London four months later, Dr. Bissell proudly emphasized the economy of the hospital's purchase explaining that "the cost had been but little more than one third of what would have been the cost here."[29]

In the meantime Bissell renewed her pleas for a galvanic battery and persuaded the board of physicians that "the hospital contained patients for whom one should be used."[30] While the board finally agreed to purchase a galvanic battery for the hospital, they nevertheless approached the purchase of such an expensive instrument cautiously. They formed a committee from among themselves to research the types of galvanic batteries and their costs. Two months later, upon the committee's recommendation, they decided to purchase one similar to "those in use in other hospitals" at a cost of $150.[31] Overall, it had taken over six months from the time Dr. Bissell first raised the subject of a galvanic battery for the doctors to actually order such a battery for the hospital.

While the doctors exercised the same financial conservatism whenever they considered purchasing new instruments, they were not always so interested in economy. Rather, their interest in economy waned when they considered a topic of greater importance to them—construction of a new surgical building. By the last decade of the nineteenth-century, the surgical ward of the NEH was no longer adequate to accommodate the increasing numbers of surgical patients. In 1893 the doctors made their first public plea for funds for a new surgical building. "The need of new and modern arrangements for surgery is now very urgent," the resident physician explained in her annual report. "The work of the surgical department has developed most rapidly during the past few years," she continued, "but to hold the reputation they have gained, our surgeons should be enabled to work under the best possible advantages which means that they should be provided with a new surgical pavilion."[32]

The Board of Directors, which had to approve major projects such as this, expressed a willingness to construct a new surgical building, but only when sufficient funds were guaranteed. The doctors, who were always cautious about expenses when considering the purchase of instruments, disapproved of the directors' financial conservatism. Dr. Marie Zakrezewska, the hospital's founder and central figure since its inception, expressed the concerns of the entire medical staff in an angry letter to the treasurer of the hospital, explaining that the hospital could lose all four of its surgeons if they were not promised better surgical facilities. "Dr. Keller remains with us only by our urgent appeal," she explained. "Dr. Berlin . . . has a large practice as a surgeon and can accommodate all her patients [elsewhere]. . . . Drs. Smith and Culbertson," she continued, "I fear will resign because they cannot be expected by the directors to work so hard . . . under such conditions in which they have to work." Without its surgeons, Zakrzewska continued, the hospital would lose the solid reputation it had built for itself. "Now you want to crush what we have gained, by an unwise retarding of what is absolutely necessary," she charged. "All right, go on and we must go on also, by taking patients to private hospitals."[33] Despite Zakrzewska's strong attack, the directors firmly refused to agree to build new surgical facilities until sufficient funds were available.

The doctors must have been especially frustrated by the directors' strong stand because these years witnessed a major expansion of the NEH in other directions. Funds were promised to the NEH for a new maternity building and a new dispensary, the former opening in 1893 and the latter in 1896. While construction on the maternity building and dispensary was underway, the doctors continued to pressure the directors for a new surgical building. In 1895 they sent the directors a formal position paper explaining the reasons for the "imperative need of a proper surgical building."[34] At the same time, they continued their appeals to the public for money. "The much needed and long-anticipated Surgical Pavilion still remains an unachieved desire," they explained in the annual report of 1895, "and must remain so until the sum required for its erection flows into the treasury."[35]

In 1898, when the $40,000 needed for construction was finally raised, the directors laid the cornerstone of the new surgical building. In announcing the event to the public, the secretary of the hospital briefly summarized the internal struggle that had preceded the building of this pavilion. "For years our surgeons have been patiently waiting for a suitable place in which to work. . . . In spite of the caution of a conservative though wise Finance Committee, which has constantly counselled, 'Wait!' the Surgical Building Fund has grown large enough to cover the cost of building."[36] Construction was completed within a year, and the surgical building of the NEH was formally opened on May 19, 1900. The new surgical building took its place alongside the hospital's new maternity building and dispensary. From the Directors' point of view, the allocation of funds for its construction signalled their understanding and acceptance of the important role surgical medicine would play at the hospital in the future. From the doctors' point of view, the new surgical building stood as a symbol of the hospital's commitment to surgery, and insured that the NEH would keep pace with the new directions of modern medicine.

The quarter century preceding the opening of the new surgical building demonstrated the hospital's need for more surgical facilities: During this twenty-five-year period, surgical practice dramatically increased at the hospital, the numbers of successful operations rose steadily as did the number of major operations. This rise in surgery at the NEH fits the picture historians have painted of the rapidly developing field of gynecological surgery in the second half of the nineteenth century. Yet, the pattern of surgical growth at the NEH deviates from this picture somewhat, for the rise of gynecological surgery at the hospital was not accompanied by a rapid accumulation of gynecological instruments. Rather, the NEH doctors accumulated surgical instruments gradually over time. They approached the acquisition of new instruments carefully, always considering their cost and seeking the most economical means of purchase.

This slow and cautious accumulation of surgical instruments at the NEH indicates that the instruments played an integral but not the central role in the rise of gynecological surgery at the hospital. Perhaps more significant in setting the pattern of gynecological surgery at the NEH were the decisions—previously uncharted by historians—which doctors made regarding what operations to perform and when. They had to determine which patients could benefit from surgery and which ones could not. They had to recognize what operations they could perform and what operations were too difficult and beyond their technical expertise. The availability of gynecological instruments certainly allowed the doctors at the NEH to offer better medical care. Yet, it was the doctors' ability to make correct decisions about when to use these instruments which ultimately determined the quality of medical care at the NEH.

Notes

[1]Pessaries were inserted into the uterus to correct a displacement of the uterus. For a discussion of uterine displacements and their use see Jonathan Henry Robinson, *A Short treatise on Prolapsus Uteri, with Some Remarks on the Various Kinds of Instruments Hitherto Employed in its Cure; Also a full description of Dr. Robinson's Improved Uterine Supporter, an instrument highly approved of by the Medical Profession* (Boston: John B. Hall's Steam Press, 186?) For a description of a particular uterine supporter see *Dr. Thompson's Uterine Truss* (Columbus: Wright and Legg, 1843).

[2]The growth of gynecological surgery went hand in hand with the rise of obstetrics and the development of obstetrical instruments. This paper will focus specifically on gynecology and its instruments. For a discussion of the transition from midwifery to obstetrics and the development of obstetrical instruments see Jane B. Donegan, *Women and Men Midwives: Medicine, Morality, and Misogyny in Early America* (Westport: Greenwood Press, 1978). See also Richard W. Wertz and Dorothy C. Wertz, *Lying-In: A History of Childbirth in America* (New York: The Free Press, 1977).

[3]James V. Ricci, M.D., *The Development of Gynecological Surgery and Instruments: A Comprehensive Review of the Evolution of Surgery and Surgical Instruments for the Treatment of Female Diseases from the Hippocratic Age to the Antiseptic Period* (Philadelphia: The Blakiston Co, 1949); Harold Speert, M.D., *Iconographia Gyniatrica: A Pictorial History of*

Obstetrics and Gynecology (Philadelphia: F.A. David, 1973), Albert Lyons and Joseph R. Petrucelli, *Medicine: An Illustrated History* (New York: Abrams, Inc., 1978).

[4]All pictures are of instruments in the collection of the Warren Anatomical Museum of the Harvard Medical School, Boston, Mass.

[5]The maternity ward of the NEH, for example, was partially supported by an annual grant of $1,000 from the Boston Lying-In Hospital Corporation. One historian has concluded that the NEH had a better medical record than other Boston hospitals because its doctors were women. See Laurie Crumpacker, "Female Patients in Four Boston Hospitals of the 1890s," paper delivered at the Berkshire Conference on the History of Women, October 26, 1974.

[6]In order to select a sample, I employed a table of random numbers. The patient records are in the New England Hospital Collection, Countway Library, Harvard University, Boston, Mass.

[7]Calculated from NEH Annual Reports.

[8]Calculated from NEH Annual Reports.

[9]Calculated from NEH Annual Reports.

[10]Speert, *A Pictorial History of Obstetrics and Gynecology*, p. 482.

[11]Calculated from NEH Annual Reports.

[12]Patient Record 38, November 18, 1880, Surgical Ward, NEH Collection, Countway Library, Boston, Mass.

[13]Patient Record 51, November 15, 1880, Surgical Ward, NEH Collection, Countway Library, Boston, Mass.

[14]Patient Record 44, October 3, 1874, Surgical Ward, NEH Collection, Countway Library, Boston, Mass.

[15]Calculated from NEH Annual Report, 1885.

[16]Calculated from NEH Annual Report, 1888.

[17]Calculated from NEH Annual Report, 1892.

[18]Calculated from NEH Annual Report, 1890.

[19]Harvey Graham, *Eternal Eve: The History of Gynecology and Obstetrics* (Garden City: Doubleday Co., 1951), p. 440.

[20]For a critical discussion of James Marion Sims see G.J. Barker-Benfield, *The Horrors of the Half-Known Life: Male Attitudes toward Women and Sexuality in Nineteenth-Century America* (New York: Harper & Row, 1976).

[21]Patient Record 8, February 5, 1874), Surgical Ward, NEH Collection, Countway Library, Boston, Mass.

[22]Patient Record 17, May 31, 1878, Surgical Ward, NEH Collection, Countway Library, Boston, Mass.

[23]Calculated from the NEH Annual Reports, 1887-1889.

[24]Calculated from NEH Annual Reports, 1882-1889.

[25]Patient record 34, July 31, Surgical Ward, NEH Collection, Countway Library, Boston, Mass.

[26]Minutes of Board of Physicians Meetings, Volume I, p. 40, May 26, 1878 in NEH Collection, Sophia Smith Archives, Smith College, Northampton, Mass.

[27]Minutes of Board of Physicians Meetings, Volume II, p 153, Oct. 7, 1887, in NEH Collection, Sophia Smith Archives, Smith College, Northampton, Mass.

[28]Minutes of Board of Physicians Meetings, Volume II, pp. 155-156, November 4, 1887, in NEH Collection, Sophia Smith Archives, Smith College, Northampton, Mass.

[29]Minutes of Board of Physicians Meetings, Volume III, p. 5, February 3, 1888 in NEH Collection, Sophia Smith Archves, Smith College, Northampton, Mass.

[30]Minutes of Board of Physicians Meetings, Volume III, p. 3, January 6, 1888 in NEH Collection, Sophia Smith Archives, Smith College, Northampton, Mass.

[31]Minutes of Board of Physicians Meetings, Volume III, p. 7, March 2, 1888, in NEH Collection, Sophia Smith Archives, Smith College, Northampton, Mass.

[32]Annual Report of the New England Hospital for Women and Children, Boston: George E. Ellis, 1893, pp. 13-14.

[33]Marie Zakrzewska to Goddard, June 6, 1893 in NEH Collection, Sophia Smith Archives, Smith College, Northampton, Mass.

[34]Statement in Regard to Need of a New Surgical Building, adopted by Physicians in meeting of June 7, 1895 in NEH Collection, Sophia Smith Archive, Northampton, Mass.

[35]Annual Report of the New England Hospital for Women and Children, Boston: George E. Ellis, 1895, p. 9.

[36]Annual Report of the New England Hospital for Women and Children, Boston: George E. Ellis, 1900, p. 9.

*I would like to thank David Gunner for allowing me to use the collection of surgical instruments at the Warren Anatomical Museum of the Harvard Medical School and for photographing the instruments, Audrey Davis for advice in the earliest stages of research, Joyce Antler for her comments on an earlier draft of this paper, and Douglas Jones for his careful readings and helpful suggestions.

This essay is drawn partially from materials collected while the author was a fellow in the Division of Medical Sciences at the Smithsonian Institution in 1975-76, during her tenure on a Rockefeller Foundation Humanities Fellowship, 1977-78, and as a fellow at the Bunting Institute of Radcliffe College, 1978-79.

Feminine Marks on the Landscape: An Atlanta Inventory

Darlene Roth

It is the rule of architecture to glorify the builder of buildings, the rule of economics to glorify the owner of them. Seldom is either party female; yet women are great consumers of buildings, inspirers of them, designers of them, even owners of them. Women's organizations are seldom taken in this context. In every community in America there are structures on the landscape which are the result of collective female efforts and testimony to what women's organizations think of their communities and how they perceive their role in them—schools, orphanages, libraries, parks, clinics, gardens, social and recreational centers, monuments, memorials, club houses, headquarters buildings, and similar institutions. Taken together and in proper sequence, these structures begin to reveal not only patterns of cultural function and values peculiar to women's organizations, but also a special chronology of city-building among American women which has been overlooked.[1]

While numerous patterns can be discerned in women's city-building, three major patterns are of concern here because they appear to be common to the general American culture: the erection of historic monuments and preservation of historic houses, the purchase of buildings for philanthropic uses, and the creation of organizational headquarters. It is my purpose to identify these patterns, to discuss their social functioning, and to give examples of each from a single landscape, that of Atlanta, Georgia, from the end of the Civil War to the outbreak of World War II.

The first and oldest pattern is the most prosaic, the most expected of women and, in some respects, the most southern pattern of the three. It reflects woman's role as "culture-bearer" and "culture-preserver" and has two components: 1) those memorials and monuments erected by women to honor dead heroes (and occasionally heroines) and to mark great historical events, and 2) those house museums and other mausoleums preserved to honor dead heroes (rarely heroines) and mark great historical events.

Since 1858, when South Carolinian Ann Pamela Cunningham established the Mt. Vernon Ladies' Association of the Union, southern women especially have been involved in all aspects of historic and cultural preservation—from the restoration of architectural masterpieces to the collection of historic documents, from the creation of patriotic societies for the reclamation of ancestors to the erection of every kind of enshrinement to their past.

In Atlanta, women spearheaded, inspired, financed or otherwise participated in the erection of a host of such monuments, beginning with the Confederate Memorial in 1873, a 65-foot, granite shaft raised in Oakland Cemetery by the Atlanta Ladies Memorial Association for the Confederate dead (Fig. 1). Other monuments followed: a copy of the Lion of Lucerne on the same cemetery grounds raised by the same organization 20 years later for the "unknown" dead; bronze markers placed at the entrance of the State Capitol by the United Daughters of the Confederacy to tell the saga of the Battle of Atlanta, and a peace monument raised in Piedmont Park by the Daughters of the American Revolution, the Gate City Guard, and other interested parties to commemorate post-Civil War national good will (in 1910!). World War I was commemorated by the Pershing Point Memorial, erected by the Service Star Legion and the Fulton County War Mothers (Fig. 2). This is the last war monument erected by a women's organization in the city, but not the last war memorial to be completed with women's support.

That distinction belongs to the largest confederate monument in the city, the Stone Mountain Memorial, the idea for which originated simultaneously in several different places. One was the Atlanta Chapter of the United Daughters of the Confederacy (UDC). Its founder, Mrs. C. Helen Plane, broached the idea to the local daughters—who favored it, of course, carried it through state convention, and on to the national convention, where it was adopted in 1915 as a project of the entire federation. The monument was plagued by scandal and tragedy for the more than 50 years it took to build, and the UDC's original influence over it was absorbed by the Stone Mountain Memorial Association, a male-dominated body. The UDC, however, never stopped supporting the endeavor which is now known as one of Atlanta's most famous landmarks and Georgia's answer to Mt. Rushmore.

The need to commemorate those who died in service to the common good is universal, but in America the expression of honor has been stronger among the vanquished than among the victors. The war memorial business thrived in the South, especially between 1870 and 1920; it was so good, in fact, that several artisans made a living specializing in just such community memorials as the UDC erected. Every courthouse square in every county in every state of the old Confederacy is marked by a statue of "Johnny Reb" or other reminders of the days when southern knighthood was allegedly in flower.[2]

The planting of trees as historic memorials became almost a standardized form of women's organizational behavior. Women's groups planted trees; Girl Scouts planted trees. In Atlanta, tree-planting became a veritable obsession as thousands were put out in the ground for every conceivable purpose. Memorial trees lined the Stone Mountain Highway and the Jefferson Davis Highway; they were placed in groves in Piedmont Park to honor mayors and authors and war heroes, made to stand in solitary splendor in school yards to do the same. President McKinley was honored with a tree, simply because he once said, "Every soldier's grave made during our unfortunate Civil War is a tribute to American valor."[3] His tree was planted in 1922. Only the marked trees have survived as living testimonies; the others have long since disappeared into the landscape, as the authors' grove in Piedmont Park, now indistinguishable from any other

Fig. 1 The first memorial erected by an Atlanta women's organization, a granite shaft placed in Oakland Cemetery by the Ladies Memorial Association.

stand of trees.

The second component of this pattern of culture "bearing" is apparent in the abundant numbers of house museums supported by women everywhere. From Mt. Vernon and the Sulgrave Manor (George Washington's ancestral home in England*) to the "Mt. Vernon" of the black race, "Cedar Hill," the home of Frederick Douglass in Washington, D.C.— all were preserved by women's groups.

The first local Atlanta effort appeared in 1909 with the move to save the Wren's Nest, Joel Chandler Harris' home. A committee of women was formed because the men were too busy to fund-raise. This body, known originally as the "Uncle Remus Memorial Association," gained title to the Harris farm in 1913 and has run it ever since. In accordance with the best female memorial philosophy, this museum is not only a monument "to genius" but also a monument "to the domestic virtues, a guarantee of the world's respect for faithful married love and for the hearthstones of the world."[4]

Cultural preservation of this kind continues, obviously, and to the Wren's Nest may be added the birthplace of Martin Luther King, Jr., as its latest manifestation in Atlanta. House museum work has been dominated by women throughout the country. Women's changing roles in historic preservation in general, in the face of growing professionalization of the field and the availability of additional public funds for its support, is an interesting story in itself, but a peripheral one to that of female patterns of city-building. While memorialization is the most usual reason for women's organizations to concern themselves with some aspect of architectural creation, the second and third patterns of women's involvement in city architecture, philanthropy and the creation of organizational buildings, engaged women's groups more directly. Philanthropic buildings—the creation of structures for others such as orphans and indigents—came first. In Atlanta, these appeared in the latter half of the nineteenth century and the first two decades of the twentieth. Later, women created structures such as organizational headquarters and club houses for themselves. The club houses began appearing in 1910, but occurred on the city landscape with greater speed and frequency in the 1920s.

Unfortunately, in Atlanta it is almost impossible to document the earlier philanthropic structures—the orphanages, nursery schools, kindergartens, old ladies' homes, poor houses, girls' clubs—which the women built between 1880 and 1920. Not a single structure remains intact in its original form and location. What remains in the record, however, is illustrative on two important points—the locations of these buildings, and their general character.

The marginality of the women's clientele was reflected in the marginal locations of the charitable institutions. In 1890, for instance, the Home of the Women's Christian Association (Baptist) was located in the old commercial section of Atlanta, on the far western edge next to the railroad

*Editor's Note: Sulgrave Manor is permanently endowed by the National Society of the Colonial Dames of America. Presidential homes such as Jefferson's Monticello and Andrew Jackson's Hermitage were also purchased and maintained by women's organizations.

tracks, while the Home for the Friendless was located actually inside the railroad gulch in a kind of no-man's land. At the same time the Home for the Incurables rented a house in a new downtown section—abandoned for commercial interest—then moved to more convenient quarters, located (somewhat morbidly) one block from Oakland Cemetery. No organization had more difficulty getting located than did Florence Critenden. After many false starts, it settled "permanently" on the old city dump in 1892, but with continued vandalism, vigilante threats, and petitions for its closure from "concerned" citizens and clergy, the Home offered no clear refuge for many years.

Other organizations such as the settlement houses and orphanages were more compatible with their neighbors. Probably the best illustration of this is the Leonard Street Orphanage, which enjoyed a mutually beneficial relationship with Spelman College for many years. As long as Spellman College ran an elementary school (until 1928), the residents of Leonard School, just next door, could attend classes free and enjoy the "protection of a private school."[5] When the orphanage closed in 1935 its building was sold to Spelman, and the College continued to use it as a nursery for neighborhood children until World War II (Fig. 3).

Regarding the general size and appearance of any of these early institutions there is little remaining evidence, but most were homes or home-like structures. The Florence Crittendon Home, with 38 rooms, was probably the largest single institution built at this time by the local women.[6] The Carrie Steele Logan Orphanage, the first black orphanage in the city, had room for 50 children. Described as a three-story brick building on a stone foundation, it was built for $5000 in 1890.[7] By contrast the first Home for Incurables was a "dingy little weatherbeaten cottage...near the very heart" of the city, which held (either at one time or altogether) 27 patients.[8] The Leonard Street Orphanage building is as instructive as any; its second structure (Fig. 3) was erected in 1916. Although it has been completely remodeled and enlarged to suit other academic purposes, it still gives the impression (especially from the front) of being an attractive home-like place. Its homey atmosphere, in fact, was a source of considerable early pride in the place.[9]

A "homey" atmosphere was an essential ingredient to these operations, and as they became larger and more institutionalilized, often unusual measures were taken to try to preserve that sense of home. The much overgrown Home for the Friendless in 1930, now heavily subsidized by the city, was reorganized and rebuilt to become "Hillside Cottages." The President that year reported on the eight cottages making up the institution; each one is a "home," she affirmed,

a complete unit caring for twenty children and two matrons and approximates a simple family home. No servants are employed but all the work done by the matrons and children, each child, thereby learning to become a useful member of his own future home.[10]

Twenty children (almost certainly of the same sex) and two "mothers" do, however, make a curious home.

Of all the early philanthropic groups, the organization with the greatest demand for facilities and the most complex needs for space was the

Fig. 3 The second building used by the Leonard Street Orphanage, built in 1916, now used by Spelman College for offices and schoolrooms.

YWCA. Within three years of its founding in 1901, the Atlanta YWCA was running a combination gymnasium-staff office-placement center-meeting room-chapel out of the second floor of a downtown commercial building. In the mid-1920s, the YW had two program buildings (one white, one black), a large boarding house, and a camp in the north Georgia woods. From the first, the YWCA has had one of the largest investments in properties of widely varying sorts, the largest number of real estate holdings per se, of any organization in the city. It is to be regretted that not one brick or board remains of any of its earliest establishments.

The relocation, transformation and ultimate disappearance of the buildings associated with the early women's charities speak eloquently of the fundamental changes which occurred in women's public activities at this time, in Atlanta as elsewhere. Not only is the demise—or in some cases the professionalization—of small-scale female philanthropy suggested thereby, so is quite a conspicuous loss of female public visibility. The lady philanthropists, once those who administered charity, became its mere supporters, its gray ladies, and fund-raisers. Their private, personalized delivery system had become dysfunctional among large scale organizations, and the women turned to another metaphorical "home."

While cultural and historic commemoration represents a more or less permanent, feminized, social concern, the shift from constituent-oriented structures to member-oriented structures represents a major change in women's organized activities nationally.

The drive for women's organizations to own their own club houses was described by one astute observer of twentieth century women's affairs as a "major modern movement" among clubwomen—"major" because it commanded a large percentage of organizational energies and funds and "modern" because it emerged in full strength after World War I.[11]

The club house was intended to do more than provide administrative and meeting space; it was to be a true "home"—but with a difference. In this home the wife was the guest; in the club house she had

shelter and living conditions that [were] comfortable and private—where a woman may have a 'room of her own' where she may exercise hospitality without the burden of preparation.[12]

The gentleman's club, with its facilities for lodging, refreshment, entertainment, and respite, was an obvious model for these club houses; so was the house museum, with its antique furniture, plaques and markers, and collections of commemorative memorabilia. So, however, was the home itself; in fact, most of the women's club houses were converted residences.

By 1940 at least half of the federated women's clubs in the state of Georgia had their own clubhouses, including the Atlanta Women's Club and suburban clubs in the neighborhoods of West End, Grant Park and Capitol Hill, as well as nearby Decatur and College Park. This number did not include the Atlanta Section of the National Council of Jewish Women, the United Daughters of the Confederacy, and both chapters of the Daughters of the American Revolution (DAR), all of which also had clubhouses.

The Atlanta Woman's Club building, while not the first woman's clubhouse acquired by an Atlanta organization, is still one of the most attractive and most informative as a "type" of building owned by women's groups (Fig. 4). The club purchased its house at 1150 Peachtree Street in 1920 for a variously quoted price (somewhere between $32,500 and $40,000). The house was originally designed after a French chateau by Atlanta architect Walter T. Downing in 1898 for the Wimbish family, who were well known in elite social circles. The club added much to the original structure to make it more suitable for club needs and aspirations: a commercial kitchen and banquet hall (for club dinners, special occasions, and a public tearoom), a swimming pool (an unintegrated "public" recreation facility), and an auditorium (equipped with acoustics to augment the female voice and a skylight which could be opened for natural lighting for daytime meetings). At the time the clubhouse was acquired, the Atlanta Woman's Club had hundreds of members and a master plan for the building's development which set the Club's property investments at well over a quarter of a million dollars.[13]

The interior of the clubhouse was outfitted with fine furnishings, most of them the gifts of members, and it was glowingly described by its president in 1940:

With its commodious entrance, living room, library, palm room, sun parlor, office, art gallery, spacious banquet hall, beautiful auditorium, and swimming pool, newly decorated during the past two years, this club home is a marvelously adaptable one, and so pleasing in architecture that there is not a woman in the club who is not proud to say "MY CLUB" and happy and anxious to share it with her friends.[14]

There was a tendency in the patriotic societies for the museum aspects of female city-building to come together with the other clubhouse aspects, as is illustrated in Atlanta by the chapter house for the Joseph Habersham Chapter of the DAR. Their building, "Habersham Hall," was intended to be a copy of the Savannah home of the Revolutionary War hero after whom the chapter was named. The exterior of the building resembles a residence, but the interior is designed expressly for meeting and entertaining. The clubhouse of the second Atlanta DAR chapter also has an exterior reminiscent of a residence, a functional interior design *and* a museum on the second floor.

There were no clubhouses in the Atlanta black community until 1947, though there were many plans and ideas for them. Even so small an organization as the elite Chautauqua Circle, a literary and social organization, dreamed of someday owning a "Greek colonial, white-columned" architectural beauty. For a long time the only exclusively female meeting space in black Atlanta was the Phillis Wheatley branch building of the YWCA; otherwise clubwomen met in homes, in churches, and in fraternal lodge buildings. In 1947 the Atlanta Federation of Colored Women's Clubs obtained a site near Atlanta University on Raymond Street (Fig. 5). On it was a residential structure which, like the other organization buildings, was adapted for club use.

As a rule, all of the structures associated with female city-building do not do much glorification of either the builders or the owners. Few are architecturally significant; many are, in fact, architecturally anonymous. The more public the structure, the further removed it is from the identity of

Fig. 4 The Atlanta Woman's Club building, occupied first by the Club in 1920, built originally for a wealthy Atlanta family in 1898

Fig. 5 The site of the Atlanta Federation of Colored Women's Clubs, bought by the Federation in 1947, now abandoned.

the organization which erected it or owns it. For example, the memorials, which signify a cause, hero, ideal, or other element external to the organization do not connote the organization itself. Yet those properties closest to the organizations, i.e., the clubhouses, are themselves not unequivocal statements of identity. The buildings do not reflect much, immediately, beyond the implicit value of the respective organizational pocketbooks and preference for location. There is little architectural symbolism or exterior decoration to convey any unique qualities about the organizations, since most clubhouses have only detached, discrete signs to announce their ownership. Few have ever had lettering actually fixed to the building facades to tell the club name. The best example of architectural personalization is the iron railing on the Joseph Habersham DAR chapter house, which inscribes "JHC" (for the chapter) in graceful but barely perceptible configurations on the balustrades and windows (Fig. 6). It is the ultimate in feminine modesty.

Fig. 6 Detail of the balustrade railing of the Joseph Habersham DAR Chapter House showing the initials of the organization.

If these buildings and structures lack significance as individual architectural statements, they do not lack significance as collective social statements. As either accolades to masculine achievements or as varieties of "home" located in or near residential areas, they are an extension of the cult of domesticity itself. Female city-building has not yet been industrial, military, governmental or commercial, but it has certainly been philanthropic. It has also been feminized in the extreme—an institutional testimony to the culture of separate spheres, when even the public activities of women took place in homelike settings. Furthermore, in their declining state (none of these buildings is in good physical condition; some have already been abandoned), they are a testament to the fragile viability of separate female institutions.

Yet, if these buildings are intentionally domestic and self-effacingly feminine, that is their exterior image only. Their interiors, replete with paintings of founders, honor rolls, photographs of club events, plaques and prizes, are more personal, more self-aggrandizing, more declarative of self and autonomous female identity. Externally, the structures bow to convention, revere the record of men; internally, they celebrate their own achievements and respect themselves. It is their own effort of which they are most proud: their leadership, the amounts of money have have raised for pet projects, the honors they have bestowed on each other, the assistance they have offered to others, the problems they have faced and solved together. In literal concrete forms, these structures are symbolic of the tensions in the female experience. The buildings publicly acquiesce to a male-dominated system while they privately revolt; though separate from the mainstream and unequal to it, yet they are visible, as long as they stand.

Notes

[1]This article is adapted in part from two previous works of the author, "Matronage: Patterns in Women's Organizations, Atlanta, Georgia, 1890-1940," (unpbl. diss., George Washington University, 1978) and "Atlanta Is A Female Noun: Evidence of City-Building Among Women," unpbl. paper (American Historical Association, Annual Meeting, Atlanta, 1975).

[2]See Steven Davis, "Johnny Reb in Perspective: The Confederate Soldier's Image in the Southern Arts," unpbl. diss. (Emory University, 1979).

[3]Quotation taken from the tree plaque; the tree is located just north of the Peace Monument near the 14th Street entrance into Piedmont Park.

[4]"The Winning of the Wren's Nest," in Julia Collier Harris, ed., The Life and Letters of Joel Chandler Harris (Boston, 1918), 601.

[5]Florence Read, The Story of Spelman College (Princeton, 1961), 214.

[6]Otto Wilson and Robert Waller Barrett, Fifty Years of Work with Girls, 1881-1933: A Story of the Florence Crittendon Homes (Alexandria, Va., 1933), 165.

[7]Rev. E.R. Carter, The Black Side (Atlanta, 1894), 35-37.

[8]Erminie Ragland (Mrs. Oscar), "The Founding of Atlanta Tuberculosis Association and the Home for Incurables," Atlanta Historical Bulletin (Oct. 1939), 258.

[9]Read, p. 274; "Miss [Amy C.] Chadwick [the director/founder] made the orphanage truly a home for the Negro girls admitted to her care,—a home to which they returned for visits and advice and encouragement long after they had jobs or homes of their own."

[10]Atlanta Federation of Women's Clubs, Yearbook, 1929-31, 30.

[11]Sophonisba Breckinridge, Women in the Twentieth Century: A Study of their Political, Social, and Ecnomic Activities (New York, 1933), 43, 82.

[13]Matronage, 350, 355; material from the National Register Nomination Form for the Atlanta Woman's Club (Georgia; Fulton County); Atlanta Constitution, May 14, 1939.

[14]Atlanta Constitution, May 14, 1939.

"Wave High the Red Bandanna": Some Handkerchiefs of the 1888 Presidential Campaign

Otto Charles Thieme

By the beginning of the eighteenth century, handkerchiefs became objects of everyday use. Various advancements in European textile technology provided an increasingly inexpensive object to a ready market. Men in particular assured the continued production of the handkerchief by adopting the habit of taking snuff; the large textile square handily prevented the spotting of clothing. Although the use of snuff became increasingly unfashionable, by the 1880s the usefulness of the handkerchief established it as a common item.

Various kinds of handkerchiefs were available in the 1880s. One of the smallest was a twelve inch silk square which women wore tucked into their belts. Larger squares of linen were sold for use by both men and women. Everyday handkerchiefs were white, solid colored or were printed with fancy borders. Hemstitching usually finished off the edges. The cotton bandanna, with its distinctive color and design, became one of the cheapest, most common forms of the nineteenth century handkerchief.

From the middle of the nineteenth century on, European manufacturers used the handkerchief as a format for new printing and dyeing techniques as well as new designs. Prints aimed at the male audience included military and political subject matter. Special events including campaigns also inspired designs. One of the earliest was printed for the presidential campaign of Andrew Jackson and at least two were printed for the 1840 campaign of William Henry Harrison. One, printed on silk, showed Harrison's log cabin birthplace with a border of barrels marked "Hard Cider" interspersed with various slogans. The elaborate design of the second, printed on cotton in either sepia or crimson dyes, centered on a finely drawn equestrian portrait of Harrison. Scenes from the General's military victories as well as peaceful accomplishments surrounded it.

Special handkerchiefs appeared in many subsequent campaigns. These items assumed an importance as a central mass communication technique in campaigning prior to the days of the electronic media and the widespread use of celluloid buttons, and played an especially important role in the presidential campaign of 1888.

The presidential campaign of 1888 centered firmly on the issue of protective tariffs. While the Democratic party supported a low tariff chiefly to provide revenue, the Republican party uncompromisingly favored a system of high protective tariffs. Not surprisingly, campaign materials focused squarely on this issue. Among the paraphernalia distributed by both parties was a group of campaign handkerchiefs. Of these, nineteen supported the Democratic candidates and thirty-one were associated with the Republican campaign. These handkerchiefs reflect both the issues of the campaign and production possibilities within the textile printing industry.

The Democratic Campaign Handkerchiefs

The Democrats convened in St. Louis on the fifth of June, 1888. The delegates adopted a platform that endorsed the views of President Cleveland, who criticized the existing high tariffs as a source of surplus revenue. The position of the party was that a surplus of over $125,000,000 lying "idle in the Federal Treasury"[1] would be spent by extravagant appropriations of the Republican party, whereas the Democrats sought frugality and the reduction of unnecessary tariff taxes. A lowered tariff would not threaten American industry. On the contrary, the Democrats felt that lower tariff taxes would cheapen foreign merchandise in the American marketplace as well as extend American markets overseas.

Cleveland easily gained renomination. Allen G. Thurman, a former senator from Ohio, and Governor Isaac P. Gray of Indiana, were both nominated to fill the vice presidential slot. During the roll call, when Thurman's victory seemed assured, a demonstration broke out. The "Indianians tore down their Gray banner, and hoisted the bandana...[sic] The bust of Cleveland, already garlanded with laurels, was decorated with a bandana, and this was the occasion for increased applause."[2]

The delegates' use of the red pocket handkerchief was more than chance; the bandanna symbolized Thurman. Early in his career he adopted the practice of using a red bandanna handkerchief after taking a pinch of snuff and continued the practice throughout his political career. Cleveland's campaign managers made the most of this picturesque feature. A campaign book entitled "Our Bandanna" was published. Five copies printed on satin sold for $250 apiece. Three hundred more were printed on rice paper and sold for $25 each, while cheaply printed copies were sold for a dime.[3] Even campaign songs such as "Wave High the Red Bandanna" underscored its use as a rallying point.

The bandanna, a commonly used item during most of the nineteenth century, had its origin in India. There in its traditional form, patterns made up of small spots were tied into cotton cloth and dyed Turkey red. When the knots were untied, the resulting design of small white diamonds on squares with tiny red centers appeared against a red background. The great popularity of the bandanna motivated the British textile industry to perfect machinery by 1815 on which four men could print more than 19,000 yards of bandannas in a ten hour day.[4] The resulting product was cheap and readily available, as advertisements of the day attest. Shortly after the Democratic convention, Daniell and Sons of New York City advertised bandanna handkerchiefs, solid red with small white motifs, at a cost of nine cents each.[5]

Seven handkerchiefs associated with the Democratic campaign used the bandanna as a design source. White diamonds used individually, in rows, or in clusters appeared on solid red backgrounds (Fig. 1).

Colors were reversed; red diamonds were printed on white backgrounds (Fig. 2). An additional handkerchief design made up of dots instead of diamonds would have been considered to be a bandanna since the design convention included many tiny, simple white spot motifs appearing on a red background.

The handkerchiefs associated with the Democratic party used more than allusions to bandannas. The need to familiarize voters with the candidates and the campaign issues justified the inclusion of not only names and images of the candidates but also slogans that coordinated with the platform adopted in St. Louis. The platform, though addressing itself to the question of tariff reform, used that term only once, usually by substituting words such as taxation or taxes for the term 'tariff.' Phrases such as "NO SURPLUS, LOW TAXES" dealt as directly with the party's stand on the tariff as did the phrase, "TARIFF REFORM, FOR REVENUE ONLY." Another oft-used phrase, "A Public Office is a Public Trust," was resurrected from Cleveland's 1884 campaign.

Fig. 1 Cleveland campaign handkerchief; 22 1/4″x24″, white cotton fabric with design roller printed in red and black. Collection of the New York Historical Society. New York, New York.

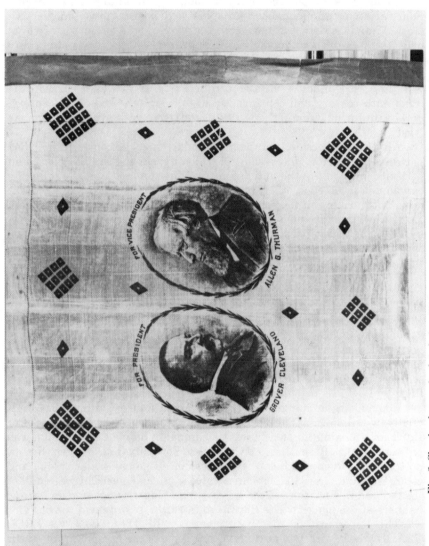

Fig. 2 Cleveland campaign handerkerchief, 22″x22″, white silk fabric with design lithographed in red, collection of the Hayward Area Historical Society, Hayward, California.

Sometimes other motifs appeared along with the phrases and protraits. Four variations of one unusual grouping were based on two brooms with crossed handles. Between them a rooster perched on a bar on top of a long pole (Fig. 3). The broom motif appeared as early as the 1876 Tilden/Hendricks Campaign where it was associated with the word "reform," and was used by Cleveland in his 1884 campaign.[6] The rooster was the first symbol of the Democratic party. It was used early in the nineteenth century and continued in use through the end of the century, despite the introduction of the donkey as the Democratic symbol by Thomas Nast.

All the Democratic campaign handkerchiefs except one included portraits of the candidates, some of which appear to have been based on portraits printed in the official convention proceedings. Usually the candidates faced each other, but not always. Two handkerchiefs present them both looking in the same direction and in one they face away from each other. Usually the large portraits were placed near the center of the handkerchief, but on three examples a small grouping is printed in one corner of the handkerchiefs (Fig. 4). Of all the Democratic handkerchiefs, this group is the most unlike the original bandannas.

The Republican Campaign Handkerchiefs

The Republican convention opened in Chicago on Tuesday, June 19, 1888. Unlike the predictability of Cleveland's nomination, eighteen candidates for the presidential nomination jockeyed for a majority position throughout the first five ballots. Following a Sunday recess, three more ballots were taken. On the eighth ballot, Benjamin Harrison, a former senator from Indiana, won the nomination. The vice presidential slot was filled by Levi P. Morton, a respected New York banker.

Republican campaign machinery worked quickly to publicize their relatively unknown candidates as well as their platform; three days after Harrison's nomination, on June 28, a campaign handkerchief design was patented by A.S. Rosenthal and Co. of New York City (Fig. 5). Even without portraits of the candidates, the political message came across loud and clear. The candidates' names were printed in red and placed in the middle of the red and white stripes of the waving flag. Slogans appeared on narrow banners at the places where they negotiated three corners of the design.

The uppermost of the three slogans, "PROTECTION VS FREE TRADE" dealt with the most important issue of the campaign: the tariff issue. The wording of the platform vigorously stated the Republican position. "We are uncompromisingly in favor of the American system of protection. We protest against the destruction, as proposed by the President and his party.... The protective system must be maintained."[7]

Of the thirty-one handkerchiefs associated with the Republican campaign, twenty-two present phrases that refer to this issue. Apprently there was no single phrase since the variety of slogans ranges from "PROTECTION TO AMERICAN LABOR AND AMERICAN INDUSTRIES," "PROTECT AMERICAN INDUSTRIES," "REPUBLICAN PROTECTION TO HOME INDUSTRIES," and "PROTECTION TO AMERICAN INDUSTRIES," to simply

Fig. 3 Cleveland campaign handkerchief; 19″x19″, white cotton fabric with design printed in red and black. Collection of the New York Historical Society, New York, New York.

"PROTECTION."

In addition to campaign slogans, the first Republican handkerchief of the campaign presented what was quickly to become the Republican answer to the Democrat's bandanna: the American flag. Campaign managers, no doubt, realized the importance of having a symbol as recognizable as the bandanna, yet unmistakeably different. The flag proved a fortunate choice; its blue and red colors added a distinctive touch to the images and its stars easily substituted for bandanna diamonds.

The connection between the flag, the tariff issue and the Republican campaign became quite clear in songs published in "The Protection

Fig. 4 Cleveland campaign handkerchief; corner detail, 21″x21½″, white silk fabric with design printed in black, probably lithographed. Collection of the Wisconsin State Historical Society, Madison, Wisconsin.

Collection of Campaign Songs for 1888." Titles such as "There's a Flag That is Known the World Over" and "Raise the Nation's Emblem, Boys," reaffirm the words of another:

Our candidates are out again, Hurrah! Hurrah!
Their banners bright with never a strain, Hurrah! Hurrah!
The Democrats, with noise and brag,
Are shaking poor old Thurman's rag,
But we will wave the flag, and carry the victory home.[8]

The association proved so effective that the design of two campaign handkerchiefs contained no mention of the candidates or their party, only a protection slogan and the flag (Figs. 6 and 7).

Fig. 5 Harrison campaign handkerchief; 19″x19½″; white silk fabric with design printed in red, probably lithographed. Collection of the Missouri Historical Society, St. Louis, Missouri.

Other slogans reflected issues incorporated into the campaign platform. The first Republican handkerchief included slogans concerned with minor, but nonetheless vote-getting issues. "AID FOR FREE SCHOOLS" directly reflected the plank in the platform stating that "the free school is the promoter of that intelligence which is to preserve us a free Nation, therefore the State or Nation, or both combined, should support free institutions of learning."[9] The second slogan supported use of surplus revenues in the national treasury for "PENSIONS FOR SOLDIERS" to "provide against the possibility that any man who honorably wore the Federal uniform shall become an inmate of an almshouse, or dependent upon private charity."[10]

A second Harrison handkerchief also derived its slogans from the campaign platform (Fig. 8). In addition to the expected "PROTECTION TO AMERICAN INDUSTRY" is the phrase "FULL VOTE, FAIR COUNT"

Fig. 6 Harrison campaign handkerchief; 17 7/8″x15½″, white silk fabric with design printed in red and blue dues, probably roller printed. Collection of the Wisconsin State Historical Society, Madison, Wisconsin.

Fig. 7 Harrison campaign handkerchief; 18″x19½″; white cotton fabric with design printed in blue and red, probably roller printed. Collection of the Wisconsin State Historical Society, Madison, Wisconsin.

Fig. 8 Harrison campaign handkerchief; 19 3/8"x19 5/8", white silk fabric with design lithographed in blue ink. Collection of the Wisconsin State Historical Society, Madison, Wisconsin.

which refers to the Republican position on the adoption of the Australian ballot. The 1888 convention desired that every citizen should be able to "cast one free ballot in public elections and have that ballot duly counted."[11] The inclusion of this somewhat secondary issue and its placement in the design above the tariff slogan may have been an attempt to win over members of one of the factions of the Labor party who included this as a plank in their platform at their May convention.

Benjamin Harrison was the grandson of president William Henry Harrison [nicknamed "Old Tippecanoe" after his participation in that famous battle in the Indian Wars of 1811]. The importance of this link with the past president was not lost on campaign supporters. They formed Tippecanoe Clubs across the country composed of men who voted for "Old Tippecanoe" in 1840. "Members wore Tippecanoe badges with portraits of William Henry Harrison, pictures of log cabins, and other devices to remind the 'old boy' of the time when nearly all cast their first votes for the Hero of Tippecanoe."[12] As the phrase "Tippecanoe and Tyler too" was associated with his grandfather, so "TIPPECANOE AND MORTON TOO" became associated with Harrison. A campaign handkerchief incorporated this phrase into its design (Fig. 9).

Printing and Construction Techniques of the Campaign Handkerchiefs
During the last quarter of the nineteenth century, the textile printing industry witnessed much experimentation with printing processes. Photography and lithography were applied to mass production. Photography on cloth proved unadaptable to industrial needs and remained a novelty of local photographers, but lithography proved useful for specialty items. In spite of innovations, roller printing maintained its position as the most important pattern printing technique. Even the age-old technique of block printing remained in use. Each of the processes had unique characteristics that facilitated their use for printing campaign handkerchiefs.

The roller printing process was ideal for printing countless yards of fabric. It required that continuous lengths of fabric be passed between one or more pairs of rollers. Each pair of rollers worked together to deposit one color of dye on the surface of the cloth. After setting, washing and finishing processes, the resulting yardage would be sold as such or cut apart and made into specialty items. Campaign handkerchiefs made from yardage were probably roller printed; these handkerchiefs tend to have solid colored backgrounds.

Campaign handkerchiefs were formed from yardage in two ways. If the design on the handkerchief was small, it was printed two abreast and the unit then repeated as yardage.[13] Individual handkerchiefs were then cut from the fabric and hemmed. Any handkerchief so produced would have three cut and hemmed sides. The remaining side, either on the right or the left, would be unhemmed since the selvedge formed an edge that would not unravel.

The second production method involved printing a design which covered the full width of the fabric from selvedge to selvedge. Handkerchiefs formed from this yardage would be hemmed only on the cut

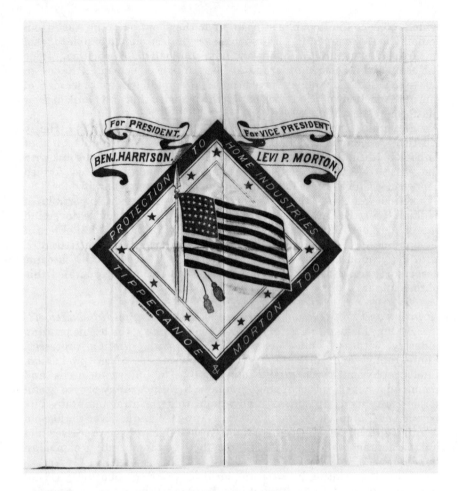

Fig. 9 Harrison campaign handkerchief; 19¾″x19½″, white silk fabric with design block printed in red and blue ink. Collection of the Missouri Historical Society, St. Louis, Missouri.

edges which were on the top and the bottom. The tightly woven selvedges formed the two side edges and were not hemmed. In this method, the width of the fabric determined the width of the handkerchief. Narrow cloth could be used for smaller handkerchiefs while the use of wider cloth resulted in larger handkerchiefs. Narrow cotton cloth was used for elaborate composition of one Harrison handkerchief (Fig. 10). A surface roller printed the large areas of red while an engraved roller produced the more detailed parts of the design in black.

The full twenty-four and one half inch width of cotton cloth was used for one of the largest of the Harrison handkerchiefs (Fig. 11). A huge circular shield forms most of the design, nearly touching the side selvedge edges. The word "PROTECTION" rendered in red against blue and white stripes is visually balanced by a forty-two star spangled blue field. The candidates'

Fig. 10 Harrison campaign handkerchief; 19¾"x19¼", white cotton fabric with design roller printed in red and black dyes. Collection of the Wisconsin State Historical Society, Madison, Wisconsin.

names and offices are located in the outer rim of the circle. Since the shield occupied most of the space, the candidates' portraits were moved into the four corners. Only this handkerchief design utilized double portraits of the candidates. Two examples of this hankerchief have been located. The one illustrated is in perfect condition and unhemmed. It shows the red and dark blue dyes full strength. Another, washed and exposed to sunlight, has faded badly in the areas dyed blue. Obviously these handkerchiefs were not made to last.

Records of the Cocheco Manufacturing Company associated with this handkerchief list it as "Style 5605, July 1888 campaign textile for Benj. Harrison and Levi Morton."[14] This is the only Harrison campaign handkerchief identified as made by an American manufacturer. The Cocheco Manufacturing Company of Dover, New Hampshire, originally known as the Dover Manufacturing Company, was one of the oldest textile producers in the United States. The firm began in 1824 to print patterns on the white cotton cloth that came from its looms. Their printed textiles

Fig. 11 Harrison campaign handkerchief, 22¾″x24½″, white cotton fabric with design roller printed in red and blue dyes. Collection of the Merrimack Valley Textile Museum, North Andover, Massachusetts.

received a silver medal at the Boston Exhibition of 1839 where their quality was favorably compared to that found on British printed textiles. In 1827 the Dover Manufacturing Company became known as Cocheco Manufacturing Company and continued to print quality dress goods, cotton furnishing fabrics, as well as specialty items such as this campaign textile.

Lithography and block printing had several advantages over roller printing. Unlike roller printing which required the use of continuous lengths of fabric, both lithography and block printing techniques could easily be used to print on prehemmed handkerchiefs. The use of inks, furthermore, while stiffening the fabric, eliminated the extra finishing processes required by the use of dye. Most importantly, the handkerchiefs produced by these processes did not have to come from large East Coast mills. Skilled pressmen and printing equipment distributed throughout the country could easily have met the needs of local campaign managers by printing on commercially available handkerchiefs.

Lithography was based on drawings done with a grease crayon or with a greasy liquid applied with a pen, brush or spattered. Areas of white could be scraped from darker areas. Occasionally, strokes of the grease crayon might be seen.

The design on a badge from the 1892 Harrison campaign for reelection printed "Wm. B. BURFORD. LITH INDS." illustrates the possibilities of lithography (Fig. 12). Printed in black ink on white silk satin, the design was made up of heavy lines and spattered gray tones. The white line on a dark ground caused by removing some of the grease from the original drawing can be seen in Harrison's beard on the campaign ribbon and on Thurman's hair and beard on the campaign handkerchief illustrated in Fig. 2. The fine textured lines of the grease crayon are visible in the portraits in Figs. 2 and 8. Photolithography, an innovative process at that time, produced subtle gray tones even in small scale designs. Printed in one corner of five different Harrison campaign handkerchiefs are small compositions with portraits which appear to rely on photolithography for their detail (Fig. 13).

Unlike lithography and roller printing, block printing does not require elaborate presses. In the block printing process the background is gouged out of a block of wood and the image to be printed remains in relief. The relief image is inked and printed on the cloth. The technique relies on bold, hard edge shapes and strong value change; there are no value changes within a color. If the carver is not careful, small chunks of the relief areas might be accidentally gouged out. If he is hurried, not all the nonrelief (background) area might be cleared out. In addition, misregistration of blocks is possible when two or more colors are used.

One handkerchief design printed by block shows gouge marks of the technique in the crisp lines used to suggest shading in streamers near the top of the diamond and in the slightly irregular quality of the outline. On both, the carving of the word "president" is sloppy since tiny residual marks were not cleared out from the background between the letters (Fig. 9). The blurred red stripes in the flag in this same print were caused by a misprint of the red block. Both block printing and lithography usually produced a colored design on a white background.

Fig. 12 Harrison campaign ribbon; 2 2/3″x7¼″, white silk satin fabric with design lithographed in black. Collection of the Wisconsin State Historical Society, Madison, Wisconsin.

Fig. 13 Harrison campaign handkerchief; 18½″x17 13/16″, white cotton fabric with design printed in black, probably lithographed. Collection of the Wisconsin State Historical Society, Madison, Wisconsin.

Many of the lithographed and block printed campaign handkerchiefs were printed on prehemmed white silk squares. Usually the designs were centered on the square; occasionally the design was printed off center or even into the borders in cases where the design was too large for the prehemmed silk square (Fig. 8).

The manufacture of the silk handkerchiefs required much hand labor. The cut edges of large squares of silk were folded back slightly to remove their unevenness. Then several threads were withdrawn from the silk about one to two inches from the edges. The slightly folded edges were then folded back to form a border of double thickness from one half to one inch wide. Hand stitching caught the first folded hem to the back of the handkerchief thus fastening the double thickness border in place. Corners were finished in several ways, although the only unusual method consisted of having a small specially dyed silk "envelope" sewn down over the existing corner (Fig. 5). Although the source of these silk squares is unknown, they were not uncommon. Handkerchiefs of the same type were used for commemorative purposes and at least one handkerchief from the 1892 campaign was printed on a similar silk square.

Prehemmed cotton handkerchiefs were also used. Some were solid white; others had narrow patterned borders. These squares were made from grid patterned yardage that produced patterns along the edges when made up into handkerchiefs. Occasionaly the same campaign design would be printed on squares having different patterned edges.

Neither Cleveland nor Benjamin Harrison was a likeable folk hero; their campaigns focused on issues rather than a cult of personality, as had the earlier Jackson and William Henry Harrison textiles. Cleveland's handkerchiefs, based on the bandanna used by the vice presidential candidate, drew their inspiration from an existing textile familiar to nearly every voter. The Harrison handkerchiefs on the other hand not only avoided any visual reference to the bandanna, but also adopted a substitute symbol. Most important are the two dated handkerchiefs: one documenting the early use of handkerchiefs during the campaign; the other firmly documenting a textile produced by a leading American textile mill. As a group the various designs offer a total picture of the campaign.

Notes

The editor would like to note that this article was accepted for publication in the Journal of American Culture in April, 1979, prior to the publication of Herbert R. Collins' *Threads of History* (Washington: Smithsonian Institution Press, 1979).

The author would like to express his appreciation to Sara Traut, whose help in the middle stages of the research proved invaluable. Research for this article was funded in part by a grant from the Helen Louise Allen Textile Collection, Madison, Wisconsin.

[1]*Official Proceedings of the National Democratic Convention* (St. Louis, 1888), 97.

[2]New York *Times*, Vol. XXXVII, No. 11474, June 8, 1888, 1.

[3]Louis Clinton Hatch, *A History of the Vice Presidency of the United States* (New York, 1934), 323.

[4]Thomas Cooper, *A Practical Treatise on Dyeing and Calico Printing* (Philadelphia, 1815), 349.

[5]New York *Times*, Vol. XXXVIII, No. 11475, June 10, 1888, 8.

[6]Otha D. Wearin, *Political Americana* (Shenandoah, Iowa, 1967), 17.

[7]George Francis Dawson, *The Republican Campaign, Textbook for 1888* (New York, 1888), 1.

[8]"Potomac," *The Protection Collection of Campaign Songs for 1888* (Washington, 1888), 5.

[9]Dawson, *The Republican Campaign Textbook*, 2.

[10]Dawson, 3.

[11]Dawson, 1.

[12]Col. Dorus M. Fox, *History of Political Parties, National Reminiscences and the Tippecanoe Movement* (Des Moines, Iowa, 1894), 309.

[13]One example known to the author is a length of uncut yardage dyed yellow and printed with a handkerchief design in red. The design, based on the Declaration of Independence, is roller printed twice per width of fabric. Collection of the Society for the Preservation of New England Antiquities, Boston, Accession number 23.593.

[14]I am indebted to Katherine R. Koob, Assistant Curator of Textiles, Merrimack Valley Textile Museum, for providing me with this information taken from records in the museum's collection.

1896 Campaign Artifacts:
A Study in Inferential Reconstruction

Roger A. Fischer

A fundamental tenet among students of material culture is that we must pay heed to things as well as to the written word in our efforts to understand the present and reconstruct the past. The small measure of success we have enjoyed in peddling this premise has come almost exclusively in those areas of research where written records are clearly insufficient, while those of us who labor in fields blessed with ample documentation are either regarded as "treasurers of trivia" or ignored altogether. It is difficult to imagine a field in which material culture has had less influence than the study of American electoral politics, especially at the presidential level, where our quadrennial rites produce a mindboggling quantity of documentary evidence for scholars. Yet every presidential race since the 1820s has also generated, used, then discarded countless campaign artifacts—from the "Old Hickory Forever" thread boxes and "Hero of New Orleans" tokens of Andrew Jackson through the buttons, bumperstickers and plastic peanuts of Jimmy Carter—that deserve attention in their own right. Properly understood, they add a welcomed dimension to our understanding of the American electoral process that cannot be gleaned from the written record alone.

The thousands of different objects manufactured and used in 1896 for the presidential campaigns of William McKinley and William Jennings Bryan comprise a good case in point. 1896 was the year that the celluloid campaign button made its debut into presidential politics, with more than one thousand different varieties of pinbacks and lapel studs turned out by such firms as Whitehead & Hoag of Newark and Baldwin & Gleason of New York to grace the lapels of McKinley and Bryan supporters.[1] The cloth campaign ribbon, in the twilight of its dominance of campaign regalia, appeared in 1896 in several hundred varieties, as did gaudy badges made by combining buttons, ribbons and metal hangers. Nearly one hundred types of metal stickpins were produced, some of them elaborate mechanical gadgets. Also manufactured and sold or given to partisans were banners, pillows, plaques, tapestries, belt buckles, bandannas, shirts, watch fobs, canes, paperweights, ashtrays, cigar holders, match safes, mugs, plates, trays, bracelet charms, spoons, rings, soap "babies," (Fig. 1), razors, mirrors, and other items bearing the names or likenesses of the Republican and Democratic standardbearers.[2] (Fig. 2) Indeed, it is possible to imagine the properly equipped McKinley or Bryan enthusiast awakening, washing, shaving, dressing, eating breakfast, enjoying a cup of coffee and a smoke, eating supper, enjoying his after-supper coffee and cigar, then undressing

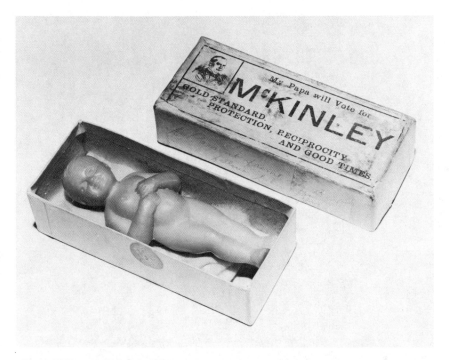

Fig. 1. William McKinley soap doll, 1896. *Photograph Courtesy of the Smithsonian Institution.*

and retiring without ever losing sight of an image of his political idol! These 1896 mementos exist today in ample quantity, treasured by curators, collectors and antiquarians and ignored by political historians. But what can they tell us?

According to scholarly accounts based upon documentary evidence, we know that the Republicans met in St. Louis in June of 1896, nominated William McKinley of Ohio and Garret Hobart of New Jersey, and endorsed a platform pledging a return to prosperity through the gold standard and a protective tariff. Three weeks later the Democrats, bitterly divided over monetary policy and the wrecked presidency of Grover Cleveland, gathered in Chicago and adopted a platform demanding the free and unlimited coinage of silver at a value of 1/16 that of gold. They then chose a ticket of Nebraska silverite William Jennings Bryan and Maine's Arthur Sewall. In the epic "battle of the standards" that followed, the Democrats waged a virtually single-issue crusade for free silver, while the Republicans based their campaign on the broader theme of prosperity through economic growth, the tariff, anti-inflationary "sound" money, and general fiscal responsibility. Flush with funds and superbly organized, McKinley was able to adopt the traditional "above the battle" pose by remaining at his home in Canton and conducting a leisurely "front-porch" campaign. Bryan was forced by an empty till and a hostile press to break sharply with tradition and take his case straight to the people, traveling more than 18,000 miles into twenty-seven states to give some six hundred speeches

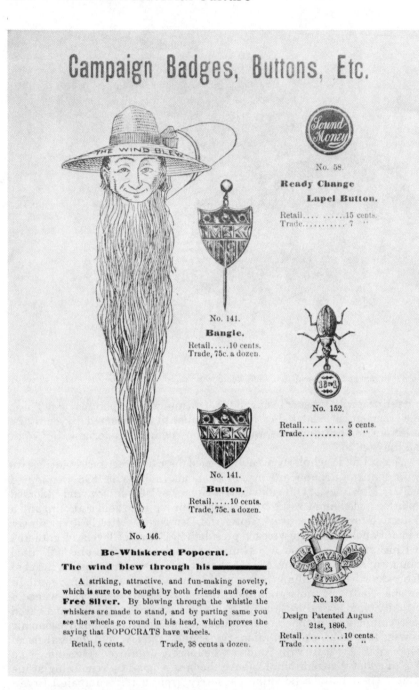

Fig. 2 A page from July, 1896, supplementary catalogue issued by The American News Company of New York, a major supplier of campaign items to political groups and vendors. Photograph by Kenneth J. Moran, University of Minnesota-Duluth.

heard by five million people, pioneering the 20th century campaign style.

The personalities and issues on both sides created extraordinary public interest, with voter turnout exceeding 95% in five key midwestern states. Bryan ran well in the South and trans-Mississippi West, winning 176 electoral votes and more than 6,500,000 popular votes, some 750,000 more than Cleveland had won with in 1892. But it was not enough, for McKinley won 7,111,607 popular votes and 271 electoral votes of every northern state from Maine to North Dakota plus seven border-South and western states, running especially strong among blue-collar and ethnic voters.[3]

Most of this can be corroborated by analysis and interpretation of 1896 campaign artifacts. It would be foolish, of course, to assert that we could duplicate in full detail the "battle of the standards" or any other election solely through artifact analysis. Language is the ultimate descriptive device and has long been the politician's main stock-in-trade. We cannot, for example, infer from artifacts McKinley's organizational superiority or leisurely campaign activities, Bryan's rationale for waging the first modern "whistlestop" campaign, or that lyrical speaking style that moved Vachel Lindsay to call Bryan "the one American Poet who could sing outdoors." Nor could artifacts replace statistics in determining the precise dimensions of the McKinley mandate or voter turnout. They can, however, help illuminate the rest of the story: the conventions, candidates, basic issues, general strategies, general indications of voter interest and participant fervor, basic indications of demographic and interest-group response, and outcome. These artifacts, however, provide evidence to substantiate some ideas that scholars have been forced to advance without documentary support and even to suggest some facets of the "battle of the standards" that historians limited to written sources have yet to discover.

It is a simple matter to determine that the Republicans met in St. Louis in June and the Democrats in Chicago in July, since places and dates were inscribed on many of the convention badges and ribbons worn by the delegates, officials and supporters of various candidates and causes. Many of these items also provide clues to the tenor of the two conventions and several of the conflicts that enlivened their proceedings. Convention badges featuring Republican hopefuls Levi Morton, Thomas B. Reed, Matt Quay, William B. Allison and Henry M. Teller give evidence that McKinley did not win nomination by default, just as badges touting Democratic contenders "Silver Dick" Bland, Claude Matthews and Horace Boies reveal that Bryan also had to overcome internal opposition. From a host of badges bearing such legends as "GRAND OLD PARTY, GOOD AS GOLD," "SOUND MONEY" and "PROTECTION" the basic nature of the Republican platform can be deduced, but two Henry Teller items—a button reading "TELLER SILVER REPUBLICAN, 16 TO 1 BY UNCLE SAM ALONE" and a ribbon reading "WE ARE AS SOLID FOR TELLER AS TELLER IS SOLID FOR SILVER"—offer evidence of at least one rift within the Republican ranks. Issue-oriented Democratic convention badges nearly all read "FREE SILVER" or "16 TO 1," a clue to the singleminded motivation of the convention and majority. That the two conventions selected the McKinley-Hobart and Bryan-Sewall tickets can be determined by a number of buttons, ribbons and badges issued during the subsequent campaign that feature the slates with party affiliation, year, or both.

To judge from the hundreds of issue-related campaign objects distributed during the four months that followed Chicago, Bryan and the Democrats made virtually no effort to broaden their ideological appeal to the electorate. Silver *was* their campaign,[4] as countless buttons, ribbons, badges, jewelry items, and other 1896 Democratic artifacts attest. Some of these items promoted silver per se. Others utilized the slogan "FREE SILVER." Even more urged "16 TO 1," the ratio between silver and gold values demanded by the Bryanites. The "silver bug" [a scarab or beetle-like creature] emerged as a ubiquitous symbol of the crusade, with dozens of different jewelry items and buttons featuring the little creatures. Other items used various combinations of these slogans and symbols. If the Democrats exhibited little imagination in shaping their propaganda, some manufacturers at least showed occasional creativity in displaying it. Attractive buttons were made symbolizing a gold center and sixteen silver coins encircling a gold piece. Clocks with hands frozen at 12:44 ("sixteen to one") were featured on several buttons and one rather imposing jewelry item, a full size replica of a pocket watch (Fig. 3).

If the Democrats made any real effort to broaden their appeal at all, their campaign artifacts did not reflect it. A button reading "SILVER — PROSPERITY" seems to have been the only campaign item designed to equate the silver issue to larger economic considerations. Two buttons—one reading "AMERICAN MONEY FOR AMERICANS" and another proclaiming "EUROPE WANTS GOLD, WE WANT SILVER"—attempted to relate silver to Americanism, an effort to make political capital out of Republican insistence that bimetallism must be negotiated through international agreement.[5] The only 1896 Bryan campaign items that might be considered issue-related in any sense that departed altogether from the silver issue were a few picture buttons that sought to portray Bryan as the champion of the people, an apparent effort to exploit the idea that McKinley was the minion of the vested interests.[6] One such button urged "FACING THE FUTURE, LET THE MAJORITY RULE," while others labeled the Nebraskan "THE TRIBUNE OF THE PEOPLE" and "THE CHOICE OF THE PEOPLE."

The ideological items distributed by the McKinley forces in 1896 provide clear evidence of a much more diverse and subtle attempt to win votes (Fig. 4). Some Republican items were simple rebuttals of Bryan's silver propaganda pieces. Several, for example, made pleas for gold per se, including one excellent caricature button portraying McKinley and Hobart pedaling to the White House on a tandem bicycle, surrounded by the legend "GOLD DIDN'T GET THERE JULY 7TH, BUT WATCH US TAKE IT THERE NOV. 3RD." "Gold bugs" surfaced in profusion as stickpins and other jewelry pieces and in the designs of buttons, easily outnumbering their silver cousins. Other McKinley items sought to lampoon "free silver" through satire. One such button dismissed the issue as "16 PARTS FOAM, 1 PART BEER," while another pictured a silver dollar featuring a rather bumpkinesque caricature of Bryan and the motto "IN GOD WE TRUST FOR THE OTHER 47 CENTS."[7] This legend was also used on a bogus silver dollar, just one of a series of "funny money" items issued by the

Fig. 3. William Jennings Bryan crusades for "free silver." *Photograph by Kenneth J. Moran, University of Minnesota-Duluth.*

Republicans to satirize Bryan's monetary beliefs.

Many issue-related McKinley items, however, reveal a Republican strategy of elevating the monetary debate above mere metallurgy by endowing the gold standard with an ethical dimension. A picture button urged "AN HONEST DOLLAR." Marching and street banners sold to local Republican groups by a Chicago distributor carried the legend "HONEST MONEY," one of them even adding "AND NATIONAL INTEGRITY" to further emphasize the innate nobility of McKinley's monetary position. The

Fig. 4. William McKinley, Prosperity's Advance Agent. *Photograph by Kenneth J. Moran, University of Minnesota-Duluth.*

most widely used of all 1896 Republican campaign devices was the motto "SOUND MONEY,"[8] which appeared on literally hundreds of McKinley buttons, ribbons and other items, often in the titles of "sound money clubs" created in many communities to work on McKinley's behalf.

Other McKinley items show that the Republicans were able to do what Bryan's Democrats were either unable or unwilling to do, diversify their economic appeal beyond the monetary issue. Many buttons and ribbons carried the legend "PROTECTION," alone or in tandem with "SOUND

MONEY," an indication of the importance the Republicans placed on the tariff question.[9] Other items pledged economic growth, especially in the industrial sector. One such button pictured a factor with the motto "OPEN MILLS NOT MINTS." Another rhymed "IN MCKINLEY WE TRUST, TO KEEP OUR MACHINES FREE OF RUST." Another button proclaimed McKinley "PROSPERITY'S ADVANCE AGENT,"[10] while many other buttons and ribbons carried the motto "PROSPERITY." Lest the point be lost on blue-collar workers, another button featured McKinley as "LEADER OF LABOR IN LIBERTY'S LAND."

If the artifacts are any indication, McKinley appears to have made a much more serious attempt than Bryan to attract the votes of industrial workers. The only known 1896 Bryan items appealing directly to the blue-collar vote were a pair of attractive "UNITED WE STAND, DIVIDED WE FALL" caricature buttons depicting Bryan shaking hands with a workingman identified as "LABOR." Characteristically, the laborer shown was a farmer tilling his field, not an industrial worker.[11]

Many McKinley items also reveal a concerted Republican effort to win votes through an appeal to patriotism. Documentary scholars invariably assert that the 1896 campaign was the first since the Civil War in which the Republicans failed to resort to "bloody shirt" demogogy—attacking the Democrats as the party of traitors and slackers while wrapping whichever former Civil War general they were running in the folds of Old Glory—as a basic component of their campaign. The artifacts would indicate, however, that these historians are not completely correct. Although no known 1896 Republican campaign items castigated Bryan (a babe in diapers when the guns roared at Sumter) or his party for ancient crimes against the Union, a host of buttons, badges, and stickpins provide ample evidence that the Republicans missed few opportunities to remind northern voters that McKinley stood in the vanguard of the tradition that had preserved the Union (Fig. 5). An abnormally large number of McKinley buttons and other items utilized flag motifs in their designs.[12] Buttons portraying McKinley as "MAJ. Wm. McKINLEY" hung from ribbon replicas of Old Glory, reminders of his service in the Union ranks. Other buttons proclaimed "THE BOYS IN BLUE ARE FOR WM. McKINLEY," a slogan used by the Grand Army of the Republic and other Union veterans' organizations for every Republican presidential nominee since Grant. If these items are any indication, it seems that the Grand Old Party's abandonment of the Civil War as campaign ammunition did not occur in 1896.[13]

Other campaign artifacts enable us to piece together a partial reconstruction of the personal activities of both standard-bearers during the autumn of 1896. A number of badges and ribbons were made to be worn by the local welcoming committees and dignitaries who greeted Bryan at his many appearances throughout the nation, as well as items sold or given out to the public to commemorate these events. Similarly, many of the Republican delegations which made the pilgrimage to McKinley's home in Canton wore items specially produced for the occasion (Fig. 6). In all likelihood, there were not enough items of this type made to establish anything approximating a day-by-day itinerary for either Bryan or McKinley, but enough of them have survived to prove that Bryan visited a

Fig. 5. Echoes of the "Bloody Shirt": Major William McKinley, Patriot. *Photography by Kenneth J. Moran, University of Minnesota-Duluth.*

Fig. 6 Badges of Republican delegation to Canton, Ohio, and of a home-town Republican club.

large number of communities in the Northeast, Midwest and South, while McKinley spent a lot of time in his home town in Ohio.[14]

Some of the 1896 campaign artifacts hold clues to the basic tenor of the campaign, as well as the climate of opinion it engendered among the people. A number of Bryan objects hint at a strident, almost bellicose crusade. Several "16 TO 1" buttons contain the motto "NO COMPROMISE." Several buttons and jewelry items depict gold bugs being impaled by pitchforks, spikes or silver arrows, often accompanied by such threats as "WHAT WE'LL DO TO GOLD BUGS." A number of Bryan buttons repeat the phrase "NO CROWN OF THORNS, NO CROSS OF GOLD" from his celebrated Chicago speech, words more appropriate for some sort of spiritual Armageddon than a contest for tenancy at 1600 Pennsylvania Avenue. That the Republicans, at least, believed that Bryan was "coming on too strong" can be inferred from several buttons and jewelry items which featured skeletons or cadavers accompanied by such mottos as "TALKED TO DEATH" or "TOO MUCH POLITICS." The electorate seems to have reacted differently, however, for indications are that the candidates, issues and campaigns on both sides generated unusual fervor among the voters. As one scholar has written, 1896 "gathered a charged excitement that sparked a lifetime's memories. Those who lived through it never forgot it."[15] The essential validity of this assertion can be inferred from the extraordinary number of 1896 campaign items that were not discarded after the day of reckoning, but were put away as treasured mementos and eventually found their way into museum and private collections.[16]

Many of the artifacts also provide some clues as to the relative popularity of the candidates among certain interest groups. Businessmen seem to have favored McKinley overwhelmingly in 1896 and their employees would appear to have tilted in the same direction, judging from the many "sound money club" items produced for business and worker groups, especially railroaders, and a virtual absence of pro-Bryan items of this type.[17] The urban press would also appear to have been solidly pro-McKinley, although too few buttons endorsing either candidate were issued to provide much proof.[18]

It is also possible to draw inferences from these objects about the regional and ethnic responses to the Bryan and McKinley campaigns. From items revealing Bryan's agrarian orientation, equation of "16 TO 1" with Americanism, and penchant for Biblical rhetoric, for example, it might be assumed that the Nebraskan ran best in the South and West, agricultural regions with the highest proportions of native-born and evangelical Protestant voters. Less speculative would be the assumption that he was especially popular in such silver-producing states as Nevada and Colorado, where "16 TO 1" promised boom times even if it proved worthless as monetary theory.[19] It would be equally logical to infer that McKinley did well generally in the Northeast and Old Midwest, running especialy strong in industrial centers and strongest of all in those manufacturing communities dependent on protection from foreign imports. There are indications in the artifacts pointing to the probability that McKinley also fared rather well among white ethnic voters alienated by Bryan's monetary radicalism, evangelical fervor, apparent indifference to blue-collar concerns, and the blatant xenophobia of "AMERICAN MONEY FOR AMERICANS."[20]

Many 1896 artifacts seem to indicate that both parties entertained more than a casual interest in winning the minds and hearts of American women, even though they voted in only a few Rocky Mountain states at that time, states in which neither Republicans nor Democrats did much campaigning because they were so safely in the Bryan column. Many of the campaign items sold or given out in 1896—cups, plates, trays, silver spoons, mirrors, pillows, bandannas, plaques, tapestries and many jewelry items, for example—appear to have been intended primarily if not exclusively for women[21] (Fig. 7). Whether or not one accepts Edith Mayo's interesting hypothesis elsewhere in this volume that the politicians may have wooed women more before they received the vote than afterwards, there is no question that these 1896 artifacts confirm that women were widely regarded as an influential factor in determining how their husbands would cast their votes. They thus lend a measure of credibility to the possibility that the anti-suffrage spokesmen of this era who insisted that women already voted indirectly were not patent hypocrites.

One point, at least, requires no speculation. That McKinley won and Bryan lost when the nation went to the polls on November 3, 1896, can be ascertained by a host of 1897 inaugural badges, buttons, ribbons and medals featuring the victorious Republicans. Further evidence can be provided with 1900 items calling for McKinley's re-electon and, by implication at least, a few post-1896 buttons satirically dismissing Bryan as a perpetual loser.[22]

The unusual quantity, diversity and ideological tenor of the 1896 McKinley and Bryan campaign items make the "battle of the standards" a very attractive test case for reconstruction through artifact analysis, but it is hardly unique in that regard. The 1900 McKinley-Bryan rematch, with many superb items inspired by the Spanish-American War, anti-trust agitation, and "full dinner pail" prosperity, lends itself to this type of exercise equally well. Others that come to mind are the "Tippecanoe and Tyler Too" campaign of William Henry Harrison in 1840, Franklin Delano Roosevelt's third term bid in 1940, the Lyndon Johnson-Barry Goldwater mismatch in 1964, and the Jimmy Carter-Gerald Ford contest in 1976. Reconstructing other elections—the two Eisenhower landslides, for example, by searching for hidden profundities in mounds of red, white and blue buttons that all say "I LIKE IKE" or something to that effect—might prove dramatically less productive.

Whether or not these bits of celluloid, metal and cloth hold clues that permit us to challenge interpretations gleaned from documentary sources, they are valuable in their own right, for they evoke the signs, sounds, feel and fervor of grassroots politics in a way that words on a page or numbers in a column cannot do. They allow us to relive vicariously that "sound money" demonstration or "free silver" rally, to experience anew the Republican rage behind "NO THIRD TERM" or "NO FRANKLIN THE FIRST," or to share again the unfulfilled dreams of "JACK ONCE MORE IN '64." In short, they help confirm the faith, shared by students of material culture, that Samuel Johnson was wrong when he wrote, "Life is surely given to us

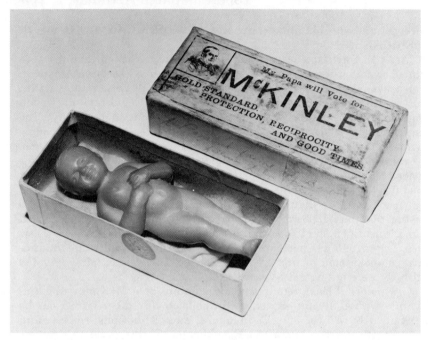

1896 women's campaign objects.

1896 women's campaign objects.

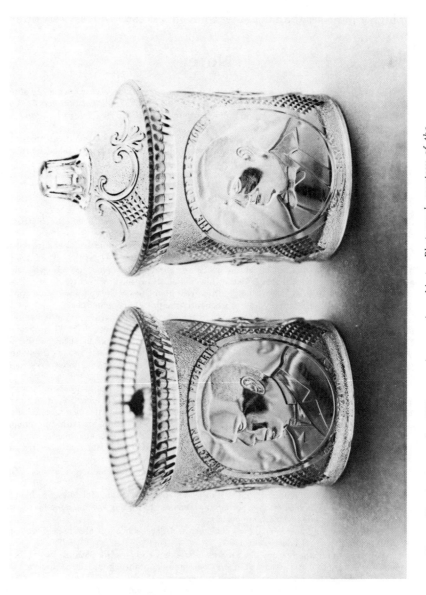

Fig. 7. Not for men only: 1896 women's campaign objects. *Photograph courtesy of the Smithsonian Institution.*

for higher purposes than to gather what our ancestors have wisely thrown away."

Notes

[1]The best collections of these can be found in Theodore L. Hake, *Encyclopedia of Political Buttons: United States, 1896-1972* (New York, 1974), 13-53; Hake, *Political Buttons: Book III, 1789-1916* (York, Pa., 1978), 138-175; and Richard Bristow, *The Illustrated Political Button Book*, 4th ed. (Santa Cruz, Ca., 1973), 11-52.

[2]Such items commonly receive token coverage at best in volumes on political Americana invariably monopolized by buttons. The best source of information on them would be the auction catalogues issued by various dealers in political collectibles

[3]See Paul W. Glad, *McKinley, Bryan, and the People* (Philadelphia, 1964); Stanley L. Jones, *The Presidential Election of 1896* (Madison, 1964); Margaret Leech, *In the Days of McKinley* (New York, 1959), 66-96; Paolo E. Coletta, *William Jennings Bryan, I: Political Evangelist, 1860-1908* (Lincoln, Neb., 1964), 99-212; and R. Hal Williams, *Years of Decision: American Politics in the 1890s* (New York, 1978), 97-127. Vachel Lindsay's marvelous poem "Bryan, Bryan, Bryan, Bryan" remains unsurpassed in conveying the tenor of the campaign.

[4]This issue evolved from a widespread belief that America's economic ills, so apparent in the depression beginning in 1893, were caused primarily by the Coinage Act of 1873. The Silverites hoped to replace this with the bimetallic system originally established in 1837, with silver accepted in unlimited quantities at 1/16 the value of gold. Since silver was currently worth only about 1/30 as much as gold, it was thought that great quantities of the metal would be minted, thus increasing the money supply and subsequently the price of commodities.

"Free silver" proved enormously popular with debt-ridden southern and western farmers, struggling for survival in the face of horrendously low cotton and grain prices. When President Cleveland in effect declared war on the concept by leading the campaign to repeal the Sherman Silver Purchase Act, enraged silverites took control of the Democratic party, setting the stage for Bryan's 1896 crusade. For a lucid, detailed account of these developments, see Jones, *Presidential Election of 1896*, 3-73.

[5]This was a compromise written into the Republican platform to placate McKinley. Something of a "closet" bimetallist in his own right, he wanted to avoid a party split on an issue he regarded as inconsequential. As a result, he was denounced by silverites as a "straddle-bug."

[6]This notion apparently emanated from McKinley's close relationship with his campaign manager, Cleveland's millionaire Marcus Alonzo Hanna, and was exploited most savagely by Homer Davenport, whose New York *Journal* cartoons featured "Dollar Mark" as a bloated giant with dollar signs on his suit and McKinley as a dwarf in Hanna's pocket.

[7]At 1896 market prices, "16 to 1" would create a silver dollar with a bullion value of only fifty-three cents.

[8]Although this term did not originate with the McKinley campaign, McKinley was fond of it and used it constantly in his orations, perhaps as a means of avoiding specific references to gold that might have alienated western supporters.

[9]The tariff had long been McKinley's pet cause and discussion of the blessings of protection invariably dominated his speeches in 1896.

[10]Although this rather catchy slogan was used extensively during McKinley's bid for the Republican nomination and remained in vogue to some extent throughout the campaign, this is the only campaign item I know of on which it appears.

[11]These items are probably an accurate reflection of Bryan's inability to seek a broader constituency, for many of his speeches in industrial centers consisted mainly of praise for the farmers. See Jones, *Presidential Election of 1896*, 313-314.

[12]Flag-oriented campaign items are a rather common phenomenon and many 1896 McKinley ones appear to have been stock designs, for identical items exist with pictures of Bryan or various candidates for local office. There is no question, however, that 1896 McKinley items utilized this motif to an unusual extent. His campaign also distributed millions of small flags, flag ribbons, and plain flag buttons to make McKinley and Old Glory interchangeable in voters' minds. See Jones, *Presidential Election of 1896*, 291-293.

[13]Ironically, the Republicans appear to have quit using the Civil War to win votes in the 1900 campaign, not because it was unethical but because they now had a new war on which to base their patriotic appeal.

[14]It is altogether possible that if ribbons and badges were catalogued with the same diligence that celluloid buttons have been, there would exist sufficient evidence to closely approximate Bryan's travels. McKinley's itinerary would remain more difficult to reconstruct, since many of the delegations that made the pilgrimage to Canton wore plain gold ribbons, standard campaign buttons, or badges merely indicating membership in the organizations they represented.

[15]Williams, *Years of Decision*, 97.

[16]In a market governed primarily by the law of supply-and-demand, 1896 items generally appear in auctions much more often than comparable ones from other elections of that era and invariably bring a lower price. It might be argued that the McKinley items are more plentiful simply because his 1896 campaign was so amply funded that an unusual quantity were made and given out. This would not, however, account for the same phenomenon with Bryan items, since his 1896 campaign was unusually poverty-stricken.

[17]These "sound money clubs" are often explained as attempts by employers to coerce their workers to support McKinley. Paolo Coletta even gives credence to stories of workers forced to sing pro-McKinley songs at "sound money" demonstrations who mumbled softly a rather contrived ditty about "millionaire employers" and "goldbugs' greed" instead. See Coletta, *William Jennings Bryan, I,* 201-202. It is difficult to reconcile this, however, with the graphic labor assertiveness during the period on other issues and with the large majorities McKinley received in almost every industrial center on election day.

[18]This problem is compounded by the fact that some newspapers issued buttons for both candidates, apparently as give-aways to boost circulation rather than endorsement items.

[19]Bryan did win 85% of the vote in Colorado, 83% in Utah, 81% in Nevada, 80% in Montana, and 78% in Idaho.

[20]Bryan did well among the solidly Democratic Irish voters in the Northeast, who occasionally referred to him as "O'Bryan" or even "O'Brien" in their literature, and at least held his own with McKinley among ethnics generally in that region except for the Jewish voters, who perceived him as anti-Semitic. His overwhelming rejection by Midwestern ethnics, however, especially Scandinavians and Germans, proved fatal for his chances of victory. See Jones, *Presidential Election of 1896,* 345-346; Coletta, *William Jennings Bryan I,* 191; Glad, *McKinley, Bryan and the People,* 204; and Williams, *Years of Decision,* 125.

[21]Without falling prey to the notion that anything delicate or decorative should be classified as "feminine," I am convinced that such items were mainly intended to please women, since wives were invariably conceded authority over home furnishings, decorations, and bric-a-brac in the Victorian household. In the case of bracelet charms, mirrors, pincushions, and articles of feminine wearing apparel, of course, no reasonable doubt exists.

[22]Perhaps the best of these is one worn by William Howard Taft's supporters in 1908 that read "VOTE FOR TAFT THIS TIME, YOU CAN VOTE FOR BRYAN ANYTIME."

Campaign Appeals to Women

Edith P. Mayo

Women's involvement and participation in America's political activities did not begin with their organized drive to obtain the vote. Women have been involved in politics since the beginning of the republic, and the major parties, Democrats, Republicans and Whigs, produced and distributed campaign items which had a special appeal for women.

The object collections in the Division of Political History of the Smithsonian Institution demonstrate a continuing presence of "women's appeal" items throughout our electoral history. In treating the subject of campaign appeals to women, it seemed logical to assume a greater effort by the parties to gain the support of a new bloc of voters constituting half the electorate—women—after the granting of suffrage than before. Judging from the campaign artifacts, this does not appear to be the case. In determining the campaign appeal to women, I have sought both general trends in campaign objects to present the type of appeal used in a particular era, and representative elections (1840, 1888, 1952) which may be examined in detail.[1]

Early campaign objects from the era of Washington through the 1824 election were predominantly clothing buttons with the candidate's name and/or patriotic slogans, ceramic tableware, and printed textiles. All are items with a distinctly "home" appeal, calculated to reinforce the intensely personal patriotic and partisan attitudes of the family. An example of such an item is a red tile mold, probably used as a decoration for the making of bread or butter, with a standing figure of John Quincy Adams and the legend: "Home Industry, Peece [sic], Liberty, J.Q. Adams" from the election of 1824.[2]

By the election of 1828, in addition to ceramics and textiles, such distinctly feminine items as sewing boxes for candidates Adams and Jackson had been added, as well as a lovely tortoise shell comb with a likeness of Old Hickory to adorn a lady's hair. During the 1828 Adams-Jackson campaign, women participated in a multitude of non-voting political activities such as rallies, parades, banquets, mass meetings and barbeques.[3] Women actively entered into the production of campaign materials themselves by sewing or decorating the elaborate (or crudely made) campaign banners of that day.

The campaign of 1840, which pitted incumbent President Martin Van Buren against William Henry Harrison, saw an unprecedented explosion of political activity, and a production of Harrison campaign items by the Whigs which went unequalled for another forty years.[4] (No women's appeal items for Van Buren were located.) Women's activities in 1840 included

Fig. 1 Ceramic tableware from early campaigns. These pieces are typical of the items produced. (Note the misspelling of Monroe's name.)

Fig. 2 Sewing box produced for the campaign of Andrew Jackson (probably 1828).

holding campaign teas, making speeches, participating in torchlight parades, letter-writing campaigns, and reportedly attending two to three day rallies by the thousands.[5] To encourage and reinforce this political activity by women, the Whigs greatly expanded the range of ceramic wares available for the home (all the Harrison "log cabin" motif.) Cream pitchers and sugar bowls, as well as cups, plates, and glassware abounded. Tablespoons with Harrison's likeness on the handle were produced, as well as women's hair brushes with the candidate on the handle. Lovely, colorful quilts, fashioned from campaign ribbons, were a very popular item. Stationery, with Harrison's likeness and log cabin motif, was plentiful. The strong women's campaign appeal by the Whigs undoubtedly encouraged increased female participation in pro-Harrison campaign activities. Whether this paid off in women's influence over the political choice of the men in their families at the polls is impossible to determine, but is an interesting point on which to speculate in view of Harrison's victory.

The campaigns between 1844 and 1888 generally reveal a very low production of women's appeal campaign items by either party fielding a candidate. Some of the earlier ceramic and textile items remain, but on a greatly reduced scale. The campaign of 1856 marked the beginning of the Republican Party. The Republicans produced a campaign medal with the likeness of their first presidential candidate, John C. Fremont, with the legend: "COL. JOHN C. FREMONT/JESSIE'S CHOICE." Jessie was Fremont's wife, daughter of the distinguished Senator, Thomas Hart

Fig. 3 Typical tableware with log cabin and hard cider motif produced for the 1840 campaign of William Henry Harrison.

Benton, of Missouri. Jessie had eloped with Fremont, marrying him against the wishes of her father, thus making the statement "Jessie's Choice" a particularly powerful one. Campaign music was also produced entitled, "We'll Give 'Em Jessie!" ("Jessie" was an euphemism of the day roughly comparable to the modern "We'll Give 'Em Hell!") While campaign objects such as medals, banners, and parade items without a particular "women's appeal" were produced for this campaign, the use of Jessie (probably intended to draw the western votes of the followers of Senator Benton) was the first use of the wife of a candidate as a "First Lady" (a term not then in use) appeal.[6]

Beginning with the "Jessie's Choice" medal at mid-century, and continuing until the end of the century, the wife of the political candidate was increasingly introduced into campaigns as the symbolic idealization of American womanhood. The Victorian "Ideal" of woman as paragon of virtue and queen of the home was touted as evidence of the elevated status of woman in society, and admirably suited to the production of First Lady appeal items.

The height of this trend may be seen in the campaign of 1888 which brought a great resurgence of campaign items related to women. The "women's appeal" by both Democrats and Republicans is that of the late Victorian Ideal of womanhood: wife, mother, helpmate, queen of the domestic scene—in short, "woman in the home." The campaign articles produced reinforce this impression. They appeal to woman in the realm of her home duties: helpmate to her husband, who makes all the political decisions, but whom she perhaps indirectly or subtly influences in his opinions.

The ceramic objects for household use, familiar from earlier campaigns, are still much in evidence: china pitchers and plates with the likenesses of candidates Cleveland and Harrison (some ceramic items now include the likenesses of candidates' wives); an amber glass cup with a likeness of Cleveland; a brown ceramic cream pitcher with a likeness of Cleveland; a glass plate bearing Harrison's image in the center. New types of household objects were introduced. Table napkins resembling the American flag with the legend "Harrison and Morton," cotton pillow cases with lithographs of the Republican candidates, and silk scarves with likenesses and names of the party hopefuls were among the new items. Campaign jewelry for women was introduced in 1888 in the form of pendants and necklaces with the candidates' portraits.

While traditional items promoting the Republican and Democratic candidates were produced in large numbers, the campaign of 1888 sounded several new notes: for the first time a woman appeared on the campaign material itself as an appeal to the public in her own right; the manufacturing and commercial interests of the country recognized the effectiveness of a campaign appeal to women as consumers.

The overwhelming majority of "new" objects were produced by the Democrats and centered, not surprisingly, on Frances Cleveland, wife of President Grover Cleveland. While it may seem to modern minds singularly inappropriate to elevate the wife of Cleveland who was a "...middle-aged, corpulent statesman, the self-confessed sire of a bastard child,"[7] no greater symbol could have availed itself for mass dissemination than Frances Folsom Cleveland, First Lady of the Land. Frances was hailed as young and beautiful, the epitome of womanly innocence and social grace. Nothing was mentioned about the double standard—indeed, public sentiment did not seem to notice there was one! For the first time a candidate's wife appeared on a campaign button—the likeness of Mrs. Cleveland. She was featured on plates, campaign ribbons, table napkins, special campaign sheet music, handkerchiefs, and playing cards. Frances Cleveland even appeared on a beautifully-colored, separate poster of her own circulated during the campaign—(the Farah Fawcett of her times!)

Reinforcing the theme of the First Lady as homemaker and helpmate is the popular literature of the time. *Cosmopolitan Magazine* of August 1888 carried an article entitled, "The Ladies of the American Court,"[8] detailing at length the glittering social gatherings and receptions held at the White House. It lauds Mrs. Cleveland as the "noble type of American womanhood" and stresses the great importance of her social and domestic role as mistress of the White House to the functioning of good government.

The nation's manufacturers and commercial interests also recognized a good thing when they saw it. A sure yardstick in the measurement of any social phenomenon is its ability to be exploited in the form of "sales" by the business community. The campaign of 1888 and Frances Folsom Cleveland presented an excellent opportunity. Though sugar-coated with Victorian idealism, the importance of women as consumers was obviously recognized. Again, it was Mrs. Cleveland who appeared for the first time on advertising cards during the campaign. One such card in color, for the Gilbert Manufacturing Company which produced cloth, depicted President and Mrs. Cleveland seated, looking at a bolt of cloth, obviously pondering whether or not to purchase it. The President is saying to his wife: "My dear, it is all right, you see the name GILBERT MANUFACTURING COMPANY." A similar appeal was made by "The Best Tonic," which was "for sale by all druggists" displaying a lovely colored portrait of Mrs. Cleveland.

The favorite of all women, however, must have been that produced by the Merrick Thread Company, which showed Frances' and Grover's portraits intertwined within a heart made of thread, held by Cherubs. The caption read: "THE THREAD THAT BINDS THE UNION" (!!)

The rematch of Cleveland and Harrison in the campaign of 1892 did not seem to produce the outpouring of women's appeal objects which the 1888 campaign had generated. No doubt, many items were still in circulation from the previous campaign.

The 1896 match of McKinley versus Bryan again saw an enormous production of campaign materials aimed directly at women. The Democrats apparently produced little material using Mrs. Bryan with the exception of a campaign poster showing Bryan with his wife and children. While Mrs. McKinley, an invalid, did not provide the Republicans with a wifely symbol nearly so appealing as Frances Cleveland, the Republicans had plenty of money and produced massive quantities of objects with a women's appeal. There were the time-honored plates and cups, silver spoons, bandannas and handkerchiefs. To these traditional objects were added metal trays, pillows

Fig. 4 Colored campaign poster of Frances Cleveland, 1888.

and pillow cases, jewelry items such as rings and bracelet charms, mirrors, tapestries, pin cushions, and a magnificent colored, silk ribbon for the "Women's McKinley Club of Canton, Ohio." (See Roger Fischer Figure 7.)

From the turn of the century until 1920, with the serious drive of the suffrage movement, came a virtual halt in the use of the candidate's wife as a First Lady appeal, and a noticeable decline in the production of campaign items appealing to women. With few exceptions such as a Teddy Bear pillow top, a plate for Mrs. Theodore Roosevelt, a few trays, coasters, and kerchiefs for William Howard Taft, a "Republican Housewives Scarf" for Harding, and sheet music for Mrs. Harding (published in March, 1921 for the Inaugural, not while her husband was still a candidate), campaign appeals to women by the parties drop to virtually nothing. No First Lady "candidates" appear on political buttons again until the 1930s. The only woman figure to appear on political buttons (and even she disappears after World War I) is the mythical Columbia—representing the soul of the nation—endorsing candiates for the presidency.

Woman suffrage might be thought to have presented the political parties with a golden opportunity to court a woman's constituency. Almost every suffrage item extant in political collections, however, was produced by a pro-suffrage women's lobby group and not by the political parties. The absence of First Lady "candidates" and women's appeal campaign items during this period suggests deep-seated confusion and ambivalence over the role of women in society and, particularly, in political life.

The enfranchisement of over half the adult population with the passage of the Nineteenth Amendment in 1920 granting full suffrage to women, would lead one to expect a concomitant party "appeal" to these new voters, perhaps on a wide variety of issues and levels. Such does not appear to have been the case. Suffragists anticipated (and professional politicans and special interest lobbies feared) that women would constitute a political entity in themselves, thus wielding a large "bloc" vote or forming a separate political party. (The latter was envisioned by Alice Paul in founding the National Woman's Party.) This woman's vote, organized as a bloc, would be able to wield great political power for the accomplishment of social reforms which the women had sought: continuance of prohibition, the passage of protective labor legislation for women and children, the furtherance of world peace, and the enactment of laws favorble to the advancement of the economic, political, and social status of women. This did not occur. Most women gradually entered into political affiliation with one of the two major political parties.

Moreover, women did not register or vote in anywhere near the numbers which were anticipated by either the suffragists or their male opponents. Though the eligible number of women voters in 1920 was estimated to be 16,000,000, only 25% of this number exercised their right to vote. For those who did, the Republicans produced a beautiful gold silk ribbon with the legend: "I CAST MY FIRST VOTE FOR THE STRAIGHT REPUBLICAN TICKET." The number of women participating in the election of 1924 was estimated to have been only slightly higher.[9]

The campaign of 1924 was characterized by an almost total lack of campaign items with any appeal to women. Only two were found in the

Political History collections: a silver thimble with red and blue edge for "Coolidge and Dawes,' and a pudding dish for "Davis." Mrs. Coolidge was not in evidence on posters or buttons. The strongly feminine appeals of the late nineteenth century, instead of persisting or increasing, had almost completely disappeared.

The majority of both men and women seemed almost embarrassed at the thought of "equality." The men, who still controlled the political machinery and decision-making, realized that they must somehow recognize woman's vote as a new political fact of life, but bent over backward not to encourage voting. They did not want to risk upsetting the status quo of the political apple cart. Most women, for their part, were neither enthusiastic nor prepared to exercise their franchise. They were faced with the prospect that voting was now a "duty" which they must "perform," but they felt there was a conflict between voting and yet remaining feminine.[10] There was also the feeling that women should now be able to "clean up" politics, but doubt was expressed that this could be accomplished.

The literature of the times, both partisan and non-partisan, sheds considerable light on these attitudes. The Republican Platform of 1924, in its section entitled "Women," stated that the Republicans "...extend our greeting to the women delegates who for the first time under Federal authorization sit with us in full equality... We welcome them not as assistants or as auxiliary representatives, but as co-partners in the great political work in which we are engaged..."[11]

These sentiments sounded noble in the platform, but it was clear from President Coolidge's acceptance speech that general public opinion still knew where "woman's place" was. Coolidge stated: "For the first time, after having the opportunity fully to organize, the women of the Nation are bringing the new force which they represent directly to bear on our political affairs. I know that the influence of womanhood will guard the home, which is the citadel of the Nation. I know it will be a protector of childhood. I know it will be on the side of humanity...I want every woman to vote."[12]

That everyone felt in some way self-conscious about the woman's vote can be seen by the popular literature then appearing in women's magazines. That women needed a "political education" was also greatly in evidence. *Good Housekeeping* ran an article by Ida Tarbell entitled, "Is Woman's Suffrage a Failure?" She pointed out that after only four years, who can truly say? Nevertheless, this lament of the "failure" of women to exercise suffrage and thereby to "clean up" politics (a prime argument for the granting of woman suffrage) was now being used as a prime deterrent to keep women from the polls. Tarbell's attitude asserted, "we must not let them intimidate us." She assured women that as they grew more accustomed to the idea of voting and experienced in political matters there would indeed be an increase in the number of women voters but "it takes time and experience to use [the vote] effectively.... The only real failure at present in woman's suffrage is the failure to exercise it.... The majority of women are probably a little booth shy, still a little awed by their responsibility, often a little afraid to talk politics because conscious that they are amateurs."[13] The article ended by urging women to exercise their new right.

"To Vote or Not To Vote," which appeared in the *Ladies' Home Journal,* urged women to think of voting not from the standpoint of participation in "politics" which had a "dirty" connotation, but as an exercise of her say in civic affairs which intimately affected all aspects of the daily life of her family.[14]

"American Women's Ineffective Use of the Vote" in *Current History Magazine* pointed out a fact which was largely ignored by other writers: most states did not separate ballots by sex. It was, therefore, impossible to determine whether the "woman's vote" had been effective or not. The authors also stated that studies had shown that women tend to support "morality" in political campaigns and speculated that the reason the difference between men and women's votes at the national level was not greater was because, at the national level, "moral" issues were not so sharply drawn and it may have been difficult for women to distinguish them.[15] [!!]

With the beginning of woman's vote, there began almost immediately a debate among political experts within the national parties and among political historians as to whether there was, in reality, such an entity as the "women's vote." The debate has continued to the present day, producing various studies which attempt to explain or analyze the phenomenon.

As early as 1928, F.R. Kent in *The Great Game of Politics* explained: "The woman's vote has changed nothing at all in politics.... If women voted...with solidarity and singleness of purpose...it is easy to see they could bring about a political revolution in the country.... But women do not and never will vote that way. There are as many varieties of women as there are of men—perhaps more. They divide and disagree in much the same way and over much the same things, and they are swayed by much the same arguments. Women neither feel alike nor think alike, and while they are no more the creatures of prejudice than are men, they do not and will not vote alike."[16] A host of other experts and studies to the present day have likewise concluded that there are no sex-related differences in voting behavior or party affiliation.[17]

Few women's appeal items, including the always-traditional buttons, scarves, or plates, appeared during the 1930s and 1940s. A kerchief promoting the Democratic stand for the repeal of Prohibition, an FDR clock, a few buttons favoring Edith Willkie for First Lady, and many attacking Eleanor Roosevelt as First Lady are what little remains. A variety of factors probably contributed to the lack of women's appeal items during this era: the Depression and World War II greatly reduced the production of campaign objects of any kind; the return of the image of "First Lady" in a negative role (Eleanor Roosevelt is the single instance in our history where the First Lady was the object of the opprobrium of a large segment of public opinion); an acceptance that there was no "woman's vote."

Despite these factors, the integration of women into political life made definite strides. Franklin Roosevelt appointed Frances Perkins as Secretary of Labor, the first woman to serve in the presidential cabinet. Eleanor Roosevelt's political involvement was widely visible but earned her widespread disdain. Among the less visible New Deal advisors whom

Roosevelt brought with him to Washington was Mary (Molly) Dewson who became the woman "admitted for the first time to [political] policy conferences." Dewson was responsible for organizing the first effective women's organization within a political party, the Women's Division of the Democratic National Committee, begun in 1933.[18] "Under Molly Dewson's leadership women were for the first time to do effective work of their own choosing in campaigns, to be taken seriously by the men as an organized and potent force on a national scale. The Women's Division of the Democratic National Committee was to serve as a pattern for women's organizations of both major parties for the next twenty years."[19]

It was Dewson's goal to organize women effectively within the party framework and make their usefulness forcefully felt in the national organization by organizing women on the local as well as the national level. The tangible results of her efforts may be seen in campaign pamphlets of 1936 entitled, "Democratic Victory" and "Dedicated to Mrs. County Leader." In this pamphlet, a new departure in the party appeal to women, Dewson declared: "You, Mrs. County Leader, are the keystone in the arch of Democratic Victory."[20] The brochure outlined specific steps for women party workers in getting out the vote and influencing the voter to cast a ballot for the Democratic candidate.

The pattern of women in both parties as the mainstay of grass roots political work (but seldom, unlike the Roosevelt administration, with access to policymaking at the top party levels) has remained until the 1970s when the women's movement began to force changes in party structure and access for women.

The post war era brought the return of a small number of items appealing to women voters. The Dewey-Truman election of 1948 saw the production of ladies' umbrellas, powder compacts, and scarves in small numbers by the Republicans. I have located no items produced by the Democrats.

By 1952, women had gradually become accustomed to their role as voters. Of the total 61,5 million people casting ballots in 1952, 30,900,000 were men and 30,300,000 were women.[21] The Republican Party, in particular, made a concerted effort to capture what had now become half of the electorate.[22] Democratic items for women were notable by their absence.

The "it's alright for women to vote" literature of the twenties had, by 1952, become a frankly partisan appeal to the woman voter. Senator Margaret Chase Smith and Mrs. India Edwards urged women to vote for the Republican and Democratic candidates respectively in articles appearing in *Woman's Home Companion*.[23] Both women stressed their candidates' views on "peace" and the status of women in government and society.

By the 50s, too, the effectiveness of the work by Molly Dewson had paid off in generous dividends for both national parties, which had built up large and efficient grass roots women's organizations. Pamphlets for women party workers were widely circulated. Highly organized telephoning, radio and television[24] parties were conducted, especially by the Republicans. Though these local women's organizations are today taken for granted by both national parties,[25] their emergence in 1952 in such abundance and such strength, with such effective organization, was little short of startling.

Fig. 5 Powder compact with likeness of Thomas E. Dewey, campaign of 1948.

The popular literature again bore this out. "Political Pilgrim's Progress—Women Organize for Action" appeared in the *Ladies' Home Journal* outlining the type of political campaigning activity conducted by both Republican and Democratic women's organizations and giving a glimpse of just how vast this network had become.[26]

Marion Sanders, a woman politician, explained the growth of this phenomenon in the highly organized modern campaign. She claimed that the largest group of women in political activity in the 1950s were the "ardent amateurs," who made up the majority of local political precinct workers. These women, who then outnumbered men in political volunteer work, staged political get-togethers, phone calling parties, and television sessions. Sanders explained that women had more free time, while their children were in school, to conduct meetings at home which their husbands, with full time jobs, could not hope to do. Women's flexible domestic schedule left time for phoning, canvassing, meetings, tea parties, driving voters to the polls, and staffing the polls themselves.[27]

Campaign objects were circulated in enormous quantities in 1952. Mass production contributed in part to the large circulation, but the recognition that an appeal to the large number of women voters was imperative cannot by any means be discounted. Campaign items with feminine appeal returned to the scene in abundance. Buttons with the picture of the candidate's wife were again circulated, though to a degree undreamed of at an earlier date.[28] The wife of the vice presidential candidate, Pat Nixon, appeared on campaign buttons for the first time in 1952 and was highly popularized.

Household items such as plates, cup and saucer sets, salt and peppers, bud vases, pitchers, cream and sugar sets, and cast iron trivets survive in enormous quantities. So too does campaign jewelry in the form of necklaces, bracelets, earrings, and pins, all bearing the likeness or name of the candidate. In addition, there are "Republican" emery boards, napkins, mirrors, combs, thimbles, corsages, compacts, and fans.

Fig. 6 Political button for Ike and Mamie Eisenhower, campaign of 1952.

Though the silk scarves of 1888 foreshadowed an appeal to women through wearing apparel, the 1952 campaign produced an almost unbelievable "apparel appeal." There were "I Like Ike" women's blouses and dresses, Republican umbrellas, "Ike and Dick" sunglasses, and to complete every well-dressed Republican woman's wardrobe, nylon stockings proclaiming to the world on both calves, "I Like Ike!" And what fashionable Republican woman would dare venture forth without her GOP perfume, "For the Scent of Victory."??

Political campaigning with a women's appeal had, however, by 1952 become more sophisticated than simple domestic objects and wearing apparel. The Republicans sought to take the appeal a step further by carrying out the themes of their campaign slanted toward women through campaign objects.

Three major campaign themes of the Republican party during the 1952 election were the Korean War, corruption or "the mess in Washington" as it was called, and a balanced budget. While these themes have universal appeal, the Republicans cleverly managed to portray each of them to women with a particularly feminine "angle." The Korean War was pictured as involving a son or a husband. A campaign comic book published by the Republican National Committee graphically portrayed a woman whose son was being shot at in Korea and a sweetheart whose boyfriend would be unable to make it to their wedding because "the war" had intervened. Ike had promised to end the war and "bring the boys home." Women were told that since Ike was a brilliant military hero and knew first-hand the horrors of war, he had not only the knowhow but the incentive to "bring the boys home." Women obviously believed this claim. According to pollster Louis Harris, "Women. . . were more disturbed about the Korean War than men in 1952. In fact, there is evidence to indicate that women were among the real prime movers in making the Korean War a major and decisive influence in the final outcome of the election."[29]

The "mess in Washington" was translated from a rather unintelligible bureaucratic problem into a rather simple matter which housewives readily understood. Cleaning up the mess in Washington was portrayed in terms of the housewife's cleaning her home. Red, white, and blue scrub pails with the slogan "Let's Clean Up With Eisenhower and Nixon," and large "Ike and Dick" brooms were widely distributed. Women were urged to help Ike, "a thrifty housekeeper," to "sweep out the mess."[30]

The problem of the balanced budget was also translated into the language of the average housewife—it was equated with her balancing of the family budget. The implication was clear: if she could do it, so could the government. A brochure produced by the Republicans displaying a housewife on the cover asked women: "How Much Did Your GROCERIES COST YOU TODAY?" It explained the rise in prices and the high cost of living by declaring that "waste, corruption, extravagance, blunders, bungling, bureaucrats and taxes are hidden in your grocery bag. . ."[31] Following this theme to its conclusion, Republicans circulated extra large "Ike and Dick" shopping bags—no doubt to show the housewife just how much she could buy if Ike were elected.

Harris again pointed out that this appeal was not by any means lost on

Fig. 7 Metal cleaning pail produced for the 1952 campaign.

women voters. Pressures on the family budget to buy more than there was money for fell largely on women. "This was a crucial fact in the 1952 elections. Women lost faith in the Democratic Party to help them financially. Polls show...women thought there was more likelihood of the Republicans keeping prices in line than the Democrats.... Women more significantly than men felt the Republican Party would bring them economic security."[32]

The great effort of the Republicans to capture the woman's vote in 1952 was not without results at the polls. Kruschke, after conducting polls in Michigan, and studying polls of others in the 1952 election, concluded that women in greater percentages than men (52% of the men and 58% of the women) voted for Eisenhower and contributed significantly to his victory.[33] Harris substantially agrees with this conclusion.[4] Kruschke's samplings are significant in finding that all the women interviewed who voted for Eisenhower mentioned as their reason one of the three "women's appeals.[35-36]

From the zenith reached in the 1952 election, campaign appeals to women have greatly receded. Buttons, plates, scarves, and jewelry in moderate quantities were produced for the Ike and Stevenson re-match in 1956, and the Nixon-Kennedy contest in 1960. The production of these items, however, came nowhere near the production of 1952. In 1964, Johnson made wise use of the "First Lady" appeal by sending the "Lady Bird Johnson Special" campaign train throughout the South (where Johnson was not popular due to his support of Civil Rights.) Lady Bird was to court votes in dulcet Southern tones. Mrs. Johnson was presented in a non-challenging light—being the supportive helping hand that good wives should be. In so doing she made the transition from campaign symbol to active partisan campaigner using the still-believed-in charm of Southern womanhood to accomplish the feat. The Republicans circulated scarves (western variety), jewelry, perfume (Gold Water), and dolls imaginatively costumed as cowgirls. But, any major campaign appeals to women through object materials seemed by the mid-sixties to have become a relic of the past.

Certainly the decision in modern campaigns to expend funds on extensive surveys and opinion polling and on exorbitantly expensive media time leaves money for production of appeal gimmicks virtually non-existent. The almost universal acceptance by political scientists, polling experts, party campaign managers, even organized women's groups that "there is no women's vote" discourages a women's appeal. The Women's Division of the Democratic National Committee has decided in 1980 not to treat women as a "special constituency" any longer because, with 50% of the convention delegates now being women (mandated by Party rule changes), "women are mainstreaming." I was assured that "not singling women out any longer is a measure of their acceptance."[37] One must wonder, reading history, if this is a wise decision. Women should consider further whether accepting, or participating in, this decision enhances their own interests. Perhaps an examination of the patterns of material culture appeal to women can be helpful in this consideration.

In three instances of a major "women's appeal" (1840, 1896, 1952), the party mounting the appeal won the election. Perhaps this is coincidence. However, women's organized networking should not be underestimated. One would guess that such party networking could only be enhanced by a group appeal. While the 1930s and '40's saw little "women's appeal" through objects by the Democrats (probably due to Depression and World War II), that Party seemed to benefit enormously from the organized efforts of the Women's Division. By 1952, the Republicans had beaten them at their own game.

While the physical items themselves appealing to women have not changed a great deal in the century and a half, there has been enormous fluctuation in the periods in which these appeals have occurred. The strongest campaign appeals to women have occurred at those times in our history when the belief in and societal enforcement of the Cult of Domesticity was at its height: mid-nineteenth century, later nineteenth century and the 1950's. Almost all the items are couched in "feminine" and "household" terms. This is hardly a coincidence.

Issues which raise substantive and legitimate questions about women's

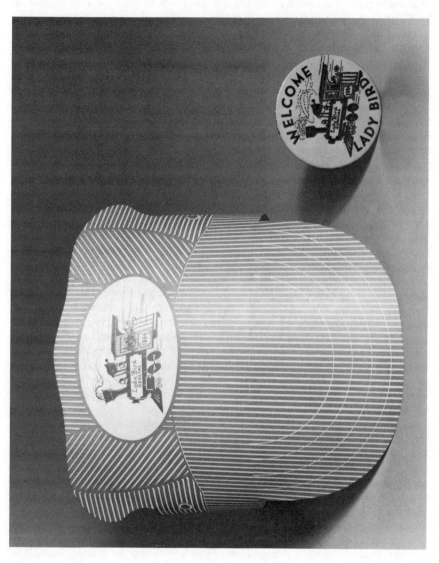

Fig. 8 Paper hat and button produced for the Lady Bird Johnson Specia̤ ⋯mpaign train tour of the Southern states, 1964.

relationship to political life, such as women's vote, do not produce an appeal by the parties which would logically be expected. Production of campaign appeal objects suggest that with suffrage, as with the Equal Rights Amendment, affirmative action in employment, child care, and abortion of the 1970's and '80's, substantive issues often are not addressed by the major parties and candidates themselves. Instead, these issues are addressed by women's social and political organizations whose feminist thrust is reflected in their objects and lobbying aimed at the parties. Women's lobby groups (pro and anti), in the suffrage era and currently, create their own appeal to women and some portion of this is translated into party policy, but rarely into campaign objects.

The entire span of "women's issues"—except those which involve the safe assumption of women in the home caring for children, or issues which can be presented in those terms—have been thought to be polarizing and divisive and are, therefore, not to be "appealed to" in terms of political paraphernalia at the risk of alienating other large aggregate groups.

Current women's issues, as with suffrage, were brought to the front not by the parties but by women's lobby groups which strongly suggests that issues which matter in women's lives are not successfully represented within the political party forum.[38] This is partly because women traditionally have lacked *real* representation or decision-making power within the party structure, and partly because real women's issues have been ignored by the parties.

The fact that "women" often do not appear as a category in political surveys and opinion polls[39] speaks powerfully to the public perception of the irrelevance of issues affecting women to the "general population." Often, not until these same issues appear in another form (will they affect "the family?" will "the state" have to pay for it? will "the government" or "taxpayers" be involved?)—as *someone else's* concern—do they merit being categorized as a voting question. Perhaps this perception helps explain why, when women now outvote men,[40] political studies continue to find lower interest, feeling of efficacy, and participation (other than voting) rates in politics among women than men.[41]

The assumption of political equality for women is a premature one at present. There continues to be a deep ambivalence toward women's role in politics and society which says on the one hand that a "women's constituency" does not exist (i.e., women are just like "everybody else;"—"mainstreaming"), but on the other mirrors a deep-rooted anxiety about appealing to "women's issues" for fear of upsetting the prevailing social order.

The concept of "mainstreaming" may be an attempt, under an inclusive-sounding catchword, to transcend sexual politics. Does it transcend sex, or merely provide another way not to deal with crucial issues, ignoring women again?

If political studies are correct that women continue to perceive candidates and issues differently, that they feel intensely about some issues which do not interest men so greatly,[42] might it not be worth consideration by the parties, in their extensive polling, to determine whether "appeals" calculated to reach the party's female constituency are worth the investment? Perhaps this would produce more equitable representation and intelligent political discussion of issues which affect over half our population.

Notes

I would like to express gratitude to my colleague, Herbert R. Collins, for his generous assistance in locating "women's appeal" objects within the Division of Political History collections. I am also indebted to Mary Lee Kallfelz for sharing with me her unpublished paper, "The Voting Behavior of American Women." Deep appreciation is also due to Constance Potter and Carol Rotundo for their excellent research assistance and unfailing support.

[1]Tangible campaign material was produced in varying quantities during the years and has survived in varying amounts, those elections closer to the present usually, but not always, having a larger number of surviving objects. From 1916 until 1932, however, few campaign objects were produced by either party, and few survive. The parties did not produce materials in equal amounts for any given campaign; hence the distribution of materials is unequal.

States do not separate or count ballots according to sex (some exceptions exist at local levels), and women's voting patterns must be estimated based on extensive polling.

[2]This item is in the campaign collections of the Division of Political History, Smithsonian Institution (DPH, SI). All campaign items noted in this paper are housed in this collection.

[3]Louise M. Young, "Women's Place in American Politics: The Historical Perspective," *Journal of Politics*, 38 (August 1976), 309.

[4]Wilcomb E. Washburn, "The Great Autumnal Madness," *Quarterly Journal of Speech*, 49 (December 1963), 417-431; Roger Fischer, "Genesis of Campaign Artifacts," unpublished manuscript.

[5]Young, 311.

[6]For a treatment of First Ladies as campaign symbols and women's political button iconography see: Edith Mayo, "Ladies and Liberation: Icon and Iconoclast in the Women's Movement," in Ray B. Browne and Marshall Fishwick, eds., *Icons of America* (Bowling Green, Ohio: The Popular Press, 1978), 209-227.

[7]William Burlie Brown, *The People's Choice: the Presidential Image in the Campaign Biography* (Baton Rouge, Louisiana, 1960), 129.

[8]Frank Carpenter, "The Ladies of the American Court," *Cosmopolitan*, V (August 1888), 321-333.

[9]Sophonisba Breckinridge, *Women in the Twentieth Century* (New York, 1933), 245-256.

[10]The seriousness and intensity of extreme role conflict in the socialization of women persists after sixty years of women's voting and is pointed out in a number of modern voting studies. See: Lynn B. Iglitzin, "The Making of the Apolitical Woman: Femininity and Sex Stereotyping in Girls," in Jane S. Jaquette, ed., *Women in Politics* (New York: John Wiley & Sons, 1974), 25-34; Robert Lane, *Political Life* (Glencoe, Ill.: Free Press, 1959), 210-212; Kirsten Amundsen, *A New Look at the Silenced Majorty: Women and American Democracy* (Englewood Cliffs, New Jersey: Prentice-Hall, 1977), 124-129, 136-139; Angus Campbell, Philip Converse, Warren Miller, Donald Stokes, *The American Voter: An Abridgment* (New York: John Wiley & Sons, 1964), 255-261; Marcia Manning Lee, "Why Few Women Hold Public Office: Democracy and Sex Roles," *Political Science Quarterly*, 91 (Summer, 1976), 297-314; Jean Lipman-Blumen, "How Ideology Shapes Women's Lives," *Scientific American*, 226(1972), 34-42; Jane S. Jaquette, "Introduction," in Jane S. Jaquette, ed., *Women in Politics* (New York: John Wiley & Sons, 1974), xix, xxvii.

[11]Republican National Committee, *Platform of the Republican Party Adopted at Cleveland, June 11, 1924.* (Washington, D.C.: 1924), 15. DPH,SI.

[12]Calvin Coolidge, *Address of Acceptance of Calvin Coolidge, August 14, 1924* (Republican National Committee, 1924), 14. DPH, SI.

[13]Ida M. Tarbell, "Is Woman's Suffrage a Failure?" *Good Housekeeping*, LXXIX (October 1924), 240-241.

[14]Alice Ames Winter, "To Vote or Not to Vote," *Ladies' Home Journal*, (October 1924), 21, 155, 157.

[15]S.A. Rice and M.M. Willey, "American Women's Ineffective Use of the Vote," *Current History Magazine*, XX (1924), 645.

[16]F.R. Kent, *The Great Game of Politics* (Garden City, New York, 1928), 172-173.

[17]See: Paul Lazarsfeld, *The People's Choice: How the Voter Makes Up His Mind in a*

Presidential Campaign (New York, 1948), 16-43. Lazarsfeld concluded that social characteristics such as religion, economic and social status, educational level, and individual personality traits determine party preference for both men and women. Therefore, women divide along the same lines as men, often voting as their husbands vote not because they are incapable of political decisions but because they have similar interests and social motivation; Edward M. Bennett and Harriet M. Goodwin, "Emotional Aspects of Political Behavior: The Woman Voter," *Genetic Psychology Monographs,* LVIII, 3-53, conclude that the two major parties are endowed by the voter with "personality" characteristics which correspond to the emotional aspects of the voter's own personality, thus determining party preference. The Democratic Party was seen as more socially conscious, the Republican as more concerned with the individual; Martin Gruberg, *Women in American Politics* (Oshkosh, Wisc.: Academia Press, 1968), Ch. 1; Campbell, et. al., 489-493; Maurice Duverger, *The Political Role of Women* (Unesco, 1955), Ch. 1; Harold F. Gosnell, *Democracy, The Threshold of Freedom* (New York: Ronald Press, 1948), Ch. 4; Lane, *Political Life;* Gabriel Almond and Sidney Verba, *The Civic Culture* (Boston, Mass.: Little, Brown, 1965); Fred Greenstein, "Sex Related Political Differences in Childhood," *Journal of Politics,* 23 (1961), 353-371; Kenneth Langton and M. Kent Jennings, "Mothers versus Fathers in the Formation of Political Attitudes," in Kenneth Langton, ed., *Political Socialization* (New York: Oxford Press, 1969); William Chafe, *The American Woman: Her Changing Social, Economic, and Political Role 1920-1970* (New York: Oxford University Press, 1972), 45.

[18]Eleanor Roosevelt, *Ladies of Courage* (New York, 1954), 18, 11.

[19]Roosevelt, 12.

[20]Mary Dewson, *Democratic Victory* (Democratic National Campaign Committee, 1936), 3. In DPH, SI.

[21]Earl Roger Kruschke, *The Woman Voter* (Washington, D.C., 1955), 4. While this participation rate was the highest for women to that date, several studies state that the percentage of women voting compared to those eligible to vote was 10% below that of males voting who were eligible. See: Lane, 210; Campbell, et. al., 255-256 found that until 1960 the voter participation rate among women was consistently below that of men by 10%.

[22]The Democratic Party produced surprisingly little campaign material of any kind for the 1952 election when compared with the tremendous output of Republican campaign material for the same year.

[23]India Edwards, "Why Vote for Stevenson," and Senator Margaret Chase Smith, "Why Vote for Eisenhower," *Woman's Home Companion* (November 1952), 38-41.

[24]The 1952 election was the first in which national television was employed. The Republicans did not fail to exploit this new campaigning medium. They produced and circulated a most interesting pamphlet, "Your Television Image," which showed marvelous insight into the problems presented by a largely unknown campaign technique. Suggestions to the candidate include how to dress to advantage for television, what colors to wear, what makeup to employ, how to stand and sit, when to walk around, and how to illustrate a speech to hold the attention of a television audience. In DPH, SI.

[25]A great deal of both local and national campaign work and organizing is still done by volunteers. Since the mid-1960s much of this work has been performed by students and young adults of both sexes brought into politics through the civil rights and anti-war movements. Indeed, Jo Freeman, *The Politics of Women's Liberation* (New York: David McKay Co., 1975) credits this phenomenon as one of the radicalizing elements in the rebirth of the feminist movement. Recent studies continue to find "a large pool of women devoting a great amount of time to politics...at the local level." Marcia Manning Lee, 303.

[26]"Political Pilgrim's Progress—Women Organize for Action," *Ladies' Home Journal,* LXIX (September 1952), 25, 162.

[27]Marion K. Sanders, *The Lady and the Vote* (Boston, 1956), 29.

[28]In this respect Stevenson was at a distinct disadvantage having been divorced.

[29]Louis Harris, *Is There a Republican Majority?* (New York, 1954), 111. For a detailed analysis see Ch. 7.

[30]Republican National Committee, *How Much Did Your Groceries Cost You Today?* (Washington, D.C., 1952), 2. In DPH, SI.

[31]*How Much Did Your Groceries Cost?,* 1.

[32]Harris, 110.

[33]Kruschke, 4.

[34]Harris, Ch. 7.

[35]Kruschke, 6-14.

[36]For an opposing view see: "Did Women Elect Eisenhower?" *U.S. News and World Report,* (May 8, 1953), 45-46.

[37]In a telephone interview with Greta Dewald of the Women's Division of the Democratic National Committee, April 9, 1980, polls by Gallup, Harris, ABC, and CBS were cited to establish that "there is no women's vote." Almost incredibly, I also learned that the League of Women Voters, the National Women's Political Caucus, the Women's Campaign Fund, the Women's Education Fund, and the National Organization for Women have never conducted polls or studies on the voting patterns of women.

[38]Jaquette, xxiv.

[39]Hazel Erskine, "The Polls: Women's Role," *Public Opinion Quarterly,* 35 (Summer 1971), 275-290; Jaquette, xxxi; Iglitzin, 31, 32, 34.

[40]Marjorie Lansing, "The American Woman: Voter and Activist," in Jane S. Jaquette, ed., *Women in Politics* (New York: John Wiley & Sons, 1974), 5-6.

[41]Amundsen, 124-129, 136-139; Lee, 297-299, 302-303; Iglitzin 25-31; Campbell, et. al., 255-261.

[42]Lee, 312-313; Susan Hansen, Linda Franz, and Margaret Netemeyer-Mays, "Women's Political Participation and Policy Preferences," *Social Science Quarterly,* 56 (March 1976), 576-590; Iglitzin, 30; Jaquette, v-xxxiii.

Toys and American Culture
Objects as Hypotheses

Bernard Mergen

Toys are the material artifacts of play. Unfortunately, there is no simple definition of play. Johan Huizinga's summary of the formal characteristics of play—"a free activity standing quite consciously outside 'ordinary' life as being 'not serious,' but at the same time absorbing the player intensely and utterly"—has been elaborated upon, but never completely rejected.[1] I think most researchers on play would agree with Brian Sutton-Smith that we need to know more about the "antecedents of play, the structure of play, the consequences of play and the relationship of all these within larger ideological frames of reference."[2] We need to know more about what happens to a person after he has played. Has he learned some of the norms and conventions of his society, or has he discovered how to manipulate them? Certainly there has been a significant change in attitudes toward play in the past century. Artists, novelists and scientists increasingly proclaim that their work is play.[3] Play is no longer merely an imitation of, or preparation for adult life, nor is it limited to games of chance, skill and strategy. Play may be a projection of unconscious feelings, but the forms of expression may owe more to custom and class than to psychology. Above all, play is not trivial.[4]

Can the study of toys contribute to an understanding of the context of play? Do American toys of the past two hundred years tell us anything about attitudes toward play? The answer to both questions is yes, if we keep in mind that toys are part of the material artifacts of a culture (sometimes abbreviated to "material culture") and as artifacts are merely approximations of cultural beliefs and values. They are hypotheses about culture which raise questions: What ideas about life, play, children, and so on, does a particular toy suggest? How was it made? How was it used? Why, if it is old, did it survive? How is it related to other objects used in play? The answers to these and other questions will be found by examining the objects themselves; by carefully observing children and adults playing with toys; by reading trade journals, catalogs, advertisements and the business records of toy makers; and by systematically applying theories of child development, games and play to the historical record of toys.

Influential theories of child development and play, such as those of Jean Piaget and Erik Erikson, tend to be strongly functional. Play contributes to intellectual and pyschological growth. Toys, therefore, have cognitive and symbolic value. Erikson repeatedly confirms the observation of William Blake: "The child's toys and the old man's reasons are the fruits of two seasons."[5] Closer examination of the writings on play with toys reveals that most psychologists have confined themselves to manufactured toys, ignoring the many objects which children (and adults) find or make to use as toys. Manufactured toys, as the historian Jac Remise has observed, are made by adults to appeal and sell to other adults.[6] This simple truth is a good reminder that the cultures of childhood may differ from the cultures of adulthood. Toys may give us insights into both cultures. I am assuming with Brian Sutton-Smith that "there are not constant and universal meanings that we can attribute to toys in general or to any particular toy. Toys are like other human artifacts insofar as they lend themselves to multifaceted human behavior. It is not surprising, therefore, that study of their history reveals that they have had many functions, and that they have often appeared both in adult ritual and in children's play at the same time."[7]

Over twenty years ago, the French sociologist Roger Caillois classified play in four types: competition, chance, vertigo and mimicry.[8] At about the same time, John Roberts and others began to study games cross-culturally using the Human Relations Area Files. Roberts classified games in three categories: physical skill, strategy and chance.[9] Splitting Caillois' competition category into play involving physical skill and play involving strategy, and his mimicry category into fantasy and imitation gives us a very useful six type division. Although most play with toys involves combinations of the types, the categories are useful for labeling the principal functions of toys thus providing a rough index of changes in the popularity of each type as measured by their appearance in toy catalogs and collections. Caillois flatly states that certain combinations do not occur. Mimicry and chance are incompatible, he writes, yet the recent popularity of the board game "Dungeons and Dragons" suggests otherwise. The outcome of this game is determined by throwing dice, while the contestants are encouraged to play the roles of fantasy characters.

Roberts originally found correlations between games of strategy and complex social organizations; and between games of chance and religious systems with benevolent gods. He and his associates speculated "that further inquiry will show that games of strategy are linked with the learning of social roles, games of chance with responsibility and achievement, and games of physical skill with self-reliance. Alternately stated, games of strategy may be related to mastery of the social system; and games of physical skill are possibly associated with the mastery both of self and of environment."[10] To repeat, most games and toys in American society serve multiple functions, but it is possible that certain types of play have been emphasized by specific subcultures, and that there have been shifts in play preferences over time. Brian Sutton-Smith has identified three such changes in the play of American children. First he discovered that from the 1890s to the 1960s, the preferred play of girls has become more like that of boys, while "boys have been steadily lowering their preference for games that have had anything to do with girls' play. So that it is by implication much more deviant behavior for a modern boy to play at, say, Dolls, Hopscotch, Jacks, Schools, Cooking, Jump rope, Musical chairs, Simon says, and Singing games than it was for a boy to play at these things in the earlier historical periods."[11]

In a second study, Sutton-Smith concluded that there are "two cultures of games"—ascriptive and achievement games. In ascriptive games, young children "imitate in very circumscribed ways the behavior of their parents. If they play together it is usually in terms of one child bossing the others.... In addition their play is strongly object-related; they cannot readily shift to something else, or improvise without the toy."[12] From five to nine years of age ascriptive games are exemplified by ritualistic songs and dances in which girls enact the practices of marriage, death and working life. Boys play games of hiding, chasing, capture and attack which vest authority in a central person who possesses greater power than the rest. Counting out formulae help to distribute power among members of the play group. Beginning about ten years of age, the central person maintains his or her role by a real exhibition of strength. Among boys, games of physical skill predominate in ascriptive game cultures.

Achievement game cultures emphasize verbal play, fantasy and individual sports such as swimming, cycling and hiking. Achievement games are associated with the rise of the middle class over the past two hundred years. This class has also extended play beyond the years of childhood. Their children are encouraged to be flexible and imaginative in their play and to carry over this adaptability into adult life. As Sutton-Smith concludes, "the type of rule games with their considerable role complexity which have developed over the past hundred years are apparently the natural successor to this increasing flexibility."[13] Although organized sports such as football and baseball are rule games with complex organizations, they also require subordination of the individual to the group. Sutton-Smith finds better evidence of the shift toward informal and individual play in contemporary toys and board games.

The third major development in children's play then is toys as instruments of role modeling. "The best-selling category of children's toys is that of games and puzzles, which involve strategy and decision-making," writes Sutton-Smith in an introduction to a catalog for an exhibit of educational toys at the Robert Hull Fleming Museum in Burlington, Vermont. After noting that games and toys have gained relatively over dolls, outdoor equipment and vehicles, he concludes that "children today spend much more time with card and board games, checkers and chess than they used to. Perhaps in an information culture, where top-level jobs have to do with marshalling facts and making critical decisions, experience in small-group interactions and decision making has become essential."[14] Although board games requiring strategy and decision making are centuries old, one careful study comparing the 1860 and 1960 versions of Milton Bradley's "The Game of Life" supports Sutton-Smith by concluding that the later version is "a fantasy of individual material advancement," while the 1860 game served both the aggressive fantasy needs of its time and the need to inculcate values such as perseverance, honor, bravery, and industry.[15]

It is difficult to gain more than a hazy impression of toys before the 1880s. A few specimens remain, but we know almost nothing of their distribution and use. Collectors such as Louis Hertz have made valuable contributions to our understanding of the early history of early toy manufacturers, but there is still much to learn. For example, do the apparently large numbers of cast iron banks and clockwork tin trains which survive from the 1870s comment on the importance of banks and railroads in American society in that period, or are they merely copies of European toys that follow conventions established generations earlier when German craftsmen began making intricate and expensive amusements for a wealthy elite? It is not until the 1880s, when toy catalogs begin to appear annually and the variety of toys increases significantly that a clearer picture emerges.

In 1883, sixteen year old George S. Parker invented his first game, the "Game of Banking." It and later games seemed to reflect the preoccupation of the Gilded Age. In 1886, the Peck & Snyder Sporting Goods Company advertised a game called "The Monopolist." "On the board," the catalog stated, "the great struggle between Capital and Labor can be fought out to the satisfaction of all parties, and, if the players are successful, they can break the Monopolist, and become Monopolists themselves."[16] "The Game of Moneta: or Money Makes Money" was offered by the Montgomery Ward Company in 1889, and a "Game of Business" came out in 1895. One of the most popular games of the period was marketed by Crandalls in 1889 under the name of "Pigs in Clover." This puzzle required the player to maneuver four marbles through a maze into a cardboard pen. Hundreds of thousands were sold and the game seems to have been especially popular in Washington, D.C., where the symbolism of the spoils system was obvious.

Games and toys were inspired by every conceivable event and subject. As early as 1844, the W. & S.B. Ives Company produced "The Game of Pope and Pagan or Siege of the Stronghold of Satan by the Christian Army." "In 1868," according to Katharine McClinton, "four games of war and patriotism were packaged together under the title "The Union Games."[17] The Chicago Columbian Exposition of 1893 was commemorated in games, puzzles and building blocks. "Sherlock Holmes" and "The Amusing Game of Innocence Abroad" appeared shortly after the books on which they were loosely based. The 1886 catalog of sporting goods and games sold by Peck & Snyder lists chess, checkers, lotto, dominoes, parcheesi, cards, bagatelle, cribbage, tetotums or spinning dice and regular dice. These games combine the elements of chance, strategy, and, sometimes, fantasy. Some can be played alone, but most require two or more players and both boys and girls can participate fully.

T.R. Croswell, in his landmark study, "Amusements of Worchester School Children," that appeared in *The Pedagogical Seminary* in 1899, confirms the impression gained from the catalogs that board games were widely present in the homes of American children, but casts some doubt on the importance of this kind of play. For example, 277 boys and 189 girls, out of a sample of 1000 each, mention playing checkers. Only 87 boys and 34 girls listed checkers as a favorite kind of play. A similar pattern occurs for dominoes, chess, puzzles, lotto, tic-tac-toe, and other games. Indeed, by the time one comes to the games of Office Boy, Around the World in 80 Days, Steeple Chase, Innocents Abroad and the Bicycle Game, the number of children even mentioning the game dwindles to one or two. A similar picture emerges with toys. Although 621 of the 1000 girls mention playing with dolls, only 233 consider it their favorite play. 188 boys mentioned wagons,

21 trains, 37 blocks, 17 wooden guns, and 2 mentioned toy soldiers.[18] Yet the collections in museums and the manufacturers catalogs create the impression that the play rooms of late 19th century American children were congested with the traffic of cast iron fire engines, circus and express wagons, clockwork trains, and columns of soldiers—wood, tin and iron.

The chief value of collections of toys such as those located at Greenfield Village and Henry Ford Museum, the Margaret Woodbury Strong Museum, and the National Museum of History and Technology, is that they provide a clearer picture of the construction of toys than can be gained from illustrations in catalogs and other advertising copy. The Kenneth Idle Collection of cast iron toys manufactured by the Kenton Hardware others; and Terry Toons, which produced toys of Kiko the Kangaroo, examples of wagons, trucks and other vehicles. These toys, now in the National Museum of History and Technology of the Smithsonian Institution, are heavy, rugged and relatively simple in construction. Wagons and cars are usually no more than a dozen pieces—the body, wheels, axles, driver and a horse or two constitute the most elaborate of these toys. Although some observers have commented on the "realism" of these toys, an equally strong case could be made for abstract or symbolic qualities. The horses are usually little more than outlines, painted one color, with a wheel mounted between the hooves of their forelegs. The wagons and cars have windows, the outline of doors, and single words such as "Ice," "Milk," and "Police" in raised letters, but they lack the small details of many early tin toys and recent plastic models.

These cast iron toys were part of two kinds of play—vertigo and fantasy. Cast iron toys do not seem to lend themselves to play involving chance, physical skill, or strategy. A case might be made for imitation, but the persistence of older forms of transportation—horse drawn farm wagons and fire engines—suggests that these toys were not intended to inspire children to imitate adult work in a literal way, but rather to imagine the romance and the excitement of unfamiliar times and places. The child who assembled his own hay wagon, buckboard, surrey, and farm animals was creating a scene for a fantasy world. Or, if he tired of that, he could pull the wheeled toys around his room, through his house, and down the street for the pure enjoyment of sound and motion. The cast iron toys of the Kenneth Idle Collection, which include Uncle Sam in a two-wheeled phaeton, the Katzenjammer Kids in a mule drawn cart, a wagon labeled "Cairo Express" pulled by an elephant, a chariot with eagle wings hitched to a camel, and numerous fire engines, beer wagons, zeppelins, trains and cap pistols, reflect changing technology and increasing affluence. Placed in the context of catalogs and *Playthings* magazine, it and other collections tell us a little about children's play and a great deal about the thinking of toy manufacturers.

Playthings, published in New York City since 1903, is an especially valuable source of information on the material culture of play. The pages of the early issues are filled with advertisements for Teddy Bears, an example of the process by which the toy industry exploited popular persons and events. By 1907, when stuffed bears of all sizes had saturated the market, manufacturers were selling Teddy Bear games, furniture and post cards.

One company sold a Teddy Bear with eyes which lit up when its right paw was raised; another created an inexpensive cloth "Teddy-Turnover," which was half girl and half Teddy, depending on which half was turned up. In five years the industry had invented and marketed virtually every conceivable kind of Teddy Bear toy. Although the Teddy Bear would remain a favorite toy and provide a staple item for many manufacturers, the pressure of competition kept the owners and managers of toy firms constantly searching for new products.

The June 1907 issue of *Playthings* carried advertisements from Milton Bradley for a reading game called "Kornelia Kinks at Jamestown," about a "little colored girl at the Exposition," and the Mather Game Company of Canton, Ohio, promoted a "Parlor Baseball Game" with endorsements by major league players. The National Game Company of St. Louis introduced the game of "Putting the Log" which requires players to maneuver a cardboard "log" around a 20" x 16" board with a pointed stick. The copy writer described it as "Unequaled for Progressive Parties," and compared its popularity to that of "Pigs in Clover." In December, the promotion of these games had been swept away by "Diabolo," a toy which required some skill and manual dexterity. Diabolo, also called "Mefisto," "Springo," "Topsy-Twirl," "The Flying Diable," and "The Whizzer," was a wooden spool which could be made to roll on a string attached to two sticks. Parker Brothers seems to have been the holder of the rights to the patent of M. Gustave Philippart, a French civil engineer, but a half dozen other companies marketed the product under other names. An article in the September issue of *Playthings* noted that the game had been introduced at Newport, Rhode Island, by Mrs. Arthur Scott Burden and Mrs. Arthur Iselin, indicating that the toy industry felt that there was a mass market ready to imitate the play of the rich. Some companies hired Frenchmen to tour the country to provide instruction on how to play. The combination of snob appeal and the authority of science (the fact that the inventor was an engineeer) is interesting in two ways. First, it was not sufficient to establish the "Diabolo" as a continuously popular toy; and second, its appeal was chiefly to older children and adults. While many board games in the previous twenty years had been designed for adults as well as children, the pages of *Playthings* reveal a trend toward toys designed principally for adults, and an increasing willingness to treat children as part of the adult world.

In 1917, Parker Brothers was offering "Militac," a war game for children along with such established favorites as "Pollyanna," and paper dolls. Another company was selling "camouflage toys," and D.C. Hughes & Co. of Chicago, advertised a "Toy Range that Actually Cooks." Over 500 advertisers appeared in the December 1917 issue of *Playthings,* their products classified under 120 categories from Aerial Toys and Air Rifles to Washers and Wooden Toys. It is difficult to draw any significant conclusions from their ads or the classification system, but in 1927, there were over 700 advertisers in over 140 categories. Whether because of internal changes within the industry, or because of changing preferences in play, certain categories expanded and others shrank, as measured by the number of firms engaged in the production of that product. Game, gun and stuffed toy manufacturers increased, while the makers of construction toys declined from 22 to 3. The ads for several horse race games imported from England appealed to those who want "a real game of chance," while a serious note was struck in an article with the headline: "Dolls Seen as Antidote for Race Suicide." Mrs. Florence Coyle, a psychologist, urged early play with dolls to prevent the dulling of maternal instincts leading to companionate marriages and "one-child mothers."[19]

A decade later, in December 1937, the number of advertisers in *Playthings* was reduced to about 250, but the 230 categories showed continued increases in games, and new expansion in airplanes, moving picture projectors and films, and playground apparatus for backyard use. A new category, "Cartoon and Movie Character Rights" listed three firms: Kay Kamen, which marketed Mickey Mouse and other Walt Disney toys; Stephen Slesinger, which handled Winnie the Pooh, Tarzan, Alley Oop, and others; and Terry Toons, which produced toys of Kiko the Kangeroo, Farmer Al Falfa, and Puddy the Pup. The late 1930s seem dominated by Disney inspired toys, while the toys and games of the 1940s follow trends in publishing, radio and motion pictures. Typical of the latter was "The Egg and I" game by the Capex Company of Evanston, Illinois, which advertised: "The Egg-citing Game of Owning a Chicken Ranch.... 25,000,000 have read the book; 25,000,000 will see the movie...and this market of many millions will be eager to buy and play this great new family game."[20] Curiously, few war toys were advertised and the number of firms listed in the toy soldiers category shrank from six to one between 1937 and 1947.

By 1957, however, military toys were returning in large numbers. Space toys began to appear, almost simultaneous with Sputnik and well in advance of the Apollo Project. Perhaps most interesting of the new toys in 1957 was "Little Miss Ginger," a busty foremother of Barbie, manufactured by Cosmopolitan Doll and Toy Company and marketed by Kathryn Kay, Inc. The ad featured sensuous full page photographs by fashion photographer Bernard Green. Television clearly dominates the toy market of 1967. Hasbro was promoting its "Flying Nun Doll" and its "Show-Biz Babies," dolls representing the Monkees, The Mamas and the Papas, Bobbie Gentry, and Herman of Herman's Hermits. The same company's G.I. Joe was already four years old, having firmly established the acceptability of doll play for boys.

G.I. Joe and the Flying Nun suggest some of the contradictions of the toy market in the 1960s. Manufacturers responded immediately to every trend in American society, from popular entertainment to Viet Nam, but they seemed unsure of what the public wanted and frightened that toy sales would decline. One significant response to these uncertain conditions was a shift to the adult leisure market. Under the headline, "A 'Leisure-Living' Setting for Toys Sales," *Playthings* told of the Gateway Sporting Goods store in Kansas City, whose owners believed that "the family that plays together often buys together." Moreover, the writer observed:

With toys and non-toys as subject material, a typical display in the Main Street outlet can be given a single theme and turned into a more realistic "scene" than would be possible with the use of toys exclusively.... For instance, Gateway will set up a tent for its camping season promotion and place near it pieces of casual-style luggage, a tape recorder, adult games (chess maybe), and a craft item or two. These would be in addition to conventional campout accessories.[21]

The decade of the 1960s saw the rise and rapid decline of war toys. Apparently encouraged by the Civil War Centennial and the escalation of American military involvement in Viet Nam, toy manufacturers increased the percentage of war toys from about 5% of all toys in 1962 to 15% in 1965. Toys of war and violence covered 30 pages of Sears' 1964 Christmas catalog. In response, Women's Strike for Peace, the Women's International League for Peace and Freedom, and the California Toy Committee organized various protests against war toys, which included demonstrations at the annual toy fair, testimony on the harmful effects of war toys on children by psychologists, and attempts to pass restrictive legislation. By 1967, the production of war toys had fallen to pre-1962 levels.[22]

By 1977, the toy industry had established a pattern of production and marketing which took advantage of fads and famous persons, and which was moving with the age pyramid toward more adult products. Computer and electronic games, radio controlled cars and airplanes, and model building tools and kits crowded traditional toys from the shelves of many retailers. It would be simple to say that toys in the 19th century were designed to help the child become an adult while the toys of the late 20th century are intended to keep grown-ups children, but the E.I. Horsman Company advertised in 1907 that their "Wondergraph instantly makes anybody, even the youngest child, a master designer and a draughtsman of the highest skill," while the Model Rectifer Company addressed the readers of *Playthings* in 1977 with the warning:

Everybody wants to sell you fun and games. We're selling survival. Fewer kids means less business. And fewer kids is what's happening in this country. To help you survive this trend, MRC offers products you can sell profitably, to a market that's growing not shrinking. A market that includes a broad spectrum of ages. Eight to eighty.[23]

While Model Rectifer sold electronic games and toys, other companies went after the "Junior Sporting Goods" market, or cashed in on media-hyped personalities. Revell announced a Billy Carter "Redneck Power Pick-up," complete with six pack. "Billy is his own man," the ad continued, "and your customers admire and love the guy!"[24]

The inescapable conclusion to any study of toys is that American children have had a wide choice of playthings for at least a century. No one type of play really dominates the toy market. Toys encouraging physical skill, such as balls, blocks, and jump ropes, seem to have a slight edge over those emphasizing imitation and fantasy, such as dolls, toy trucks, and play houses, but the evidence, based on the number of companies selling these products is not conclusive. Children find uses for toys that manufacturers never anticipate. Neither the surviving toy nor the catalog can answer the ultimate question about the meaning of play to children. For that, we need to look at toys in the context of all play.

The children of 17th, 18th and early 19th century America—children seen dimly in the collections of folklorists, in autobiographies, and in the testimony of ex-slaves—played games of skill, strategy, chance, vertigo, imitation and fantasy without any material artifacts.[25] Perhaps their very lack of toys made them more sociable, more cooperative, than children made possessive, isolated by abundance, but there is no strong evidence for this conclusion. Indeed, I think the opposite is true. Toys are central in the rituals of family and community. They are bought and used to mark important moments in the life cycle; to commemorate seasonal changes and yearly ceremonies. That they are also ephemeral, that they are used to fill otherwise empty time, does not lessen their symbolic importance in the social structure. Ultimately, the fragments saved in attics, by collectors, and by museums are holy relics of a culture that believes that childhood is a happy, remote, and sacred time.

Notes

[1]Johan Huizinga, *Homo Ludens: A Study of the Play Element in Culture* (Boston: Beacon, 1950).

[2]Brian Sutton-Smith, "Towards an Anthropology of Play," in *Studies in the Anthropology of Play: Papers in Memory of B. Allan Tindall,* edited by Phillips Stevens, Jr. (West Point, N.Y.: Leisure Press, 1977), 230.

[3]See for example, Jacques Ehrmann, ed., *Game, Play, Literature* (Boston: Beacon, 1971) and Richard Burke, " 'Work' and 'Play'," *Ethics,* 82 (1971), 33-47.

[4]See the review of various theories of play in Helen Schwartzman, *Transformations: The Anthropology of Children's Play* (New York: Plenum Press, 1978).

[5]Erik Erikson, *Toys and Reasons* (New York: Norton, 1977).

[6]Jac Remise, *The Golden Age of Toys* (Greenwich, Connecticut: New York Graphic Society, 1967), 11.

[7]Brian Sutton-Smith, "Toys for Object and Role Mastery," in *Educational Toys in America: 1800 to the Present,* edited by Karen Hewitt and Louise Roomet (Burlington, VT.: The Robert Hull Fleming Museum, 1979), 11.

[8]Roger Caillois, *Man, Play, and Games* (London: Thames and Hudson, 1962).

[9]John M. Roberts, Malcolm J. Arth, and Robert R. Bush, "Games in Culture," *American Anthropologist,* 61 (1959), 597-605.

[10]Roberts, et al., 604.

[11]Brian Sutton-Smith and B.G. Rosenberg, "Sixty Years of Historical Change in the Game Preferences of American Children," *Journal of American Folklore* 74 (1961), 17-46; reprinted in Sutton-Smith, *The Folkgames of Children* (Austin, Texas: Univ. of Texas Press, 1972), 280.

[12]Sutton-Smith, *Folkgames,* 299.

[13]Sutton-Smith, *Folkgames,* 308.

[14]Sutton-Smith, "Toys for Object and Role Mastery," 23.

[15]Thomas A. Burns, "The Game of Life: Idealism, Reality and Fantasy in the Nineteenth- and Twentieth-Century Versions of a Milton Bradley Game," *The Canadian Review of American Studies* 9 (1978), 50-83.

[16]*Sporting Goods, Peck & Snyder, 1886* (Princeton: The Pyne Press, 1971), n.p.

[17]Katherine McClinton, *Antiques of American Childhood* (New York: Bramhall House, 1970), 227.

[18]T.R. Croswell, "Amusements of Worcester School Children," *The Pedagogical Seminary,* 6 (Sept., 1898), 314-371.

[19]*Playthings,* 25 (Dec., 1927), 251.

[20]*Playthings,* 45 (Sept., 1947), 45-46.

[21]*Playthings,* 65 (Dec., 1967), 35.

[22]Carol Andreas, "War Toys and the Peace Movement," *Journal of Social Issues,* 25 (1969), 83-99.

[23]*Playthings,* 5 (May 1907), 3; *ibid.,* 75 (May 1977), inside cover.

[24]*Playthings,* 75 (Dec., 1977), 9-12.

[25]See for example, William Wells Newell, *Games and Songs of American Children* (New York: Harper & Bros., 1883), reprinted by Dover Books, 1963; Dorothy Howard, *Dorothy's World: Childhood in Sabine Bottom 1902-1910* (Englewood Cliffs, N.J.: Prentice-Hall, 1977); and George Rawick, ed., *The American Slave: A Composite Autobiography,* 19 volumes, Supplement Series 1, 12 volumes (Westport, Conn.: Greenwood Press, 1972 and 1977).

Embellishing a Life of Labor: An Interpretation of the Material Culture of American Working-Class Homes, 1885-1915

Lizabeth A. Cohen

The material life of American urban workers from 1885 to 1915, as revealed in patterns of home furnishings and organizations of domestic space, provides a new way of understanding the historical development of working-class culture. While in recent years historians have pursued the often elusive lives of working people, they have almost totally ignored domestic settings, and the material culture within them, as sources. Instead, historical investigation has focused on the workplace and local community. Only a few sociologists have examined home environments for evidence of the values and social identities of workers.[1]

Historians have examined working-class homes primarily in the context of the Progressive Era housing reform movement. The keen interest that these early twentieth-century social reformers displayed in workers' home environment, however, should alert us to the significance of the home, the most private and independent world of the worker, in expressing the working-class family's social identity and interaction with middle-class culture.

Studies of the material culture of the working-class home have much to contribute to our understanding of workers' experience beyond the outlines sketched by social historians who have quantified occupations and family events such as births, marriages and deaths. Although workers were often constrained in their household activities and consumption by low incomes and scarcity in housing options, they still made revealing choices in the process of ordering their personal environments.

This essay explores developments in the consumption preferences of urban working-class families from 1885 to 1915 and interprets how these choices reflected and affected worker social identity. My investigation of working-class homes places them in the context of the material standards of the larger society in which the workers lived. Only a comparison between working-class and middle-class homes can elucidate the degree to which working-class material culture was distinctive or part of a larger cultural system.

During the period 1885-1915 new people joined the ranks of the American working class as industry expanded.[2] Foreign-born and native American workers commonly shared the experience of having recently left rural, small town settings for the urban industrial workplace. This study examines the homes both immigrant and native American workers made within the city environment.

I will first trace the development of interior styles among the middle class during this period, probing particularly how esthetic trends reflected middle-class social attitudes. While the middle class was by no means a clear-cut group with uniform tastes, still its trend setters and reflectors, such as popular magazines and home decoration advice books, articulated a consistent set of standards. Second, I will examine efforts by reformers and institutions to influence the tastes of workers toward these middle-class norms. Finally, I will analyze working-class homes in the light of workers' experiences and values and in relation to middle-class society.

Herbert Gutman urged at the close of his seminal essay on the intergration of pre-industrial peoples into nineteenth- and early twentieth-century America that "much remains to be learned about the transition of native and foreign-born American men and women to industrial society, and how that transition affected such persons and the society in which they entered."[3] The study of the material life of American working people as expressed in consumption patterns and the arrangement of domestic interiors may offer some new insights toward that goal. Workers who left no private written records may speak to us through the artifacts of their homes.

The Changing Look of the Middle-Class Home

American homes from the 1840s through the 1880s mirrored the nation's transformation from an agricultural to an industrial society. Just as industrialization affected people and places in the country in different ways and at various rates, so too homes reflected an individual's or family's degree of integration into the industrial economy. Location, occupation and financial status all affected the quantity and quality of consumption. The middle classes, with a status and income often attributable to an expanded economy and the mechanized means of production, were the most enthusiastic purchasers of mass-produced objects for their homes.[4] Meanwhile, technologically-advanced products were less abundant in the houses of those who lived more self-sufficient economic lives.

The home served as an accurate indicator of one's relationship to the industrial economy not by accident but as a result of the Victorians' contradictory attitude toward economic and technological change. Enthusiasm for, as well as anxiety toward, industrialization provoked both an appetite for new products and a need to incorporate them carefully into private life. At the same time that new kinds of objects transformed the home, the Victorians loudly proclaimed the sanctity of the family refuge in a menacing, changing world. As John Ruskin wrote:

This is the true nature of home—it is the place of peace; the shelter, not only from injury, but from all terror, doubt and division. In so far as it is not this, it is not home; so far as the anxieties of the outer life penetrate into it, and the inconsistently-minded, unloved, or hostile society of the outer world is allowed by either husband or wife to cross the threshold, it ceases to be a home.[5]

The home embodied a contradiction as both the arena for and refuge from technological penetration. Insofar as people could tolerate this contradictory domestic environment, the home provided a setting for gradual adaptation to a technological and commercial world.

The parlor best represented this accommodation to industrial life. As the room reserved for greeting and entertaining those beyond the family circle, the parlor permitted controlled interaction with the outside world. Similarly, a typical parlor overflowed with store-bought mass-produced objects, carefully arranged by family members: wall-to-wall carpeting enclosed by papered and bordered walls and ceilings; upholstered furniture topped with antimacassars; shawl-draped center tables displaying carefully arranged souvenir albums and alabaster scuptures; shelves and small stands overloaded with bric-a-brac and purchased mementos. Technology made much of this decor possible: carpeting, wallpaper, and textiles were ever cheaper and more elaborate, and the invention of the spiral spring encouraged the mass distribution of upholstered furniture. Artificial covering of surfaces and structural frames thus replaced the painted walls and floors and the hard wood furniture of an earlier era.[6]

After about 1885, popular magazines, home decoration manuals and architectural journals revealed a gradual but dramatic rejection of the cluttered spaces of the Victorian home in favor of two stylistic trends unified around a common concern for traditional American symbols. The Colonial Revival and the Arts and Crafts Movement both sought an American esthetic to replace European-inspired and technologically sophisticated styles. In the early twentieth century, an up-to-date middle-class family almost anywhere in America most likely lived in a Colonial Revival house, perhaps along newly extended trolley lines, or in a craftsman-style bungalow, often in a recently developed housing tract.[7]

The Colonial Revival had its debut at the Philadelphia Centennial Exposition in 1876 amid the salute to American technological progress; the style reached full maturity in the 1920s with the opening of the American Wing of the Metropolitan Museum of Art in New York and the restoration of Williamsburg.[8] Middle-class Americans encountered the Colonial Revival style more intimately, however, not at these public sites, but within their own homes and neighborhoods. Just as house construction had dominated colonial American building, the domestic setting most engaged the attention of the revival style. While for some people Colonial Revival meant "accurately" recreating early American interiors replete with spinning wheels and antique furniture, for most middle-class Americans, adoption entailed purchasing new, usually mass-produced items in the colonial style, such as a house or parlor set.

The Arts and Crafts Movement, also referred to at the time as the "craftsman" or "mission" style, evolved concurrently with the Colonial Revival. Exteriors and interiors boasted natural materials such as wood, shingle and greenery, exposed structural elements and surfaces, and open, flexible spaces. Elbert Hubbard's Roycraft Industries, Henry L. Wilson's Bungalow House Plan business, and similar firms popularized on a mass level the unique work of such artists as furniture-maker Gustav Stickley and architects Greene and Greene.

This craftsman style, justified in contradictory terms, met varied pressures of the day. On the one hand, the style depended on technological innovations in heating, lighting and windowglass and was merchandised as a solution to the household problems of dust, germs and inefficiency.[9] On the other hand, the Arts and Crafts Movement invoked and sought to replicate such traditional American symbols as the farmhouse and its furnishings. In the Hingham, Massachusetts Arts and Crafts Society, as elsewhere in the country,

bits of old needlework and embroidery were brought down from dusty attics for admiration and imitation. Chairs and tables, of exquisite design and honest purpose, took the place of flimsy and overdecorated furniture.[10]

Middle-class people's attraction to the Colonial Revival and Arts and Crafts Movement corresponded to prevailing social attitudes, particularly toward workers and immigrants. Nativism, anti-industrialism, and a propensity toward environmental solutions for social problems were values incorporated into the new esthetic. Patriotic organizations such as the Daughters of the American Revolution and the National Society of Colonial Dames, both formed in the early 1890s, frequently encouraged the preservation of colonial artifacts and buildings.[11] Architects and client congregations found in the Colonial Revival an appropriate architecture for Protestant churches to replace the Catholic-associated Gothic style.[12] Founders of the Society for the Preservation of New England Antiquities blamed immigrant residents for the destruction of historical areas like Boston's North End.[13] Outspoken xenophobes like Henry Ford, Abbott Lawrence Lowell and Henry Cabot Lodge were important patrons of the preservation and Colonial Revival movements.[14]

The Arts and Crafts style satisfied the anti-industrial instincts of many middle-class Americans. Montgomery Schuyler, organizer of an arts and crafts production studio outside Philadelphia, argued that this new style was not only wholesome, but it revived the accomplishment of the colonial craftsman, "an educated and thinking being" who loved his work without demanding a wage or labor union membership.[15] Instruction manuals for making mission furniture at home encouraged the de-mechanization of furniture-making. Earlier, middle-class Victorians had handled ambivalence toward industrialism by monitoring, while increasing, their interaction with industrial products within the home. Now, the next generation was employing technological advances to restrain and deny the extent to which industrialism affected private life.

Supporters of the craftsman and Colonial Revival styles had confidence in the moral effect of this new physical environment. Stickley's *Craftsman Magazine* declared in a 1903 issue:

Luxurious surroundings ... suggest and induce idleness. Complex forms and costly materials have an influence upon life which tells a sad story in history. On the other hand, chasteness and restraint in form, simple, but artistic materials are equally expressive of the character of the people who use them.[16]

The new domestic ideal represented a search for a truly American environment, in Stickley's words, "American homes exclusively for American needs."[17]

Spreading the Middle-Class Message

Progressive Era reformers seized upon this new American domestic esthetic, contributing to its popularity and using it to assist in their campaigns to "uplift," "modernize" and "Americanize." Though social reform efforts in this period were broad in scope, a surprising range of reformers made use of the new styles as they sought to transform people's home environments in order to promote social improvement and cultural homogeneity. Often behind their pleas for cleaner, simpler, more sanitary homes for working people lay a desire to encourage more middle-class American environments. In a twist that would have shocked any colonial farmer, the "early American look" became linked with a dust-, germ-, and disease-free scientific ideal. Reformers and associated organizations made efforts to influence workers in their homes, their neighborhoods, and their workplaces through promulgating domestic models; elsewhere, workers encountered these new middle-class style standards more indirectly.*

Both public institutions and privately-funded organizations conveyed the new esthetic to working-class girls within model classrooms created for housekeeping instruction. By the 1890s, particularly in urban areas, domestic science classes in public schools promoted ideal domestic environments. Similarly, settlement houses in workers' neighborhoods fostered middle-class home standards through "Housekeeping Centers."

In a guide to planning Housekeeping Centers, *Housekeeping Notes: How To Furnish and Keep House in a Tenement Flat: A Series of Lessons Prepared for Use in the Association of Practical Housekeeping Centers of New York,* reformer Mabel Kittredge perfectly stated the new esthetic. The section "Suitable Furnishing for a Model Housekeeping Flat or Home for Five People" recommended wood-stained and uncluttered furniture surfaces, iron beds with mattresses, and un-upholstered chairs. Walls must be painted, not papered; floors should be oak stained; window seats must be built in for storage; shelves should replace bulky sideboards ("the latter being too large for an ordinary tenement room; cheap sideboards are also very ugly"); screens provide privacy in bedrooms; a few good pictures should grace the walls, but only in the living room.[18] One settlement worker who gave domestic science instruction observed, "The purpose in our work is to help those in our classes to learn what is the true American home ideal, and then do what we can to make it possible for them to realize it for themselves."[19] (Fig. 1)

Settlement workers further promoted middle-class styles through the appearance of the house itself. Furnishing the settlement house interior became a self-conscious process for its residents. In a letter to her sister, a young Jane Adams exclaimed,

Madame Mason gave us an elegant old oak side-board... and we indulged in a set of heavy leather covered chairs and a 16″ cut oak table. Our antique oak book case and my writing desk completes it.[20]

*Editor's Note: See: Robert J. Schurk, "The American Arts , and Crafts Movement and Progressivism: Reform on Two Fronts," unpublished Masters thesis at Bowling Green State University, Bowling Green, Ohio. This paper explores the shared themes of the Progressive movement in politics and the Arts & Crafts movement in objects: morality and honesty, anti-materialism, efficiency and economy, nature and conservation, health and strength, and education.

Fig. 1 Illustrations to "Homemaking in a Model Flat" by Mabel Kittredge, *Charities and the Commons,* 4 November, 1905, 176.

Edith Barrows, a settlement worker in Boston's South End House, recorded in her diary, "The pretty green sitting-room with its crackling fire and gay rugs and simple early American furniture is a good setting for all that transpires. I find that it has a spiritual and, I think, almost a physical reaction in the neighborhood."[21] Settlement workers hoped that community patrons would incorporate the styles observed at the house into the furnishing of their own homes (Fig. 2).

Industries were also involved in the business of setting standards for workers' homes through company housing, welfare programs and the creation of domestic-like spaces in the factory.

Companies sought to communicate middle-class values through housing provided for workers. Frequently, individual entrances, even in multiple or attached dwellings, sought to reinforce nuclear family privacy.[22] Interiors promoted the specialization of rooms in an effort to discourage the taking in of boarders and to enforce a middle-class pattern of living revolving around parlor, kitchen, dining room and bedrooms.

Some companies offered employees welfare programs which also affirmed middle-class domestic standards. Amoskeag Mills' employee benefits, for example, included a Textile Club (established to compete with ethnic organizations), a Textile School, a Cooking School, and a Home Nursing Service.[23]

Within the factory, workers were frequently treated to domestic-like environments deliberately planned along middle-class esthetic lines. Employee lounges and lunchrooms were an innovation in the early twentieth century and frequently provided models for light, airy rooms with hardwood floors and simple furniture (Fig. 3). Thus, McCormick Harvesting Machine Company hired a social worker to survey factories nationwide and recommend proper recreation, education, luncheon and lounge facilities, which they proceeded to install.[24]

In the minds of the reformers, simple, mission-style furniture and colonial objects, associated with the agrarian world of the pre-industrial craftsman, seemed the obvious—and most appropriate—material arrangement for all Americans, particularly for industrial workers newly arrived from rural areas. And they tried with a vengeance to impose it.

Despite the missionary zeal of middle-class reformers, however, they did not succeed very well in communicating new standards for domestic interiors to workers. In part, they were responsible for their own failure through ineffective organizational techniques and flawed programs.[25] Yet these shortcomings notwithstanding, workers seem to have actively rejected the means and messages of the reformers.

Although working-class people patronized settlement houses, employee lounges and other model environments, many did so on their own terms, partaking of the recreational facilities and resources without taking the social message to heart.[26]

Some working-class people did make objections known directly to the reformers. Miss Jane E. Robbin, M.D., reported that during her first year at the College Settlement another resident encountered a patient on a home visit who said "that she had had her breakfast, that she did not want anything, and that she did not like strange people poking around in her

Fig. 2. Interior of Hull House, Chicago, 1895. From *Hull House Maps and Papers* (New York: Crowell, 1895).

Fig. 3. Recreation room in the McCreary Store, Pittsburgh, Pennsylvania, c. 1907. By Lewis Hine. From *Women and the Trades*, by Elizabeth Beardsley Butler (New York: Russell Sage

bureau drawer anyway."[27] Others used more tact in rejecting the attentions of reformers. A Boston settlement worker recalled her neighbors' response to a circulating collection of photographs of famous paintings:

South End House had a loan collection of photographs of paintings which were given to the House to use in acquainting our friends with great works of art. These were sent from tenement to tenement to stay for a period of time and then removed while others took their place. The "Holy Pictures," as all of the Madonnas were called, were always mildly welcomed, but the lack of color made them unattractive, and the "unholy" pictures were usually tucked away to await the visitor's return. Some of our earliest calls became very informal... when the visitor joined the whole family in a hunt, often ending by finding us all on our knees when the missing photographs were drawn from beneath the bed or bureau.[28]

More than working-class rejection of middle-class tastes, however, separated the worlds of the worker and the reformer. Workers' homes themselves hold the key to the nature and sources of their material preferences, apparently at odds with those held by the middle class. This conflict of value systems was powerfully perceived by a young participant in settlement house programs when she was faced with furnishing her own home at marriage.

We had many opportunities to talk quite naturally of some of the problems of home-making and house-furnishing [wrote settlement worker Esther Barrows].... The lack of plush and stuffed furniture [in our house] was a surprise to many, whose first thought would have been just that. One of our club girls who was about to be married sat down to discuss the matter in relation to her own new home. She seemed convinced by all the arguments brought forward to prove its undesirability from the point of view of hygiene and cleanliness. Months afterward she invited us to her home, much later than would have seemed natural, and as she greeted us rather fearfully she said, "Here it is, but you must remember you have had your plush days." Her small livingroom was overfilled by the inevitable "parlor set," while plush curtains hung at the windows and on either side of the door. The lesson learned by us from this incident was never to be forgotten.[29]

A commitment to a classless America, achievable through educational and environmental solutions to social problems, blinded settlement workers like Esther Barrows to the strength of workers' own culture. Reformers had little conception of how deeply rooted these material values were in working-class life.[30]

The Working Class Becomes 'At Home' in Urban America

A lack of opportunities in both housing and neighborhood selection marked the living conditions of workers in this period. Whether home was an urban slum or a model tenement block, a milltown shack settlement or company housing, families frequently lived in substandard housing far below the quality that middle-class residents enjoyed, and had few alternative options. Furthermore, workers found themselves forced into low-rent districts separated from middle-class residential neighborhoods. Proximity to other working-class people of similar job and income status typified workers' experience more than the ethnic isolation we commonly associate with working-class life. Often, ethnic enclaves were no more than islands of a few blocks within a working-class community.[31] Limitations of housing choices, however, may have encouraged workers to value interior spaces even more.

Within these working-class neighborhoods and homes, workers expressed a distinctive set of material values. An examination of attitudes toward home ownership; space allocation within the house or flat; the covering of the structural shell—floors, walls and windows; furniture selection; and decorative details illuminates the meanings workers attached to the artifacts of their homes.

The view that workers should own their homes provided a rare convergence of opinion between reformers and working people, though each group advocated home ownership for different reasons. Some reformers felt that a home-owning working class would be more dependable and less revolutionary, and thus America would be "preserved" as a classless society. Others hoped that meeting mortgage payments in America might discourage immigrants from sending money home, and hence stem the tide of further immigration.[32] In short, reformers saw home ownership as a strategy for directing worker ambition along acceptable middle-class lines.

Workers, on the other hand, sought to purchase homes for reasons more consistent with their previous cultural experience than with American middle-class values.[33] In Russia, even poor Jews often had owned the rooms in which they lived.[34] Jews in many cases left Eastern Europe in response to Tsarist regulations prohibiting their ownership of property and interfering in their livelihoods as artisans, merchants and businessmen.[35] Emigration to America was a way of resisting "peasantizing" forces for these people. Recent work on Italian immigrants has shown that they likewise came to America hoping to preserve their traditional society and to resist efforts at making them laborers.[36] They viewed a sojourn in the States as a way of subsidizing the purchase of a home upon return to Italy.[37] Many Italians both in Europe and America sacrificed in order to leave their children a legacy of land, which supports David Riesman's theory that pre-industrial families trained and encouraged their children to "succeed them" rather than to "succeed" by rising in the social system.[38] In America, owning a home allowed Italians to uphold traditional community ties by renting apartments to their relatives or paesani, and in less urban areas, to grow the fresh vegetables necessary to maintain a traditional diet.[39] Furthermore, Slavic immigrants, property-less peasants in the old country, eagerly sought homes in America to satisfy long-standing ambitions.[40] Native American workers, moreover, descended from a tradition that equated private property ownership with full citizenship and promised all deserving, hard-working persons a piece of land. Thus, working-class people of many backgrounds sent mother and children to work, took in boarders, made the home a workshop, and sacrificed proper diet in order to save and buy a house, compromises too severe to substantiate some historians' claims that workers were merely pursuing upward social mobility toward middle-class goals.[41]

Once workers occupied purchased homes or rented flats their attitudes toward the utilization of interior space diverged markedly from those of the middle class. Reformers advocated a careful allocation of domestic space to create sharp divisions between public and family interactions and to separate family members from one another within the house. Reformers often blamed working-class people for contributing to unnecessary overcrowding and violations of privacy by huddling in the kitchen, for example, while other rooms were left vacant.[42]

While the middle classes were better equipped with, and could more easily afford, housewide heating and lighting than the working classes, a difference of attitudes toward home living was more at issue. Many people from rural backgrounds were used to sharing a bedroom—and sometimes even a bed—with other family members.[43] And for those working people whose homes were also their workplaces, the middle-class ethos of the home as an environment detached from the economic world was particularly inappropriate. Jewish, Irish, Italian and Slavic women frequently took in boarders and laundry, did homework, and assisted in family stores often adjoining their living quarters. For former farmers and self-employed artisans and merchants, this integration of home and work seemed normal.[44] Among Southern Italian women, doing tenement homework in groups sustained "cortile" (shared housekeeping) relationships endangered in the American environment of more isolated homes.[45]

The reformer ideal of the kitchen as an efficient laboratory servicing other parts of the house found little acceptance among workers. Even when workers had a parlor, they often preferred to socialize in their kitchens. Mary Antin fondly recalled frequent visits in her married sister's kitchen in East Boston where after dinner dishes were washed,

> Frieda took out her sewing, and I took a book; and the lamp was between us, shining on the table, on the large brown roses on the wall, on the green and brown diamonds of the oil cloth on the floor ... on the shining stove in the corner. It was such a pleasant kitchen—such a cosy, friendly room—that when Frieda and I were left alone I was perfectly happy just to sit there. Frieda had a beautiful parlor, with plush chairs and a velvet carpet and gilt picture frames; but we preferred the homely, homelike kitchen.[46]

When investigators surveyed working-class people for their housing preferences in 1920, most still rejected small kitchens or kitchenettes in favor of ones large enough for dining.[47] Workers kept their old-world hearths burning bright in their new American homes.[48]

Reformers applauded all attempts by workers to create parlors in their homes. They viewed such spaces as evidence of civilization, self-respect and assumption of middle-class standards.[49] A home with a parlor was more likely, they felt, to instill the middle-class image of the family as an emotional, sentimental unit. Margaret Byington's investigation of Homestead workers' homes reflected this bias:

> It has been said that the first evidence of the growth of the social instinct in any family is the desire to have a parlor. In Homestead this ambition has in many cases been attained. Not every family, it is true, can afford one, yet among my English-speaking acquaintances even the six families each of whom lived in three rooms attempted to have at least the semblance of a room devoted to sociability.[50]

Worker interest in creating parlor space at home varied, though often it correlated with occupational status. People who did little income-producing work at home, such as Jews and native Americans, most often established sitting rooms. Among Italians and Slavs, where men frequently had low status jobs and women brought work into the home, the combination living room/kitchen, so similar to their European homes, survived the longest. When George Kracha left the Homestead steel mills and established his own butcher business, his home soon reflected his change in status in a way that his neighbors all recognized:

> They still lived in Cherry Alley and much as they had always lived, though Elena no longer kept boarders.... Kracha had bought new furniture and the room adjoining the kitchen, where the girls had slept, was now a parlor. Its chief glories were a tasseled couch, a matching chair with an ingenious footrest that slid out like a drawer from inside the chair itself, and an immense oil lamp suspended from the ceiling by gilt chains. The lampshade was made of pieces of colored glass leaded together like a church window; it seemed to fill the room and was one of the most impressive objects Cherry Lane had ever seen. On the walls were colored lithographs in elaborate gilt frames of the Holy Family and of the Virgin with a dagger through her exposed heart. Drying ribbons of Easter palm were stuck behind them. On the floor was flowered oilcloth.[51]

Kracha'a adoption of a parlor, however, did not entail acceptance of middle-class modes of furnishing. Rather, his parlor presented an elaborate collage of traditional and technological symbols.

Nevertheless, reformers were not mistaken in recognizing a relationship between the presence of a parlor and some acculturation to middle-class ways. The expression of sentiment toward family and community through consumption involved in "parlorization" could indicate a favorable nod to middle-class values. For many workers, though, their usage of kitchen and parlor still respected long-established patterns of sociability. As Mary Antin's comment indicated, people with parlors did not necessarily abandon a preference for the kitchen. Likewise, workers' parlors frequently doubled as sleeping rooms at night.[52] Often when workers accommodated middle-class concepts of space in their homes, they imbued them with different social expectations. For example, Byington noted that even when a native American worker in Homestead had a dining room, "it did not live up to its name."

> In five-room houses we find an anomaly known as the "dining room." Though a full set of dining room furniture, sideboard, table and dining chairs, are usually in evidence, they are rarely used at meals. The family sewing is frequently done there, the machine standing in the corner by the window; and sometimes, too, the ironing, to escape the heat of the kitchen; but rarely is the room used for breakfast, dinner or supper. The kitchen is the important room of the house.[53]

Whereas the middle-class home provided a setting for a wide range of complex interactions related to work, family and community, and therefore required distinctions between private and public space, workers conceived of home as a private realm distinct from the public world. Because workers only invited close friends and family inside, the kitchen provided an appropriate setting for most exchange. Relationships with more distant acquaintances took place in the neighborhood—on the street or within shops, saloons or churches. The transference of these traditional patterns of socializing from an intimate pre-industrial community to the city had the impact of increasing the isolation of the working-class home. It is not surprising, therefore, that historians have noted that among many immigrant groups, the American home became a haven as it had never been in the old world.[54]

When addressing working-class people, reformers justified the new esthetic primarily in terms of cleanliness; specifically they promoted a simple house shell free of "dust-collecting" carpets, drapes and wallpaper. For most working-class people, however, these decorative treatments were signs of taste and status that they hated to forsake. In almost all European rural societies, as in comparable places in America, only upper-class people had carpets and curtains.[55] Workers embraced the accessibility of these products in urban America with delight.[56] In her autobiography, Mary Antin significantly remarked, "we had *achieved* a carpet since Chelsea days."[57] Given alien and institutional-looking housing facades, curtained windows were often a family's only way to make a personal statement to the world passing by.[58] Wallpaper—the worst demon of all to reformers—was for workers a privilege possible with prosperity and a relief from otherwise dull home walls. The behavior of one family occupying company housing which prohibited wallpaper near U.S. Steel's Gary, Indiana plant spoke for many others:

"If you'll give us the colors we want, Sophie will do the painting herself." This broken up into foreign-sounding English, ended the parley with the company decorator.... And in the "box" occupied by her family she had her way. Outside it remained like all the rest in the row, but indoors, with stencil designs, such as she had learned to make at school, she painted the walls with borders at the top and panels running down to the floor.[59]

This young girl replicated in paint the borders and backgrounds of wallpaper design; though learned in school, this long-standing form of rural folk art satisfied the esthetic tastes and status needs of her family (Fig. 4).

Workers' selection of furniture perhaps best demonstrates their struggle to satisfy both traditional and new expectations with products available on the mass market. The middle-class preference for colonial-inspired, natural wood furniture, built-ins and antiseptic iron bedsteads satisfied neither of these needs.

As indicated earlier by Mabel Kittredge's despair in her *Housekeeping Notes* at "cheap" and "ugly" sideboards, workers valued case pieces like bureaus, chiffoniers and buffets. This preference evolved out of a long tradition of dowry chests and precious wardrobes, often the only substantial furniture in rural homes. Workers, however, did not necessarily consider their acquisition of such furnishings in urban America a conscious perpetuation of traditional material values. An uncomprehending settlement worker noted that

There were the Dipskis, who displayed a buffet among other new possessions, and on the top of it rested a large cut-glass punch bowl. Mrs. Dipski said proudly, "And so I become American," as she waved her hand toward the huge piece of furniture, which took an inordinately large place in her small room.[60]

While reformers counseled against unhealthy wood bed frames as vermin-infested and expensive, feather bedding for causing overheating of the body, and fancy linens as unsanitary, working-class people sought to bring all three items into their homes.[61] Byington found a "high puffy bed with one feather tick to sleep on and another to cover" typical of native American homes in Homestead.[62] An observer in Lawrence, Massachusetts

Fig. 4 "Where Some of the Surplus Goes," 1907. By Lewis Hine. From *Homestead: Households of a Mill Town* by Margaret Byington (New York: Russell Sage Foundation, 1910).

in 1912 described the interior of an Italian mill-worker's home as boasting "pleasant vistas of spotless beds rising high to enormous heights and crowned with crotchet-edged pillows"[63] (Fig. 5).

Immigrants carried feather bedding with them on the long trek to America more frequently than any other single item.[64] Antin recalled her Russian neighbor's warnings before the family departed for the United States.

"In America they sleep on hard mattresses, even in winter. Haveh Mirel, Yachne the dressmaker's daughter, who emigrated to New York two years ago, wrote her mother that she got up from childbed with sore sides, because she had no featherbed."[65]

Jews, Italians, Slavs and most other groups shared a native experience which prized feather bedding and viewed "the bed"—unveiled at marriage—as an emotional symbol of future family happiness.[66] The bed was the dominant feature of most peasant homes, often overpowering all other furniture, which usually was very minimal. Elizabeth Hasonovitz nostalgically remembered her mother in Russia, "bending over a boxful of goose feather, separating the down, preparing pillows for her daughters' future homes."[67] Italian marriage rituals prescribed that the bride's trousseau would provide hand-sewn, heavily embroidered linens along with the marital bed. Pride often produced beds so high that a stool was needed to climb into them.[68]

At least for Italians, the bed played a part in the rituals of death as well. While in Italian villages an elaborate funeral bed commonly was carried into the public square, in America, Italian families laid out their dead ceremoniously at home.[69]

The embellished bed, then, was an important family symbol of birth, marriage and death, not an object to abandon easily.

We have seen throughout this essay that workers' homes were crowded with plush, upholstered furniture, a taste which may have emerged out of valuing fluffy, elaborately decorated beds. As the parlor appeared on the home scene, workers brought traditional bed-associated standards to their newly acquired and prized possessions. Well aware of this working-class market for Victorian style furniture, Grand Rapids furniture factories produced their cheapest lines in styles no longer fashionable among middle-class consumers.[70]

Since domestic reformers were promoting a simpler esthetic at the turn of the century, they denounced workers' taste for ornamentation. Photographs of working-class homes nevertheless reveal the persistence of abundant images on the walls (if only cheap prints, torn-out magazine illustrations and free merchant calendars), objects on tabletops, and layering in fabric and fancy paper of surface areas such as mantels, furniture and cabinet shelves.

The fabric valance which appears in almost every photograph of a working-class interior demonstrates how a traditional symbol took on new applications in the American environment of industrial textile manufacture (Fig. 6). In cultures such as the Italian, for example, where people treasured the elaborate bed, they adorned it with as much decorative detailing as possible. In fact, it was often the only object warranting such

Fig. 5 "Finishing Pants," c. 1900. By Jacob Riis. The Museum of the City of New York.

Fig. 6 Nurse with Polish immigrant mother and child, c. 1910. Chicago Historical Society.

art and expense in the home. A visitor to Sicily in 1905 shared with his travelogue readers a peek into a typical home where

you are greeted by a bed, good enough for a person with a thousand a year, of full double width, with ends of handsomely carved walnut wood or massive brass. The counterpane which sweeps down to the floor is either hand-knitted, of enormous weight, or made of strips of linen joined together with valuable lace, over which is thrown the yellow quilt so handy for decoration. The show pillows are even finer, being smaller.[71]

Under this spread, women fastened a piece of embroidered linen in a deep frill to cover any part of the bed's frame which might show. Even when families could afford attractive, wood frame bedsteads, they still used this "turnialettu," or valance, its original purpose forgotten.[72] In America, where fabric was cheap, the valance of gathered fabric found even more applications, adorning every possible surface and exposed area; in the 1930s Phyllis Williams even discovered valences over washing machines in second-generation Italian-American homes.[73] Fabric was draped and decoratively placed in a multitude of other ways as well. A French-Canadian woman who ran a boarding house for shoe factory workers in Lynn thus adorned the inexpensive craftsman-style Morris Chairs in her cluttered parlor with "inappropriate" antimacassars, an affront to any Arts and Crafts devotee (Fig. 7).

While workers brought distinctive cultural heritages to bear on the furnishing of their urban-American homes, much less variety in material preferences resulted than one might have expected. Common pre-industrial small town experience, limits to the preferred and affordable merchandise available for purchase, and mixed ethnic worker communities seem to have encouraged a surprisingly consistent American working-class material ethos that was distinct from that of the middle class. The speed with which a particular working-class family forged a material transition to industrial life depended on numerous factors, among them the intent and length of the family's stay in urban America, prior economic and social experience, and financial resources.

Once workers achieved a certain basic level of economic stability, their homes began to reflect this distinctive material ethos. While working-class people at the time may not have viewed their choices in reified terms, their set of preferences seems not arbitrary but a recurrent, symbolic pattern; not a simple emulation of middle-class Victorian standards with a time lag due to delayed prosperity, but rather a creative compromise forged in making a transition between two very different social and economic worlds. This working-class ethos of material values, inspired by rural values and reinforced within the urban neighborhood, departed in almost every way from esthetics favored by the middle class and promoted by the domestic reformers. Ironically, while middle-class people viewed the appearance of working-class homes as unsanitary, tasteless and un-American, workers in fact felt that their new material world represented acculturation to American urban ways. Through the purchase of mass-produced objects, they struggled to come to terms with this industrial society.

Material acculturation occurred as an individual or family made peace between traditional and new world needs. While many workers must have

Fig. 7 "The Window Side of Miss K's Parlour at Lynn, Mass." c. 1903. From *The Woman Who Toils: Being the Experiences of Two Gentlewomen as Factory Girls* by Mrs. John Van Worst and Marie Van Vorst (New York: Doubleday, Page & Company, 1903).

realized their home decor differed from the styles promoted by the middle class, they still felt they had adapted to their new environment and had advanced far beyond their former conditions. While the middle-class person and reformer could not see it, the working-class homes steeped in comfort and covers stood as a symbol of being at home in industrial America.

At the turn of the century, the homes of both the middle class and the working class reflected the transitions in their respective social experience. On the one hand, middle-class people rejected Victorian decor for a simpler, more "American" esthetic, which they tried to impose on workers. On the other hand, the working class found in the ornate Victorian furnishing style an appropriate transition to industrial life. The "Victorian solution" was not an inevitable stage working people had to pass through, but a circumstance of need finding available product. Furniture in the Victorian style persisted even as the Colonial Revival and Arts and Crafts dominated middle-class tastes. The old style well suited workers' rural based material values, while satisfying their desire to adapt to mass produced goods, just as it had for the middle class several generations earlier. The contrast in middle-class and working-class tastes in this period suggests that working-class culture indeed had an integrity of its own.

Further historical research may explain the recent findings of sociologists studying contemporary working-class material life. Lee Rainwater and David Coplovitz, for example, have discovered distinctive patterns in working-class domestic values: a preference for plush and new furnishings over used ones; a taste for modern products such as appliances; the valuing of the interior over the exterior appearance of the house; and a common conception of home as a private haven for the working-class family.[74] While these sociologists do not attempt to explain the historical development of material choices, connections to workers' homes in the 1885-1915 period are striking and warrant investigation.

The decades discussed in this essay, when waves of new workers were integrated into an expanding industrial society, may have served as the formative stage for the development of a working-class culture. We have seen how the transitional interior created by workers during this period, as they adjusted to twentieth-century American life, satisfied some ambivalence toward the urban, industrial world. Within this material compromise, traditional cultural values and new consumer benefits could coexist. If workers' homes throughout the twentieth century continued to reflect the attributes of this initial transition, as Rainwater's and Coplovitz's studies tentatively suggest, we may have evidence that contradictions still lie at the core of the American working-class identity. Workers may have reified and passed down this transitional style, or a contradictory attitude toward industrial society may continue to inform their domestic selections. In either case, working-class material values have emerged through both resistance and adaptation to the social environment and have remained distinct from those of the middle class. The chief legacy of this contradiction may be a worker population which on the one hand boasts a unique and discernible material culture and on the other hand does not identify itself forthrightly as a working class.

Notes

I would like to thank Kenneth Ames for his initial encouragement of this project and Laurence Levine for his invaluable criticism.

[1]See Lee Rainwater, *Workingman's Wife: Her Personality, World and Life Style* (New York: Oceana Publications, Inc., 1959); Lee Rainwater, "Fear and the House as Haven in the Lower Class," *Journal of the American Institute of Planners* 32 (January 1966), 23-31; Dennis Chapman, *The Home and Social Status* (London: Routledge & Kegan Paul; New York: Gross Press, 1955); Marc Fried, *The World of the Urban Working Class* (Cambridge: Harvard Univ. Press, 1973); Michael Young and Peter Willmott, *The Symmetrical Family: A Study of Work and Leisure in the London Region* (London: Routledge & Kegan Paul, 1973; London: Penguin Books, 1975).

[2]All historians who study "the working class" struggle with how to define it. While I am convinced the experience of class is complex, I will adopt a simple definition for the purposes of this essay and use "working class" to refer to skilled and unskilled workers. This essay will explore the extent to which people in the manual trades developed a distinctive material culture.

[3]Herbert Gutman, *Work, Culture and Society in Industrializing America* (New York: Vintage Books, 1977), 3-78.

[4]Siegfried Gideon, *Mechanization Takes Command* (New York: Norton Library, 1969), 365.

[5]John Ruskin, "Of Queen's Gardens," *Sesame and Lilies* (London: 1864; New York: Metropolitan Pub. Co., 1871), quoted in Gwendolyn Wright, "Making the Model Home: Domestic Architecture and Cultural Conflict in Chicago, 1873-1913." Diss. Univ. of California, Berkeley, 1978, p. 21.

[6]Gideon, *Mechanization*, 384.

[7]See Sam Bass Warner, Jr., *Streetcar Suburbs* (Cambridge: Harvard Univ. Press, 1962); photographs of newly-developed areas in almost every town or city in America during this period.

[8]John Rhoads, *The Colonial Revival* (New York: Garland Publishing, Inc., 1977).

[9]Barbara Ehrenreich and Deirdre English, "The Manufacture of Housework," *Socialist Revolution* 26 (Oct.-Dec., 1975), 5-40.

[10]C. Chester Lane, "Hingham Arts and Crafts" in Rhoads, *Colonial Revival*, p. 367. Even though American Arts and Crafts designers like Stickley were inspired by William Morris's English Arts and Crafts Movement, their debt to this source did not receive much attention in America. Stickley conveniently equated the American colonial experience with the medieval heritage being revived by the British.

[11]Rhoads, *Colonial Revival*, 416.

[12]Rhoads, 207.   [13]Rhoads, 517.

[14]Rhoads, 524; see also Barbara Solomon, *Ancestors and Immigrants* (Cambridge, Harvard Univ. Press, 1956).

[15]Rhoads, *Colonial Revival*, 390.

[16]*The Craftsman Magazine* (July 1903) in Rhoads, *Colonial Revival*, 285; also 412, 834.

[17]Gustav Stickly, "Als Ik Kan: 'Made in America' " in Rhoads, *Colonial Revival*, 488.

[18]Mabel Kittredge, *Housekeeping Notes* (Boston: Whitcomb & Barrows, 1911), 1-13.

[19]College Settlements Association, *Annual Report 1902* (New York: 1902), 37.

[20]Jane Addams, Letter to Sarah Alice Addams Haldeman, 13 Sept., 1889. Courtesy of Jane Addams Papers Project, Hull House, Chicago, Illinois.

[21]Esther Barrows, *Neighbors All: A Settlement Notebook* (Boston: Houghton Mifflin, 1929), 37.

[22]Roy Lubove, *The Progressives and the Slums: Tenement House Reform in New York City, 1890-1917* (Pittsburgh: Univ. of Pittsburgh Press, 1962), 163.

[23]Tamara Hareven and Randolph Langenbach, *Amoskeag: Life and Work in an American Factory City* (New York: Pantheon, 1978).

[24]Gerd Korman, *Industrialization, Immigrants and Americanization* (Madison: Univ. of Wisconsin Press, 1967), 88.

[25]See Maxine Seller, "The Education of the Immigrant Woman, 1900 to 1935," *Journal of Urban History* (May 1978); John Daniels, *Americanization via the Neighborhood* (New York: Harper & Bros., 1920); Sophonisba Breckinridge, *New Homes for Old* (New York: Harper & Bros., 1921).

[26]Herbert Gans, *The Urban Villagers* (New York: The Free Press, 1962), 152-153.

[27]Jane E. Robbins, M.D., "The First Year at the College Settlement," *The Survey* 27 (24 Feb.,

1912), 1801.

[28]Barrows, *Neighbors*, 7-8.

[29]Barrows, 40-41.

[30]Here and elsewhere in the paper, "material values" refers to preferences in the selection and arrangement of objects of material culture.

[31]See Stephen Thernstrom and Peter R. Knights, "Men in Motion," *Journal of Interdisciplinary History* (Autumn 1970), 7-35; Humbert S. Nelli, *Italians in Chicago, 1880-1930* (New York: Oxford Univ. Press, 1970); Madelon Powers, "Faces along the Bar: The Saloon in Working-Class Life, 1890-1920," University of California, Berkeley, California, 1979. Madelon Powers has found that "neighborhood saloons" drew together mixed ethnic groups living in the same residential areas.

[32]Rhoads, *Colonial Revival*, 716; Lubove, *Progressives*, 23-24.

[33]James Henretta, "The Study of Social Mobility," *Labor History* 18 (Spring 1977), 165-178.

[34]Philip Cowen, *Memories of an American Jew* (New York: International Press, 1932), 231.

[35]See Moses Rischin, *The Promised City* (Cambridge: Harvard Univ. Press, 1962), 22; Eli Ginzberg and Hyman Berman, eds., *The American Worker in the Twentieth Century: A History through Autobiographies* (New York: The Free Press, 1963), 12.

[36]John Briggs, *An Italian Passage: Italians in Three American Cities, 1890-1930* (New Haven: Yale Univ. Press, 1978).

[37]Pascal D'Angelo,*Son of Italy* (New York: Macmillan, 1924), 50.

[38]David Riesman, *The Lonely Crowd: A Study of the Changing American Character* (New Haven: Yale Univ. Press, 1950), 40, 17-18 in James Henretta, "Families and Farms: Mentalite in Pre-Industrial America," *William and Mary Quarterly* 35 (Jan., 1978), 30.

[39]Phyllis Williams, *South Italian Folkways in Europe and America* (New Haven: Yale Univ. Press, 1938), 50.

[40]Peter Roberts, *The Anthracite Coal Communities* (New York: Macmillan, 1904), 43.

[41]See Stephen Thernstrom, *Poverty and Progress* (New York: Atheneum, 1971); John Modell, "Patterns of Consumption, Acculturation, and Family Income Strategies in Late Nineteenth Century America," in Hareven and Vinovskis, *Family and Population in Nineteenth-Century America* (Princeton: Princeton Univ. Press, 1978), 206-240; Virginia Yans-McLaughlin, *Family and Community: Italian Immigrants in Buffalo 1880-1930* (Ithaca: Cornell Univ. Press, 1977), for sacrifices made toward buying a house.

[42]Edith Abbott and Sophonisba Breckinridge, *The Tenements of Chicago, 1908-1935* (Chicago: Univ. of Chicago Press, 1936), 263-64.

[43]D'Angelo, *Son*, 5.

[44]See Sydelle Kramer and Jenny Masur, eds., *Jewish Grandmothers* (Boston: Beacon Press, 1976); Mary Antin, *Promised Land* (Boston: Houghton Mifflin, 1912; Sentry Edition, 1969).

[45]Donna Gabaccia, "Housing and Household Work in Sicily and New York, 1890-1910," Univ. of Michigan, Ann Arbor, 18.

[46]Antin, *Promised Land*, 337.

[47]Morris Knowles, *Industrial Housing* (New York: McGraw-Hill, 1920), 295.

[48]Donald Cole, *Immigrant City: Lawrence, Massachusetts, 1845-1921* (Chapel Hill: Univ. of North Carolina Press, 1963), 107.

[49]Robert Woods, *The City Wilderness*(Boston: Houghton Mifflin, 1898; New York: Arno Press, 1970), 102.

[50]Margaret Byington, *Homestead: The Households of a Mill Town* (New York: Russell Sage Foundation, 1910), 55.

[51]Thomas Bell, *Out of This Furnace* (Boston: Little, Brown, 1941), 62.

[52]See Rose Cohen, *Out of the Shadow* (New York, 1918), 196-97 in Judith Smith, "Our Own Kind," *Radical History Review* 17 (Spring 1978), 113; William Elsing, "Life in New York Tenement Houses," in Robert Woods, *Poor in Great Cities* (New York: Scribner's Sons, 1895), 50.

[53]Byington, *Homestead*, 56.

[54]Williams, *Folkways*, 17; Yans-McLaughlin, *Buffalo Italians*, 223; Nelli, *Chicago Italians*, 6.

[55]Inventory Research at Old Sturbridge Village on Western Massachusetts homes, 1790-1840, revealed a similar pattern; carpets and curtains were rare and precious.

[56]Carlo Bianco, *The Two Rosetos* (Bloomington: Indiana Univ. Press, 1974), 14; Williams, *Folkways*, 43.

[57]Antin, *Promised Land*, 274 (emphasis is mine).

[58]Robert Roberts, *The Classic Slum* (London: Penguin, 1971), 33.

[59]Graham Taylor, *Satellite Cities* (New York: D. Appleton, 1915; New York: Arno Press, 1970), 194.

[60]Barrows, *Neighbors*, 70.

[61]*Reports of the President's Homes Commission* (Washington: Govt. Printing Office, 1909), 117.

[62]Byington, *Homestead,* in Ginzberg, *American Worker*, 46.

[63]Cole, *Lawrence,* 107.

[64]See Thomas Wheeler, ed., *The Immigrant Experience* (New York: Dial Press, 1971; London: Penguin, 1977), 20, 155; Cowen, *Memories*, 233.

[65]Antin, *Promised Land*, 164.

[66]Williams, *Folkways,* 86.

[67]Elizabeth Hasonovitz, *One of Them* (Boston: Houghton Mifflin, 1918), 6.

[68]Williams, *Folkways,* 42.

[69]Bianco, *Two Rosetos*, 124.

[70]Kenneth Ames, "Grand Rapids Furniture at the Time of the Centennial," *Winterthur Portfolio 10,* 42.

[71]Douglas Sladen and Norma Latimer, *Queer Things about Sicily* (London: Anthony Treherne, 1905), 85.

[72]Williams, *Folkways*, 42-43.

[73]Williams, 47.

[74]Rainwater, *Workingman's Wife*; Rainwater, "House as Haven"; David Coplovitz, "The Problem of the Blue-Collar Consumer," in Arthur Shostak and William Gomberg, eds., *Blue Collar World: Studies of the American Worker* (Englewood Cliffs: Prentice-Hall, 1964).

Furniture, the American Revolution and the Modern Antique

Michael N. Shute

Early American furniture was one bright cultural manifestation of colonial ideals. But to speak of ideals seems, today, to invite a moral lecture. "Ideals" of American society glow, when they glow at all, elusively, and to many, inaccessibly, especially when we perceive those ideals in the light of our present century. Values that once seemed grand—the Puritan errand, the attempt to construct varied kinds of culture in the wilderness, exploration, discovery—seem corroded and corrosive when seen in their historical consequences. We now see these values in their protean, complex and uncertain relation to the disorienting conditions of our present life. It is possible that no themes are so American as those which involve, as Henry James remarked (Preface to *What Maisie Knew*)

a "bright hard medal, of so strange an alloy, one face of which is somebody's right and ease and the other somebody's pain and wrong."

Now wood is not an alloy, but it can be shaped in a way that describes the human reality sketched by James. That shaping is part of our discussion, set primarily in Boston, Philadelphia and London before the American Revolution, continuing with a few quickly-marked paths to the antiques market of the present and ending with some speculation about a Revolutionary chair in the troubled and extreme improbability of our own time.

We have not yet recognized the historical importance of the artistic value of American furniture. Historians and students of the decorative arts have described colonial furniture craft in different ways. Historians have seen the Revolutionary activity of artisans, including cabinetmakers, chairmakers and other furniture artisans who advanced the cause of American independence, especially in cities like Boston and Philadelphia. And students of the decorative arts and antiques have delved with some sublety into the differences between furniture made in different colonies, between furniture made in the countryside and that produced in the cities, and between British and American furniture craft. Now, however, it is necessary to make some more general but discriminatory judgments about the aesthetic quality of colonial furniture and its puzzling relation to American and British culture.

Artisans of all sorts were of course directly involved in the Revolutionary struggle. They served on resistance committees and discussed the cause in taverns. But the growing sense of independence which these revolutionary activities reflect can be seen also in the day-to-day work of the artisans, as they fashioned their own aesthetic standards from the Old World patterns.[1]

These standards were exhibited in products which filled eighteenth-century American homes, particularly the urban middle-class homes which supplied much of the leadership for Independence. By fashioning aesthetic values, artisans identified themselves as a discrete group whose continuity made possible serious commitment to the Revolutionary struggle. But the aesthetic ambience itself contributed to the differentiation of American culture from the British. This difference (exemplified by an American chair, like that of figure #1, for example) enhanced the feeling of Americans that they were indeed a separate people.

And in their implicit but intentional struggle to create artistic norms in their work, in their transcendence of simple initiation of British patterns, craftsmen suggested the creativity of American culture as a whole. To be sure, aesthetic differences from Europe in the area of urban furniture craft (and others) tended to recede after the Revolution. And, to be sure, post-Revolutionary American distinction in art tended toward the dissonance of the literary American Renaissance rather than the harmony of pre-Revolutionary furniture. But these post-Revolutionary developments serve to make the pre-Revolutionary difference more intriguing.[2] Some understanding of that difference also helps clarify the way in which the Revolution demarcated early American culture from the life and culture which came later.

Crafts were of great use in eighteenth-century America.[3] In a society struggling to establish both its control over the wilderness and, then, rudimentary structures of urban life (efforts which continued in many ways through the Revolution), painting, sculpture, music and even reading and writing were luxuries. Homes had to be furnished, however, and their furnishing provided greater opportunities for choices, including aesthetic choices, than did, for example, the selection of a painting (painting in the pre-Revolutionary period consisted largely of portraits). Crafts were obvious vehicles for those with creative aspirations, because the products of craftsmanship were in constant demand. Native American painters (like John Singleton Copley) tended to return to Europe, while artisans from Europe migrated to America throughout the colonial period. For both artisans and users of their products, craftwork could be the vehicle for the disposition and refinement of taste, manner and values.

Furniture makers were intimately involved in this fashioning of value. Furniture was necessary and could not be easily or inexpensively imported (although importation did occur). Wood was plentiful in America, and furniture artisans arrived with the first settlers.[4] These makers of cabinets, chairs, tables and lowboys strove from the beginning for "durability, utility, and aesthetic beauty."[5]

For the most part, American furniture makers—particularly the most important "high-style" craftsmen of Boston and Philadelphia—used British patterns as a basis for their own creative work. It has been said that American furniture differed from that of the "old world" primarily by its "treatment" and use ... of borrowings from Europe.[6] But, from this special

Fig. 1 Sidechair, Chippendale Style
(Courtesy, Museum of Fine Arts, Boston)

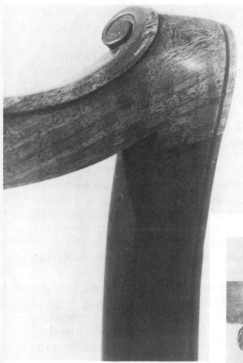

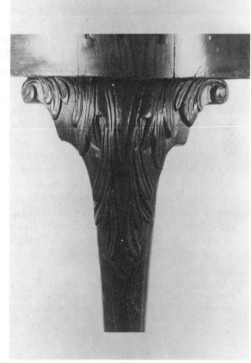

"treatment" and "use" emerged distinctive American values which represented an indigenous pre-Revolutionary culture, separated from the European tradition that had nurtured it.

Craftsmen and homemakers alike did depend greatly upon the English. Many pieces of colonial furniture such as cupboards differ so slightly from their English counterparts "as to confuse experts."[7] Settlers who could afford it did in fact sometimes use furniture imported from England. Virginians and Marylanders often had their furniture ornamented in England and sent to America to be set up.[8] Virginians, steady traders with England, bartered tobacco for English furnishings.[9]

But most colonists could not afford to import their furniture, so artisans in America began by patterning their work after the English's.[10] In the early years of the colonies, artisans who had themselves been trained in Europe worked from memory of English styles.[11] Regularly arriving immigrant craftsmen insured "the transit of new modes, inventions, and techniques."[12] When memory failed the English born artisan and when the American-bred cabinetmaker and chairmaker sought models for their own work, they turned most often to English and other European manuals, the most prominent of which was to be Chippendale's *Director.**[13]

The distinctiveness of pre-Revolutionary American furniture emerged analagously to, as well as out of, the historical development of English furniture patterns inherited from medieval culture. Medieval furniture makers, working in the usually unarticulated ethos of their societies, had been reluctant to meddle with God's nature. These craftsmen revered the environment that they found. They therefore substituted the apparently self-evident, balanced and "self-sufficient forms of geometry for the flowing line" suggested by much classical art.[20] The Renaissance and the Enlightenment promoted the resurrection of that "flowing line" in new ways, but in the early and mid-seventeenth centuries, Western furniture still held to many of the old patterns. This was particularly true in the colonies. The earliest colonial furniture was very simple; it was constructed on straightforward additive principles. One part was pegged or pinned to another. The whole was simply the sum of these agglomerated parts. Wilderness conditions—the need to focus on subsistence and survival— made simplicity paramount. Artisans did balance geometric forms—

---

*Although furniture makers depended mainly on English patterns as the model for their work, continental influences were also felt. Palatine Germans in the "Pennsylvania Dutch" country brought their own ethnic styles, the most prominent of which is "Gaudy Dutch," an adherence to a medieval kind of allegorical description which befit the cultural proclivities of these settlers.[14] Spanish styles influenced some colonial furniture.[15] Dutch styles could be seen in the furniture in the Hudson Valley.[16]

The Dutch contributed also to the unique group of furniture makers centered in Newport, Rhode Island. The "blockfront" furniture makers developed by the Townsends and Goddards was fashioned partly in the mode of English craft (of the Queen Anne period).[17] But it had also other traits not shared with highboys and lowboys in England and America. Townsend and Goddard used large, thick planks of expensive woods to construct their highboys and lowboys. It seems likely that circumstances of trade made possible this style, which originated partly in Holland:[18] Newport's advantageous position in relation to the slave trade allowed its artisans to obtain the wood they wanted for less than half of what Philadelphia craftsmen might pay.[19] In this unusual example of colonial experimentation, a practical circumstance involving the price of lumber enabled artisans to combine and mold "old world" concepts into forms of their own choosing.

rectangular blocks of wood, for example—but did little to shape them individually or to integrate them with one another. Craftsmen copied God's most manifestly "perfect" forms. Following Aristotelian philosophy rather than ancient Greek sculpture and poetry, the European middle ages detected a moral superiority in such static shapes as the rectangle and the square: it would not tamper with those shapes. The massive verticality of early colonial chairs, many of which could have easily taken their place in medieval castles,[21] was striking. (See the Baronial Oak Chair #2).

(The Puritans had their own quasi-medieval patterns for decorating their furniture. Puritans designed their interiors so that "color and pattern and ornament ran riot everywhere."[22] And such proclivities of the English colonists were rivalled by the colonists from other European countries—for example by the colorful flourish with which the "Pennsylvania Dutch" decorated their furniture in archetypal patterns. This impulse marked the almost mystical appeal of ornamentation, suited to their view of art as the product of unconscious composition and the reflection of a natural order, a view which diminished the need for and the value of man's own creative intrusion.)

The structure that medieval culture gave to art permitted great achievements; the aesthetic and useful solidity of American "baronial oak" furniture is a minor—but not insignificant—outgrowth. But other forces, which had started centuries before the enlightenment and which centered in urban life, thrust toward new approaches. With the predominance of cultural centers like London and Paris, in societies more receptive as a whole to urban needs, art began to take new forms. The ambiguities and greater spontaneity of urban life pointed away from the rigid spatial categorization of geometric shape. New scientific recognition of motion, of course, cut through the categories of horizontal and vertical to gain greater understanding of curvature (particularly irregular or imperfect curves) through calculus. Art could take steps to transcend the "perfect" circle, the square, and so forth. New desires for individual autonomy and humanistic assertion promoted new ways of establishing a new kind of fullness based on the "flowing line" in carving solid raw material.

In English furniture this movement is dated particularly from the "William and Mary" school of the late seventeenth century, continuing through "Queen Anne" and then "Chippendale" in the late eighteenth century. In the colonies this development of the "flowing line" met with particular success. Illustration #3, a scalloped Boston tea table making a sensuous use of fluid design, is an example of this success, as is Illustration #4, another tea table made in Philadelphia. Both of these examples of American virtuosity date roughly from the middle eighteenth century. Boston and Philadelphia differed in crucial respects from ancient Athens, Renaissance Florence and enlightened London, all of which had achieved dynamic creative innovation. But, like them, these American cities were maritime havens in cultural ferment. They were, furthermore, without a weighty feudal past and the critical implications of that past.

If earlier artisans formed furniture simply by adding one pre-existing shape to another, the newer craftwork showed that the furniture maker more actively controlled his environment and could create new proportions. Whatever the conscious intention artisans brought to their shops, they

Fig. 2 Baronial Oak Chair.

began to behave more deliberately, as if they were engaged in acts of self-creation.[23]

One mark of this change was the substitution of "more easily worked walnut" for the "ponderous solidity of oak."[24] The artisan, both here and in England, began to shape wood according to his inner sense of symmetry and balance and aesthetic unity. In his furniture, the artist employed human and animal traits like the padded foot characteristic of the Queen Anne style. This foot developed late in the Queen Anne period into the lifelike ball and claw which marks the Chippendale period (padded feet in table illustration #5, ball and claw in scallopped table 3#, also table #4).

The ball and claw (and the scroll foot of #1 Hingham side chair) culminated the humanistic artisanship which had begun crudely in William and Mary. In transmuting animal and human characteristics into artistic shape in the service of the craftwork—a chair for example—the new design decisively transcended many aspects of medieval art and philosophy. Medieval artists and thinkers followed ideas of Aristotle (and the ancient physician Galen) in ascribing some human traits like purpose, to nature; to the shape of an animal or the human body, for example. Shedding this animism, the modern artisan now turned this process around, molding "natural" forms into the delicately-turned contours of art.

Although the William and Mary style still tended toward two-dimensionalism and verticalism, the Chippendale style expanded the padded foot of Queen Anne furniture to three dimensions. Straight legs were replaced in the Queen Anne period by the cabriole leg, for which the shape of the human leg itself was the model. Here again man became recognizable in his furniture, but less because it was a human leg that was being copied than because the furniture made imaginative use of the natural leg or the animal foot. Rather than simply reproducing those forms, the artisans changed them in organic relation to the larger craftwork. And, with its proportional subtlety, linear grace, inward unity and compactness, the furniture now became like post medieval art.

Like each individual human being, a chair became a distinguishably organic entity. Its parts could not easily be seen as separate (as could the parts of previous additive structures). Proportion affected not only the linear outline of the piece of furniture but its whole structure. The splats of chairs became, during the eighteenth century, no longer "solids pierced by wholes" (open geometric shapes) but composed designs (as in example #1).[25] Other parts of the chair were "curved to repeat and reinforce the major outlines."[27] Furniture began to look more like sculptured art than ever before, giving the impression, with geometrical divisions removed and sinuosity accented, that each piece was a "single visual unit."[28] The sculptured quality of the Chippendale style came partly as mahogany replaced walnut, as walnut had replaced oak. Mahogany "handled with the precision of moulded clay or poured metal, polished like classical bronze or oiled marble."[29]

While this furniture established its own internal aesthetic identity, it was also useful. Shaped for a sensuous unity, the Windsor chair also fitted the curvature of the human back, as baronial oak had never done. The Windsor chair was attractive and easy to sit in. (See Windsor chair, example #6). And because its delicately curled designs were often elegant as well, it

Fig. 3
Tea Table
Courtesy, Museum of Fine Arts, Boston

Fig. 4
Tip Top Table
Courtesy, Museum of Fine Arts, Boston

Fig. 5
Cherry "Tuckaway"
Courtesy, Museum of Fine Arts, Boston

Fig. 6
Arm Chair, Windsor
Courtesy, The Metropolitan Museum of Art, Gift of Mrs. Russell Sage, 1909.

Fig. 7
Arm Chair, Chippendale
Courtesy, The Metropolitan Museum of Art, Cadwalader Fund, 1918.

lent finish to a sitting room that disconnected ornament could only mime.

The internalization of proportion and life into pieces of furniture reflected two characteristics not always viewed as compatible: spontaneity and order. The new furniture had the authenticity of spontaneous action upon patterns and raw materials. But it was also well defined and regulated, as shown by the harmonious and comfortable lines of the Windsor chair. Although craftsmen did not follow a geometric blueprint, the patternmaker and the craftsmen found in their work a plan, an order. This order and spontaneity bespoke an artistic quality in the craft process. Could the less culturally and technologically advanced American colonies do anything but follow their mother country in this matter of art? Yes. Although the colonies consistently lagged behind in the adoption of new styles, colonial craftsmen, particularly in Boston and Philadelphia, applied their art in a more sophisticated way, with a panache more consistent with the spirit of the new aesthetic approach than the English were able to offer.

One colonial resident of New York said in the eighteenth century that although his city followed London fashions in furniture closely, "by the time we adopt them, they become disused in England."[30] This was hardly unique to New York. Most colonial artisans lagged considerably behind the English, especially in the advance from Queen Anne to Chippendale.[31] This tendency was of course more pronounced in the countryside and smaller towns than in the cities. The Queen Anne style predominated in Suffield, Connecticut, until 1790, some forty years after it had been outdated in England.[32]

However much the colonists may have lagged behind the British chronologically, numbers of them proved to be adept in implementing new styles.[33] The heart of the new style in furniture was its definite unity, manifested in three-dimensional fullness and proportional relationships rather than in ornamentation. In this respect the American colonial craftsmen appear to have outdone their British tutors, if one judges by the "high style" furniture so often used in British and American homes. The British tended still to rely—even after their major break from more medieval tendencies—upon the embellishment of surfaces with "ornate carving," while the Americans, in their version of the Queen Anne chair, imparted grace "to the very forms of furniture by shaping the lines into subtle curves," giving their work a "natural, almost organic appearance."[34] The "gilt" characteristic of British pieces was rare in the colonies.[35] The products of the "American chair and cabinet-maker were distinguished by their fullness of linear rhythm."[36] Americans improved the style of the Windsor chair.[37] And they tended to avoid the confusion of Chinese and rococo decoration which often marked British furniture.[38] (See example #7).

An uneven development marked the cultural relation between England and America in the area of furniture crafts. The master taught, and continued to teach, and kept well ahead of the student, but once each lesson was learned the student excelled at its implementation. What needs explanation is not why England with its tradition and cultural resources was the teacher but why the student leaped ahead in applying eighteenth-century designs. Surely, the greater ornateness in British furniture resulted partly from England's greater wealth and from the existence of a privileged, self-indulgent aristocracy perpetuated from feudalism by its links to new commercial order. This is part of the answer. But other answers, related to the tenor of colonial society, in comparison with England, are also suggested by the clarity with which colonial artisans honed their tools on raw wood.

The community of colonial artisans started from Old World patterns and created a newly free, and full, altered design in accordance with an inner sense of creative unity. They were preceded by the settlers John Winthrop, William Penn and others guided by an inner conviction of earthly mission, fused with the necessary communal cooperation. Taming the wilderness, these settlers altered their external environment just as craftsmen set to work upon their raw materials. Early Puritanism accented congregational aspects of religious life and convenantal aspects of religious thought:[39] as we shall see, an important feature of craft life was to be its cooperative aspect. An emphasis on mission in the wilderness resulted also in sensitivity, channeled partly through religious, family and communal associations, to nature and the uses of nature: artisans were to express that by their intimate and free contact with wood. Finally, the Puritan "mission" contained a tension between creativity and aggression. Colonists were often unappreciative of the rights and virtues of the Indians, for example. They were themselves "savage" toward what they discovered in the new world. Aggression may have been internally rationalized by Old Testament sanctions favoring violence. But, of course, the tribes in Exodus also crafted the tabernacle in a wilderness and the Puritans likewise contributed to new world artisanship.

The emphasis on an earthly community hewn from the wilderness could only accentuate an impression that man was indeed creating a discrete existence from previously established patterns. American Puritans believed that one could know God through one's own works. They combatted Armenian and antinomian heresies which separated man's work from God's intentions, heresies which divorced the calling of constructive worldly activity from an overall divine plan. This concern to know one's calling began in Protestant Europe and was reinforced by the need to carve a place in the wilderness here. That concern could not help but help create a suitable religious background for artistic initiative in defining the calling.[40]

The primary habitat of the Queen Anne and Chippendale artisans, however, was the urban cultural centers, first of all Boston and Philadelphia. In these cities an artisan shop often contained the work of many kinds of craftsmen, and sometimes the work of only one individual. Whatever background religious culture provided for American artisanship, social reality in these cities (increasingly secular in their everyday ethos) assured the artisan's place. Because the urban centers of the colonies were newer, more recently shaped from trees and stones, the urban dwellers were more conscious of the transformation of raw material into the things they lived with daily: their wharves and streets, for example. In consequence, the social status of colonial craftsmen was different from that of their European counterparts. An artisan was regarded with esteem, almost as an artist would have been regarded in England, and craftsmen enjoyed greater security and freedom of association in the colonies than either the European medieval artisan or the emerging commercial entrepreneur (on either side of the Atlantic). The artisans' guilds which had burgeoned in England in feudal times had given craftsmen some security of social position. But guild restrictions had curtailed the artisan's freedom. The coming industrial society—omens of which existed in Britain to a far greater extent than in eighteenth-century America—offered social mobility and freedom from the social structure of aristocracy. But industrialism created restrictive hierarchies of its own while it simultaneously caught would-be artists up in an accumulative ethos and process of hectic technological change which reduced their sense of identity and order, and hence their autonomy in dealing with nature, with raw material. In England, residual aristocratic hierarchy found a place in new commercial, pre-industrial processes, insuring a culture with elements of each. Eighteenth-century America differed from both these worlds.[41]

The northern and middle colonies especially were havens for small entrepreneurs and landowners, individuals in a community. The condition of the crafts, including the furniture crafts, demonstrates this fact. No trade guilds existed at the beginning of the eighteenth century. Craft regulation gained little foothold in America. In 1718 Philadelphia allowed incorporation of crafts but only cordwainers and tailers availed themselves of the privilege and their organizations soon died out. Early in the eighteenth century New York and Philadelphia "clung to the medieval custom of requiring those who desired to conduct a trade or craft within their limits to pay a fee or take out a 'freedom'." By 1740 that regulation was on the decline everywhere.[42]

Craftsmen could feel much of that independence and self-confidence upon which the more deliberate construction of the "flowing line" was predicated. Various aspects of practical life abetted this condition. The shortage of labor, for example, made it difficult to maintain apprenticeship provisions of the Elizabethan Statute of Artifices, especially the seven-year indenture requirement. Masters resorted frequently to four- and three-year apprenticeships.[43] And a wide range of geographical opportunity awaited the urban apprentice who tired of his waiting period. He could easily move to the next town or to smaller villages.[44] This movement occurred often inland in New England where trade for furniture was not easily arranged and where settlers of new towns often planned to include artisans in their number.[45] Within two generations in the eighteenth-century, the craftsmen Dunlaps of New Hampshire spread their residences and businesses to five communities in that state.[46] All of the small towns in the Hartford area possessed cabinet shops.[47] Furniture makers could also combine their craft with farming, a common practice in the rural areas of Massachusetts and other states.[48] Opportunities for Northern artisans also increased and the old apprentice system declined accordingly because the South lacked furniture craftsmen and therefore sought a coastal trade in furniture which particularly profited New England.[39]

These conditions, especially the absence of a centralized hierarchy in furniture crafts, permitted the growth of many small establishments in the same trade, which in turn facilitated the application of new methods and individual skill. Artisans benefitted from this climate of personal freedom to impart their own order to their work. They also derived security and new

ideas from their relations with their fellow workers and with the broader
social climate, in which colonies began to cooperate with one another.
Cooperation among artisans existed alongside competition between them.
Few serious pressures for consolidation existed in the eighteenth century.
Competition of a cut throat sort did not therefore characterize craft trade.
"Improvements made at one shop in a given community rapidly became the
common property of the craft"[50] (a benefit less likely to occur where self-
perpetuating interests or hierarchies might block improvement). Craftsmen
exercised artistic and financial independence but they did so in the context
of a community. They often had shops and residences in a common locale[51]
and maintained friendships with others working in their craft. Thomas
Elfe, a Charleston furniture maker, lent other local furniture makers money
for their own businesses.[52]

Colonial craftsmen were integral members of their society. Artisans
naturally traded with others both in and beyond their own area. In 1769, for
example, Philadelphia craftsmen sold 768 Windsor chairs to buyers in other
colonies. Such trade helped to create bonds of taste as well as commerce,
contributing to intercolonial solidarity.[53] Appropriate to an economy
oriented to small trade, craftsmen were often important and occasionally
wealthy citizens who participated in public life and held public office,[54]
although less frequently than did merchants and lawyers. Colonial culture
had a distinct social structure; artisans, as a group, were not at the top.[55]
These artisans were flexible in their business and social relations. William
Savery, a prominent Philadelphia carver who became a city assessor in
1754, did not hesitate to make chicken coops and to repair chairs as well as
to create them.[56]

As members of their middle class community, craftsmen contributed
outside their workplace to the Revolutionary atmosphere. Apart from
trading, participating in politics and making chicken coops, they mingled
with other citizens in taverns and literary and benevolent societies. There
they discussed matters of community interest with "shopkeepers,
politicians, professional men, and journeymen."[57] These contacts
strengthened community sentiment in cities like Boston and Philadelphia,
which in turn made possible a fruitful non-commercial relation with other
colonial areas. Artisans protested against English trade restrictions
throughout the 1760s and 1770s. At times they joined with groups led by
merchants and at times encouraged those groups to stand firm in their
resistance.[58]

The social freedom of American artisans contributed to artistic
freedom, producing a harmonious fullness and delicacy of proportion, as
well as an integrity of design, in the very process of developing and
interpreting British styles. In the British milieu vestiges of medieval
hierarchies had been integrated into emerging industrial patterns. This
kind of historical continuity had strengths and weaknesses; in furniture
craft it permitted British industrial culture to absorb artifice of the past,
while it promoted its own artifice of the present. Bound by the past, British
furniture makers thus ornamented indulgently. In doing so, they gained
new ties to the past precisely as they inhibited the individual quality of their
work: they ornamented superabundantly as if they were carving the present
onto the past. (See again example #7.) American furniture makers,

with no similar attachment to the past, stripped away ornament. They concentrated on the integrity of the design, pouring their creative resources into a fulness of proportion which they embellished sometimes delicately, but almost always harmoniously, with their own flourishes. (Here, see again the Windsor chairs and scalloped table.)

Of course such differences between American and English craftsmen and their products were not universal. The centrality of small trade and the fuller development of British patterns by American craftsmen prevailed mainly in New England and the middle colonies. Except for Charleston, which had its own community of cabinetmakers,[59] and the cooperative colony of Moravians in North Carolina,[60] the South produced little furniture. Some Southern areas relied heavily upon importation; in colonial Virginia, it seemed "that English homes have been transplanted but have suffered no change."[61]

The only American colony outside the South which had an "aristocracy" of sorts was New York, from which emerged substantial loyalist sentiment in 1776. New York furniture not surprisingly bore a much closer resemblance to Old World originals than did the products of other colonies. New York Chippendale chairs, for instance, tended to be direct copies of their English counterparts.[62] New York's ornate "spider" gateleg tables were closely patterned after the British.[63] In general New York furniture was more ornamented and heavier than that of the other colonies.[64] And New York craftsmen often omitted from their furniture qualities with which the craftsmen of other colonies developed a more sophisticated realization of the Chippendale ideal. In many Philadelphia and Boston chairs, the contour of the leg carvings developed out of the inner profiles of the chairs—thus, the external proportions in turn penetrated the very body of the chair #1). New York chairs often lacked this unity.[65]

Those small trade areas of New England and the middle colonies in which furniture craft gained distinction were important centers of Revolutionary sentiment and activity. Artisans contributed in their own way to that sentiment by establishing an aesthetic autonomy from England. To some extent, the act of modifying British patterns was itself an act of separation. Each "deviation" by an artisan, "though it was not an overt act of refusal, was nevertheless a step toward independence."[66].

In their work artisans significantly fostered a sense of American identity. They helped shape values that contributed to the political and social struggles for independence. At this time, before industrialization, that pleasing surface which art lends to craft comported, in fact, with Revolutionary society as a whole: that society had its own inner life and its own organic unity—a unity which Edmund Burke noticed and which, as a social order, provided a point of reference for James Madison's theories of balance and reconciliation between groups.

Craftsmen naturally participated in a larger network of communities whose very looseness and inner variegation facilitated cooperation between groups: craftsmen mingled freely with merchants, for the most part. This network of communities included families like that of John and Abigail Adams and groups of families, around which "production and limited exchange" flourished. Craftsmen, of course, did business with such families but, also, craft as a business sometimes served as the central line of continuity for extended, continuous family structure, as was the case with the Dunlaps and others.[67]

Through its artisans this internally-confident society produced an aesthetic with its own inner life. Striving for a "flowing line" in their furniture craftsmen shaped raw material and reshaped aesthetic boundaries in the same way that colonists made Boston and Philadelphia into capitals of culture and exchange. The flowing lines of their chairs and cabinets suggested the fluidity of colonial life. This achievement also marked the ease with which enlightened principles had already become indelibly part of the experience of Americans, enabling them to make the apparently paradoxical revolutionary American claim, partly in the name of Enlightenment philosophy, to the full rights enjoyed by British citizens.[68] The "puzzle" of distinctive American furniture-making derived from British patterns, therefore found its "solution" in that "paradox" of the Revolution itself.

By making its distinctiveness palpable in the form of everyday furnishings artisans gave substance to that "elaborate map of social reality," that "pattern" of enlightenment values, "that made life comprehensible." When the British disrupted this work by "acts of power deemed arbitrary, degrading and uncontrollable" craftsmen were not last to react. British coercion threatened the self-reliance of American craft shops as it violated other voluntary spiritual and practical modes of American life. Craftsmen then joined in the political acts of separation as they had already joined in aesthetic acts of separation through their work.

Artisans affirmed the autonomy of their new world through the cooperative calling of revolution. Their vitality added to the exploratory "freshness and boldness" which followed the Revolution: the conviction in the next decade, through the Confederation period, that despite turmoil, "young energetic, daring, hopeful, imaginative men had taken charge and were drawing their power directly from the soil of the society they ruled."[70]

But if craftsmen had won a victory, the effects of that victory were ambiguous. A half-century after the Revolution, American furniture came to resemble British furniture (and increasingly, French furniture as well) more than ever before. It depended more on external ornamentation than on fluidity of structure, delicacy of contour, and fullness of proportion. (See example #8, sidechair, 1790-1800 Philadelphia—the beginnings of "hodge podge" design.) Some of the new furniture revealed seeds of struggling with new forms, a positive note inherited from the vitality of the furniture craft tradition which culminated in American Chippendale.

Much of this struggle however resulted in hodge-podge carvings which contained new artistic qualities more buried than alive. Much of it was modelled, somewhat self-consciously, on "classical" forms (a "classicism" ersatz contrasted to the pre—Revolutionary furniture). In its hodge-podge of ornamentation, Americans—producers and users—may have gained a tie to the European past and an olio effect more suitable to their way of perceiving things in a confusing world ushered in by industrialization—this effect may have been more comforting and hence of some real value. At any rate, from the standpoint of the previous craft, furniture now became more simply decorative and less aesthetically ambitious. It was more saleable in the marketplace than practical for the user: chairs, for example,

Fig. 8
Painted Oval Back Chair
Courtesy, Museum of Fine Arts, Boston.

were less shaped to fit the back and hence, less comfortable. As American culture, now the emblem of a nation, now needed external justification, greater external formality in the furniture replaced internal character and responsiveness to physical need.

To some extent, these traits simply continued rudimentary reliance upon British patterns. Early in the eighteenth century, British design, fashioned in a more fully industrial culture, began to emphasize styles less fluid and more external than it had during the evolution from William and Mary through Chippendale. But the reduction of the American difference marked also fundamental changes, changes facilitated by Revolutionary expansion in American culture itself. American furniture developed a more simply emulative relation to the British as class divisions became more delineated in the new world. The new American commercial classes, given their head in the post-Revolutionary decades, had little indigenous culture upon which to fall back. Aristocratic culture of the old world, embodied in designs of newer industrial society and attempting to display ties to the classical world, could help satisfy the yearnings for cultural status which accompanied the new commercial hierarchical status. Artists and rebels like Thoreau would come to view this yearning, with its accompanying ornateness, as pretension; it might also be viewed as a desire for attachment and roots which might not be satisfied by the slender reed of differentiated American artisanship, and the "tradition" of indigenously American pre-Revolutionary community.

At any rate, that community now vanished as "large mass production factories" emerged in the nineteenth century to replace "the small individual craft shops of the seventeenth and eighteenth centuries."[71]

Industrial change had begun quietly before the Revolution. This change included the germs of factory life and the expansion of the division of labor in the furniture trade. American commercial and manufacturing growth, beginning modestly to rival the British, contributed its share to Revolutionary tension. Independence spurred and made necessary such industrial growth.

Eventually, of course, industrialization changed everything. Artisans themselves wanted to become merchants and to profit as merchants were doing. "Buying and selling offered the greatest opportunity to make money and to rise in the social scale."[72] Successful craftsmen were ambitious, alert to possibilities of expansion like controlling their own sources of lumber.[73] One sign of impending social change was the tensions between artisans and merchants, even as they worked together.[74] But whatever distinctiveness craftsmen felt from merchants as a group, they sought often to emulate them individually.

Those merchants for their part had previously supported artistic craft products like American Chippendale by their patronage. Now, however, they wanted to become manufacturers, investing in systems of production which would transform the manufacture of goods like furniture.[75] Post-Revolutionary American expansion accelerated both the mercantile ambitions of craftsmen successful enough to afford it and the manufacturing enterprise of merchants.[76]

"With the rise of the factor," as Richard Morris has noted,

the transition from custom work to wholesale order work, and the concentration of workers in certain expanding industries served to bring about more distinct class stratifications. This period was marked by a decline of the apprenticeship system; inexpert workmen now came into competition with skilled journeymen, as middlemen now pitted master against master, giving their orders to the lowest cost producer.[77]

The Chippendale artisan and the artisans' shops, with their variety of turners, carvers and other skilled workers, had created a product whose aesthetic and utilitarian qualities were governed by personal adaptation of English patterns to suit the needs and values of the colonial community. Now industrial tendencies undercut the very survival of artisans. They were replaced on the one hand by manufacturers, who catered to a wider standardized market devaluing artistic considerations, and on the other by workers. The latter had

much the same status as those who lay the brick for the walls, saw timber for bargeboards ... all alike are hired by the job, work impersonally and anonymously.[78]

As artisans became either manufacturers or laborers, aesthetic issues arise in the more formal contexts of art: William Rush (1756-1833), apprentice to a Philadelphia carver, became not a carver himself but an important early American sculptor.[79]

The divorce of usefulness from beauty had now begun in America, just as it had begun in England a century earlier. Eighteenth-century American furniture makers had moved in an atmosphere with little conscious awareness of displacement and conflict gathering within, of those processes which were to transform the craft product. American intellectuals of the Revolutionary period were, in some ways, as blurred in their vision of American development and the American-British relation as they were acute in prescribing Revolutionary cures. Both John Adams and Thomas Paine, moderate and radical, strongly attacked English feudal hierarchies, which were in fact vestigial, existing primarily in the sway of burgeoning industrial and commercial development. Adams and Paine viewed these hierarchies as a primary feature of colonialist interference. Although their perceptions were partially accurate, they failed to fully recognize the growing sources of mercantile conflict, sources which in America were to lead, in the process of maturation, to restrictive hierarchies of their own.[80]

Furniture makers shielded themselves by their craft from impending historical reality. Using British patterns they divorced themselves from the architectonic medieval past, as did Paine and Adams. The lines of their furniture moved undeviatingly toward a whole, reflecting the harmony of eighteenth-century middle class life and separating themselves from conflict and displacement, from those tensions which, for example, may have contributed to the sporadic but meteoric popularity of religious evangelism. This work showed little sign or presentiment of the crisis of industrial culture which the transitional world of the artisan was introducing. Subtlety and inwardness, it might almost be possible to say the absence of self-consciousness, were characteristic of American Chippendale, heightening its sense of flow and innocence. That furniture presents itself in unhindered symmetry, pointing to its own interiority (see illustrations of Boston or Philadelphia pre-Revolutionary Chippendale). If intellectual craftsmen like Adams and Paine did not consciously perceive the disruptive potential beneath the Revolutionary surface, the carver internalizing awareness so completely into modelled wood cannot have made that perception. His textures bespoke primitive suspension from imminent change cultivated within the very culture which made his work possible.

More than half a century later this innocence and this particular kind of primitiveness had vanished. In passing from the center of practical life to arenas of its own, art gained insights into different aspects of reality. A distinctive national art emerged in the literature of the American Renaissance, in the works of Herman Melville, Nathaniel Hawthorne and Henry David Thoreau, for example, which marked the end of man's rapport with external natural and social reality. The aesthetic insight of this Renaissance has been labelled a "shock of recognition."[81] Among the aspects of life it recognized were pain and displacement. It reacted to the separation of art from social function and from previously unhindered contact with nature and the aesthetic material which nature provided. This Renaissance thus gave birth to an American angularity and dissonance, sometimes as sharply mannered as had been the innocence of Chippendale. In his *Bartleby the Scrivener*, for instance, Melville presented a character "refusing ... to be a character."[82] Bartleby's "I prefer not to" embodies an obsessive search for an inner life which had been blithely assumed in the age of Chippendale.

Because furniture became something of a commodity, and American artistic distinction manifested itself so much in literature during the nineteenth century, it is useful to include literary works in our discussion of pre-Revolutionary furniture and its ultimate course. In his year at Walden Pond, Thoreau tried to reunite craft with nature. In concluding *Walden*, Thoreau provides one frame through which we may perceive the departure of early American furniture from the public mind and marketplace, and a frame which might perhaps introduce us to the problem of the reappearance of that furniture in the twentieth century. Thoreau's work speaks of the displacement resulting from the loss that the passing of the artisans represented. He remarks on the legacy of the past amidst the technological extravagance of his nineteenth-century present:

Who knows what beautiful and winged life, whose egg has been buried for ages under many concentric layers of woodenness in the dead, dry life of society, deposited at first in the alburnum of the green and living tree, which has been gradually converted into the semblance of its well-seasoned tomb,—heard perchance gnawing out now for years by the astonished family of man, as they sat round the festive board,—may unexpectedly come forth from amidst society's most trivial and hand-selled furniture, to enjoy its perfect summer life at last![83]

Into what setting does Thoreau's egg of "beautiful and winged life" fit later, when the modern antique emerges as a popular commodity in the twentieth century?* By the early twentieth century American artists had begun to recreate ties to society which were not harmonious but which were not purely angular and dissonant. The novels of Theodore Dreiser for example were based on the growing sense that an American urban community did exist, however internally conflicted.

One hero of early twentieth-century art was the hunchback Randolph Bourne, who emerged from involvement with labor activity to call for new kinds of communities in which art could thrive, including an ethnically diverse America. Bourne called therefore for an art publicly relevant—one whose ultimate sanction was not sociological but was rather the approval of "that imagined audience of perfect comprehenders." This juxtaposition of appeals to social community with appeals to absolute higher authority sounded a note of one kind of apparent anomaly for this century. Bourne's physical appearance marked another. This apostle of beauty appeared to his post-World War I public, in the words of John Dos Passos, as

a tiny twisted unscared ghost in a black cloak hopping along the grimy old brick and brownstone streets still left in downtown New York, crying out in a shrill soundless giggle: *War is the health of the state.*[85]

After Bourne there were others who attended to the need for artistic integrity and for a community in which individual initiative would reinforce collaboration in the search for that integrity: this kind of reinforcement had helped to make pre-Revolutionary furniture possible. This search followed varied paths, including that of the immigrant child Henry Roth, whose point of reference for community was ethnic, in part; and midwesterner F. Scott Fitzgerald, conspicuously concerned with the flow and rupture of history. At the time of this renewed artistic stress on issues of community and history there appeared that older eighteenth-century American Chippendale which helped once to create an American difference.

In this century, particularly its second and third quarters, when ideals have seemed to be most soiled, American Chippendale has been once again in the public eye: it became important once again, but in the modern retail market (rather than in the community market places where colonial urban residents often traded) and in the home (although more in certain kinds of homes than others). The 1920s marked one moment of redefinition for the middle class and upper middle class in America, and for their new kinds of life, including leisure activities, including activities we might regard as saturnalian and ritualistically-acquisitive, and also activities we might view as reflecting simply normal desires for a better life. This new middle

---

*It had not yet emerged in the late nineteenth century as one romantic novel testifies. Rachel tells Charley he'll break her heart by using her new chair: he replies "You mean I'll break my back." "It was only bought for ornament," she says, "with commendable candor .... You may sit in the sleepy hollow chair, and I'll take the willow-rocker; but don't you dare to desecrate my family chairs by doing anything but admire them from afar." Ultimately, if Charley had felt about Rachel as Rachel had felt about the chair, the novel might not have been able to appear more prominently in the nineteenth century market than American Chippendale.[84]

class aura included a nostalgia for the past, partly of course an alloy of hollow sentimentality, an ornament to the myopia of modern mass sensibility. This nostalgia, however, embodied also a desire for historical roots, for a fragment of a memory which could be cherished as more than an echo of the past, to reaffirm one's existence—partly through ties to others— in the hectic milieu of present life. (Through the furniture Americans in a confusing industrial age could create bonds to older communities and ideals.) This idealistic yearning for the past is also very modern. Thus the Chippendale chair and tea table moved to the center of attention at cocktail parties and even to be used in everyday family life in the twentieth century, in the lives of families which felt the value of these objects as antiques, comforts and prestige.

There is a certain necessary tension between these antiques, as products of stable community, individual artisanship and historical continuity, and their new setting in the modern world. Removed from its hiding place in a New England attic, trucked to Houston or Marin County, a Chippendale chair comes face to face with the twentieth century, the century of holocaust and other advanced horrors. From a historical and artistic standpoint the tension may be suggested by Chair #1.This classic Chippendale, with its balloon-shaped seat, is one of many kinds of antiques which have become popular and prestigious in recent decades.

This chair is made primarily of walnut. It is replete with historical connections: it was made by artisan Peter Oliver, one of the leaders of the Boston Tea Party. (A brass plate affixed to the bottom of the seat reads "Oliver-Boston Tea Party.") Eventually this chair passed to the American justice Oliver Wendell Holmes and his family. The chair has a heavy pierced splat (on illustration #1) and accented scroll terminals at the base of that splat. Its top rail is bowed. Its seat rails are let into the upper blocks of the front legs, which curve at the back to follow the outer line of the seat frame. The stiff cabriole front legs have a rather squarish knee carved boldly with foliage. These legs terminate in molded scroll feet. The rear legs of this chair, projecting strength by their very gentle curvature, hold the ground, as their padded feet expand to one side and to the rear. This particular chair comes from a small group of chairs, one of many groups of eighteenth-century American chairs which have been described by experts in the decorative arts as "unusual."[86]

This chair breathes historical continuity and exemplifies the classic artistry of Chippendale: its integrity, its grace, fluidity and assertiveness. It developed from the fluidity and coherence of colonial community and initiative. It is desired today for these reasons, among others.

But this chair, rooted in history and community, seems at variance with the modern American milieu in which it has become popular. Today a disquiet, perhaps a pervasive quiet, seems present in American life more than ever before. If only by their nostalgic yearnings, Americans show their worry about what many social critics have seen as the deracination of ethnic, family and other communities, and the severing of present existence and understanding from the past: this more than continues the atomization de Tocqueville noticed in post-Revolutionary industrial society. Partly in reaction to the anomic conditions of the present, buyers of artifacts turn to the aesthetic resources of the past, touching through time and space the well settled personal coherence that created a Revolutionary culture.

What may we say about this juxtaposition of antique to modern life? Take Oliver's chair, with its stately bulk. Entering the room, a boy reaches for the ear of the chair, that substantial sculptured ear whose corners are curved with a small scroll (#1A). His fingers come to a stop on the scroll, as his hand grips tightly this ear itself, tightly so that his knuckles show white. His fingers press into the curves of the scroll; and after a second, as his fingers begin to move around those curves, exploring them, his grip relaxes, his hand lingering on the ear.

In our ambiance, Oliver's chair may be the trace of an ideal whose singularity of presence justifies the discontinuities around it: perhaps Hawthorne's "moon, creating, like the imaginative power, a beautiful strangeness in familiar objects," giving "romance to a scene that might not have possessed it in the light of day."[87] Victorian hodgepodge might be more fitting to the present.

But this view of the chair need not exclude others. Might this chair be the slight intrusion, by indirection, of a classic irony, an ancient justice tempered and unfolding out of the American past, to mock the present? And, listening to other words of Henry James, we may describe this thick ear, touched by the boy as

flourishing, to a degree, at the cost of many conventions and properties, even decencies, really keeping the torch of virtue alive in an air tending infinitely to smother it; really in short making confusion worse confounded by drawing some stray fragrance of an ideal across the scene of selfishness, by sowing on barren strands, through the mere fact of presence, the seed of the moral life.[88]

The propriety of James' words, for our view of the present-condition of this chair, depends partly upon changes in society and culture, perhaps fundamental changes, which are now occurring. Those changes bear on the ability of American culture to rebuild its affirmative ties to the past, in the milieu I described and others. About this possibility there will be no comment here. To forecast the future, we need, to paraphrase Woody Allen, not a historian but a magician.

Notes

[1]Carl Bridenbaugh, *The Colonial Craftsman* (Chicago: Phoenix, 1951), passim, and Charles S. Olton, *Artisans for Independence: Philadelphia Mechanics and the American Revolution* (Syracuse: Syracuse Univ. Press, 1975), passim, and others.

[2]This esssay touches on the relation between American and British craft aesthetics and culture, historically and against their social background. These issues have not been without traditional and continuing interest. An example of recent comment is Patricia Kane and Charles Montgomery, eds., *American Art: 1750-1800, Towards Independence* (Boston: New York Graphic Society, 1976), which stemmed from an exhibit in the Yale University Art Gallery. This volume includes an essay by Neil Harris, "The Making of an American Culture, 1700-1800," 22-21, which posits "newness" and "innovation." The volume includes also an essay by J.H. Plumb, "America and England: 1720-1820, The Fusion of Cultures," which assumes closeness to the British. Differences and similarities both in fact existed. Part of the task of the present essay is to help delineate some particular features of those differences and similarities and of the relation in which they stood to each other. It is unnecessary for historians and critics to bind themselves either by the view that American culture simply extended the Enlightenment, or by the portrait in Daniel Boorstin, *The Americans: The Colonial Experience* (New York: Random House, 1958) of extreme negativism and innovation towards European culture. Louis Hartz, *The Liberal Tradition in America* (New York: Harcourt, Brace and World, 1955), provided one basis for

evaluation by depicting colonial society as defined critically by the absence of feudal tradition. Historical explication of tangible reality such as furniture can help indicate contours of what was overtly present on the colonial scene. Colonists attempted to implement originally European values in a different soil and changes occurred in the process. Henry E. May, *The Enlightenment in America* (New York: Oxford, 1976) recognizes the particularity with which Americans used a common European intellectual heritage.

[3]Boorstin, *Americans* tends to view utility as being opposed to enduring value, including philosophic and aesthetic value. Part of this confusion results from the fact that colonial culture tended towards implicitness rather than externalization of its philosophy. Boorstin is overly restrained in acknowledging implicit value and its distinction from explicit philosophy. Much of his work therefore seems to suggest that colonists had no deeper values: that value and considerations of utility were mutually exclusive. This obscures one virtue of his work: the perception that colonial culture felt little need for, and perhaps also could not afford, an "old world" extermalization in philosophic and aesthetic areas among others.

[4]Thomas H. Ormsbee, *The Story of American Furniture* (New York: Macmillan, 1934), 33.

[5]Harold Sack, "Authenticity in American Furniture," *Art in America* No. 2 (1960), 73.

[6]Alan Gowans, *Images of American Living, Four Centuries of Architecture and Furniture as Cultural Expression* (Philadelphia and New York: Lippincott, 1964), 12.

[7]R.T.H. Halsey and Elizabeth Tower, *The Homes of Our Ancestors* (Garden City: 1937), 32.

[8]Newton W. Elwell, *Architecture, Furniture and Interiors of Maryland and Virginia During the Eighteenth Century* (1897), Introduction.

[9]Meyric R. Rogers, *American Interior Designs—The Traditions and Development of Domestic Design from Colonial Times to the Present* (New York: Norton, 1947), 36. But early in the 18th century "Boston merchants usually relied on Bostonians for their home furnishings." Brock Jobe, "The Boston Furniture Industry 1720-1740," *Publications of the Colonial Society of Massachusetts*, Vol. 48 (1974, Boston Colonial Society of Massachusetts), p. 5.

[10]*Ibid.*, 39-40, Rogers, *American Interior*.

[11]Bridenbaugh, *Craftsman*, 68.

[12]*Ibid.*, 69.

[13]For example, *The Furniture Designs of Chippendale, Hepplewhite and Sheraton* arranged by J. Munro Bell (New York: Robert McBride and Co., 1938) includes the 1754 edition of Chippendale's *The Gentleman and Cabinet Maker's Director*, although later editions may have been still more popular. Ethel Hall Bjorkoe, *The Cabinetmakers of America* (Garden City, New York: Doubleday, 1957), 11. "Eighteenth-Century American Chairs and their English Background," *Connoisseur*, American edition (June 1955), 234; Joseph Downs "Furniture at the Forum in Williamsburg: Regional Characteristics of American Furniture," *Antiques* (June 1949), 439. Craftsmen of the larger cities and those who made more elegant furniture relied often on English manuals but so did those of smaller towns and those who constructed "common furniture." The Windsor chair, for example, was built strongly and inexpensively enough to be a practical "common" chair. See Thomas H. Ormsbee, *The Windsor Chair* (Deerfield Books, 1962), 17. Once again, in regard to works of history such as Boorstin, *Americans*, positing extreme separation of American culture from the British, failure to recognize reliance upon Old World manuals (and other examples of continuity and acquaintance of colonists with modes of their past) confuses and obscures the critically valid recognition of an American difference. See note 3 above.

[14]Gowans, *Images*, 86. See below for discussion of medieval themes in early colonial stages of English based furniture.

[15]Halsey and Tower, *Homes*, 37.

[16]Downs, "Furniture," 436.

[17]F. de N. Schroeder, "Makers of Tradition: John Goddard," *Interiors* (1950), 101.

[18]Helen Comstock, *American Furniture, Seventeenth, Eighteenth and Nineteenth Century Styles* (New York: Viking, 1962), 127; E. Wenham "English and American Furniture in the 18th Century," *Antiques* (Oct. 1949), 265; E.S. Holloway, "Furniture Exclusively American," *Antiques* (May 1933).

[19]Schroeder, "Makers."

[20]This formulation describing medieval epic fits patterns of furniture described here. Robert Harrison, tr. *The Song of Roland* (New York: Mentor, New American Library, 1970), Introduction, 45-46. Furniture followed the lines of the culture as a whole.

[21]Gowans, *Images*, 1-110. For examples of the "baronial oak" furniture of New England, striking in its massiveness, see Esther Singleton, *The Furniture of Our Forefathers*, 2 vols. (New York: Doubleday, Page and Co., 1901), I, 164. For other illustrations and commentary on medieval patterns in early colonial furniture, see Ormsbee, *Windsor*, 192-93; Wallace Nutting, *Furniture*

Treasury, 3 vols. (New York: Macmillan, 1948-49), II, figures 1774, 1788, 1789, 1790. "The Jacobean 'wainscot' chair," writes Oliver W. Larkin, "was built like its medieval prototypes, and its paneled back, topped by Flemish scrolls and Italian finials, was a hodgepodge of carved motives both geometric and floral." *Art and Life in America* (New York: Holt, Rinehart and Winston, 1964), 17. From this "hodgepodge," 18th century furnituremakers would in time create new kinds of order. The extent to which furniture patterns embodied philosophical culture up to this time is revealed in Arthur O. Lovejoy's discussion of philosophical verticality in *The Great Chain of Being* (New York: Harper Torchbooks, 1965), *passim*. Almost until the Enlightenment itself the notion of mankind, not only its creations, was embedded in the idea of reproducing divine forms: the very term "anthropology" connoted the Aristotelian class "man" in its most general sense of a copy of God. OED, s.v. "Anthropology ... sb."

   [22]On Dutch cupboards, chests and mirrors were painted "fruits, flowers and ribbons,.. tulips ... and parrots." Larkin, *Art and Life*, 17. For Puritans, see Gowans, *Images*, 64.

   [23]Jacob Burckhardt remarked that the Renaissance state had become a "work of art." *The Civilization of the Renaissance in Italy* 2 vols. (New York: Harper Torchbooks, 1958), I. It is possible that the work of artisanship, in its artistic aspects, became with Chippendale a work of man deliberately differentiated from his environment by acting upon it.

   [24]Gowans, *Images*, 128. See also Rogers, *American Interior*, 63.

   [25]Gowans, *Images*, 152 and Ormsbee, *Story*, 173-175.

   [26]R. Susswein, "Pre-Revolutionary Furniture Makers of New York City," *Antiques* (Jan. 1934).

   [7]Gowans, *Images*, 140.

   [8]*Ibid.*, 140.

   [9]*Ibid.*, 152. Also Rogers, *American Interior*, 63. "Walnut and mahogany were the favorite woods of the Philadelphia men" in the mid-eighteenth century. Bjorkoe, *Cabinetmakers*, 11. But other woods also proved popular in America, often woods with some of the same possibilities as walnut, for example. *Ibid.*, 9-10. Also Charles S. Parsons, "The Dunlap Cabinetmakers," in *The Dunlaps and Their Furniture*, The Currier Gallery of Art, (Manchester, New Hampshire, Lew A. Cummings Co., Inc., 1970), p. 19; Nancy E. Richards, "Furniture of the Lower Connecticut River Valley," *Winterthur Portfolio*, 4, 1968 (Henry Francis Du Pont Winterthur Museum, University Press of Virginia), p. 25 who states that the Hartford furniture makers of the mid-eighteenth century worked primarily in cherry with some mahogany. Mahogany in America was especially popular for bureau tables, Nancy A. Goyne, "The Bureau Table in America," *Wint. Port.* III, 1967, 28. Increasingly mahogany gained acceptance in the eighteenth-century colonies. It was "easy to saw, suitable to the turner's lathe, adaptable to the carver's tool, appropriate for gluing ...." Willilam MacPherson Hornor Jr., *Blue Book: Philadelphia Furniture William Penn to George Washington, With Special Reference to the Philadelphia-Chippendale School* (Philadelphia, 1935), 85.

   [30]Cited by Singleton, *Furniture*, I, 283.

   [31]John T. Kirk, *American Chairs: Queen Anne and Chippendale* (New York: Knopf, 1972), 6 and passim. Also, "Eighteenth-Century American Chairs and Their English Background," *Connoisseur*, American Edition (Sept. 1947), 45.

I want to thank Leon Gonshery for his help in the early research for this article and in understanding the values of early American furniture.

Food for Thought:
Comestible Communication and
Contemporary Southern Culture

Stephen A. Smith

"Next to fried foods," confessed Walter Hines Page, "the South has suffered most from oratory."[1] While Page might well have been right, what he might not have realized is that Southern food, fried and otherwise, often functions rhetorically as a medium through which contemporary Southerners define themselves and their region just as clearly as they do through oratory. The idea of a Southern rhetorical and gastronomical geography defined by the foodways of the South has often escaped the attention of rhetorical critics as well, but the symbolic and communicative functions of food have not gone unnoticed by other discipines. As Roland Barthes noted, food is a "system of communication, a body of images, a protocol of usages, situations, and behaviors."[2] Other scholars have contended that "cultural traits, social institutions, national history, and individual attitudes cannot be entirely understood without an understanding of how these have meshed with our varied and peculiar modes of eating," suggesting that "as an integral part of a wider popular culture, dietary customs and the attitudes and values they embody are active agents in their own right, helping to fashion the particular tone and direction of society."[3]

In the contemporary South, certain foodways are very pronounced, and the discussion of them is a regional pastime. This study will examine the comestible communication of the region and explicate the role of foodways as rhetorical ritual in defining and determining the attitudes and values of the contemporary South. First, it will identify a variety of foods and methods of preparation which Southerners have proclaimed to be distinctive to the region and analyze the critical and commercial communication regarding these foods. Second, it will demonstrate the ways in which these foodways serve as ritual in constructing and reinforcing a contemporary Southern mythology. Finally, it will clarify the social and cultural values contained in and communicated through the mythology. Hopefully, such an effort will contribute not only to a better understanding of an often overlooked form of communcation but will also encourage other scholars to take a broader view of communcation forms in contemporary culture.

Of History, Hogs and Hominy

"Whatever else the world has thought of that fabulous land below the Mason-Dixon line, it has granted us one supreme achievement—Southern cooking, which, like the South herself, is not one but many," wrote folklorists Jack and Olivia Solomon. "The number of cookbooks on the market purporting to be Southern is astounding. In fact, cookbooks outsell everything but the Holy Bible ...."[4] Each year the folks from *Southern Living* magazine load their kitchen equipment into a van to conduct promotional cooking schools, the culinary equivalent of religious tent revivals, in forty major markets throughout the South.[5] Among the reasons for such emphasis, suggested geographer Sam Bowers Hilliard, is that "nowhere in the nation has a cultural trait become so outstanding nor certain foods so identified with a single area as in the South."[6]

Most public myths have at least some basis in fact, and the contemporary emphasis on distinctive Southern foods is no exception. In an excellent study of food production and consumption in the antebellum South entitled *Hogmeat and Hoecake*, Hilliard has documented some rather dramatic regional differences which suggest that corn, rather than cotton, deserved the title of "king." In 1840, the nation produced 22.1 bushels of corn per capita; the figures were 54.3 bushes per capita in Tennessee, 32.6 in Iowa, and 2.5 in Massachusetts.[7] Much of the corn was for direct human consumption, and even as late as the 1930s Rupert R. Vance discovered that consumption of corn in the South was approximately five times that of the rest of the nation.[8] Furthermore, corn was frequently converted to live hogs or liquid before consumption in the South. Precise figures for moonshine production were understandably unavailable, but the data on pork production underscore the early regional differences. In 1840, Arkansas produced 4.03 hogs per capita, while Iowa produced 2.43 and Massachusett's production was .19 per capita.[9]

The early regional differences in food consumption reflected differing conditions of soil, climate and culture, but the continuing modern differences, in view of the vast improvements in preservation and transportation, must be seen as being more the result of distinct social and cultural factors. One example which highlights these contemporary differences can be found in searching the cuisine guides in the Yellow Pages of telephone directories. The Atlanta directory boasts 28 barbecue locations, 7 southern style restaurants and 5 soul foods listings. By contrast, the Boston Area Yellow Pages has 26 pages of restaurant listings, but not a single entry in these three categories—and not a single advertisement pictures a smiling pig or a walking catfish. The Manhattan Consumer Yellow Pages has 29 pages of restaurant listings, but the cuisine guide doesn't even have a barbecue heading. The single entry under soul food is Jack's Nest which claims "Bar-B-Q Ribs and Chitterlings Our Specialty," but it is an obvious fraud since "chittlins" is misspelled.[10]

In both fact and fantasy, pork has always been the mainstay of Southern food. Hams were first exported from Virginia in the 1630s, and since that time the Old Dominion has had to fight with North Carolina, Kentucky, Tennessee and Arkansas for bragging rights for the best hams. Whether touted as Tidewater hams or peanut-fed Smithfields, Virginia must now face the competition from the roadside, hickory smoked, sugar cured "country" hams of the less refined states of the region. Old Hickory House in Atlanta advertises a "Country Boy Breakfast" of homemade bisquits, country gravy and country ham," a fairly country fare for a 16-

store chain.[11] In Tennessee, Bethea's Restaurant, which advertises that it has been serving Chattanooga since 1936, offers a time-honored menu of "genuine country ham ... hot bisquits, sawmill gravy ... fried corn bread hoe cakes."[12] While ham is the leading item at such locations, these restaurants are also offering the customer a rural "slice of life" to compete with McEgg.

In addition to hams, Southern hogs yield excellent bacon which can be hickory smoked and sugar cured to serve as Yankee bait, especially in the mountain regions where plantation mansions are in short supply. For local consumption, cookbooks and restaurants offer the Southerner pickled pigs feet, souse, brains, tongue, chittlins, cracklins for cornbread, ham hocks for beans and hog jowls for blackeyed peas.

Another traditional Southern meat, possum, has been a regional favorite since the American revolution. At an early Christmas feast in 1778, Louisville celebrants enjoyed a spread which put the Pilgrims' Thanksgiving to shame. Seven different meats, ranging from coon to wild turkey, were served, but witnesses suggested that a large baked possum was the most desired entree at the event.[13] Even today, some Southerners tout the epicurean superiority of "roast possum, gleaming like a greasy baby on a platter, with sweet potatoes."[14] While early Southerners often consumed possums because they were plentiful, relatively easy to catch, and high in calories, more recently the meat of this marsupial has achieved symbolic status as "put on" for shocking Yankee visitors and immigrants. One contemporary writer, for example, offered a recipe for pureed possum juleps.[15]

Among the fried foods, "Southern fried chicken" has been foremost in the national imagination since the 1930s when the first waves of motorcar tourists noticed highway signs and roadside cafe marquees advertising the specialty of the house.[16] Fried chicken is quite prominent in the Southern Eucharest, and contemporary food writers have alleged symbolic consubstantiation with assertions that "fried chicken is a summer afternoon in the South."[17] Even restaurant chains have been wise enough to adopt this theme. An advertisement for a Dallas establishment claims, "Reminiscent of the South in the 1940s, Dixie House serves panfried chicken as good as your grandmother made—or better."[18]

Historically, fried chicken was a luxury item on the Southern table, usually served only on holidays or on Sunday afternoon when the preacher came to dinner.[19] Today it is a regular menu item, both at home and on the road, and the degree of its cultural significance can be appreciated when one realizes that such diverse figures as Colonel Harlan Sanders in his white planter's suit, Minnie Pearl of Grand Ole Opry fame and black recording artist Aretha Franklin have all started chicken franchises. The U.S. Department of Commerce counts thirty franchise firms specializing in chicken, and departmental estimates for 1983 are for gross sales of almost $4 billion at 8,683 outlets. New Orleans-based Popeye's alone has an advertising budget of $8-$10 million annually, an account which was formerly placed by a New York agency and recently went to a Chicago firm.[20]

Some Southern chauvinists, however, have been outraged by the fast food sacrilege perpetrated by John Y. Brown through Colonel Sanders.

"Southern Fried" used to be a kind of culinary shibboleth pertaining to Southern tastes in comestibles, especially chicken, but the Kentucky Colonel and other chicken profiteers, in the interest of haste, standardized the flavor and the texture to an ecumenical blah acceptable from Bangor to Phoenix that has robbed fried chicken not only of its tradition but has made a proud local habitation and a name a national perversity," said Bill Terry. "Chrome and stainless steel cooking baskets are not substitutes for an iron skillet."[21]

On the other hand, Terry signed, "I am happy to say that Southern fried catfish and the quality that blessed the old days have survived uncorrupted by mass demand and the traducers of all things genuine—Madison Avenue and the marketing blitz."[22] That is to say, Terry felt that the South's own myths about catfish were, for the time being, temporarily safe from those of the New York ad agencies. Other Southerners seemed to share that view. "You come all the way to Florida and what are you doing for dinner? You're going to International Drive to search through the plastic-and-neon blight until you find a place that reminds you of dining on the unlimited-access commercial strip back home. Come on. Just for once forget Bun 'N' Run, Smorgybrothers, the International House of Krinkle Kut French Fries and the like. Take a 10-minute drive to less than bustling downtown St. Cloud and try some real Florida food at the Catfish Place," advised Rob Morse, restaurant critic for *The Orlando Sentinel.* "Visitors owe it to themselves to at least try the catfish—a fish unappreciated by those from trout and salmon country. With American regional food all the rage, it would be a pity to come to this region and not try its foremost fish."[23]

Another food editor, remembering a passage from Mark Twain's *Huckleberry Finn*, suggested that fishing for catfish and the catfish's lifestyle seemed to be appropriate icons to epitomize the leisurely pace of life in the South, and he praised the simple environment of independently owned catfish restaurants across the South.[24] The catfish shrines and rituals, however, are beginning to be affected: David Beard's Catfish King covers east Texas and the Hush Puppy restaurant chain now counts seventeen franchised locations throughout the sunbelt. One writer was dismayed at having to pass "all manner of fast catfish shacks and brand new, gaudily nautical, all-you-can-eat catfish palaces" to get to his favorite haunt, "a white hulk of a building by a wooded stream" two miles outside Columbia, Mississippi that was "so isolated and wet and green that you think you have escaped civilization as completely as Huck."[23]

Modern catfish farming in the South is approaching the scale of agribusiness, and modern processing plants can now electronically sort fish by two-ounce weight increments.[26] Paul Greenberg, a Southerner fearful that even the Southern catfish ritual was giving way to the influence of mass society, questioned the impact of recent changes on future generations. "Nowadays," he said, "sitting in air-conditioned, mass fabricated restaurants, eating frozen catfish and processed hushpuppies put on the menu that very day by some thoughtful computer in Cincinnati ..., one wonders: Will the next generation know what it was to go out in the heat of summer for a ride in the old chevy with the windows down and Hank Williams or Garner Ted Armstrong on the radio ...? Or to stop at a flyspecked watermelon stand to get a quarter of a melon for two bits and linger there, spitting out the seeds."[27]

The rhetoric and ritual of regional culinary communication are probably best exemplified by the barbeque cult which has almost as many local chapters as the Southern Baptist Association. One native observer advised prospective immigrants, "If you don't like barbeque, don't move to the South; in some sections, you might starve. If you can't find a barbeque joint in the phone book, you're not in the South."[28] Moreover, "southern people, as everyone knows, take their barbecue very seriously," said a writer in *Southern Exposure.* "The ritual of barbecuing has endless variations from region to region, or even town to town. Yet in each locale, the resident experts will assure you that theirs is the only way, the only method yielding what is termed 'true barbecue'."[29] Each self-anointed priest of barbeque claims to have special secrets about the type of pit, type of wood, cut of meat (some even prefer beef or chicken over pork), the use of tomatoes, wet versus dry cooking, the correct spelling of the word, and the recipes for sauce. "Somewhat like religious tenets, barbecue sauces are touted as being essential while, at the same time, being declared unknowable."[30]

The Rib in Dallas maintaining a "Barbecue Hall of Fame" featuring pictures and biographical sketches of outstanding barbecue chefs and promoters; Sikes' Bar-B-Q in Columbia, South Carolina boasting of being the "4th Annual World's International Bar-B-Q Champion"; and the Kentucky Smokehouse Bar-B-Q in Lexington, advertising "real hickory smoked pit cooked barbecue sliced in Henry's original sauce," provide examples of the mediated bragging dialogue. In Montgomery, Alabama one restaurant claims "honest to goodness home style real pit barbecue," and Luther's in Lafayette, Louisiana, advertises "slow smoked barbeque meats." In Atlanta, Bourne's advertises to customers that their food is prepared "the old Southern way," and another boasts of "real pit barbecue ... slowly cooked over hickory logs" and suggests that one can "put some South in ya mouth at Old Hickory House." In Greensboro, North Carolina, Stamey's says their barbecue is "pit cooked the old fashioned way," and Lil' Annies Country Bar-B-Q in Orlando, Florida advertises "North Carolina Pit Barbecue."[31] Barbeque joints also seem to have a way with monikers which rival their methods with meats. Morgan's Sho Nuf in Fayetteville, Arkansas, Grunt and Moo Barbecue in Montgomery, Piggie Park Barbeque in Columbia, South Carolina, Pig Out, Inc. in Greensboro, Smokey's in Columbus, Georgia, Fat Willie's Hawg House and Papa Doc's Pig Palace in Charlotte, and Fat Boy's in Orlando are establishments which could not have possibly been named by J. Walter Thompson.

An essential ingredient in the persuasive media strategy is the effort to create an environment which reflects the mythic culture of the region. Luther's invites patrons to "come experience our rustic atmosphere," Lil' Annie's proclaims its "cozy country atmosphere," and the Bar-B-Que Pit in Montgomery says "Ya'll Come" and offers "Homestyle Cooking Daily"— but it is reduced to admitting it is located "Directly Behind Wendy's."[32] Even the faster food establishments do their best to maintain a traditional, rural atmosphere; for example, Baretta's Famous Bar-B-Q Drive-In, mentions the fact that it has been serving Memphis since 1933, and Uncle Jones' Bar-B-Q in Orlando, which has a "Drive-Thru," reminds customers of "Home Cooked Flavor in Every Bite."[33]

Noting the ritualistic nature of barbeque, an article in *Southern Living* suggested that Southerners "revere legendary barbecue haunts as if they were shrines." Reinforcing and confirming the tendency to idealize the vernacular, "some say the best barbecue is found in cafes belonging to an architectural classification that we shall call Barbecue Primitive Style. These are often barbecue eateries identified by torn screen doors, scratched and dented furniture, cough syrup calendars, potato chip racks, sometimes a jukebox, and always a counter, producing an ambience similar to a county-line beer joint."[34] As advice to the novice barbeque customer, one old hand recommended a parking lot survey. "If you can spot an equal number of Mercedes sedans and Ford pickups, you've found a very good place. Too many expensive new cars and the joint is likely to be fake; too many pickups and its liable to be a dive. Balance is the key word. Beware of new buildings. Everything in a barbeque joint, including the help, should be old. It simply takes a certain amount of seasoning to get good barbeque, and that goes for the building as well as the food."[35]

With regard to vegetables, corn was and is, of course, the foremost vegetable of the South—don't be mislead by the Chicago Board of Trade into believing it is a grain. Other leading vegetables of the antebellum frontier were sweet potatoes and turnips, and they continue to be among the favorites of Southern cooks.[36] The Blue Plate Special at almost any cafe on a Southern courthouse square will include sweet taters, turnip greens, hominy, blackeyed peas, fried okra, a slice of onion, cornbread, a big glass of iced tea and sweet potato pie or a piece of watermelon. Other regional vegetable dishes are poke sallet, crowder peas, collards, cowpeas and fried squash. Southerners seldom express a preference for vegetable quiche. One expatriate in New York expressed his distaste for "artichokes, various raw fish, trick lettuces, suspect sauces, and other outright inedibles" frequently served in Manhattan, and he suffered the ridicule of his female companion. A gentleman to the last, he said he "made nary a public judgment when his Yankee-based lady failed the tests of such basic staples as turnip-green pie ... or possum and taters."[37]

There is some empirical evidence that Southerners do consume certain foods more frequently than do folks in other regions. For example, during the summer months the average Southern family eats almost a pound of okra each week, and in all seasons they consume more than three times as much okra as people in other regions.[38] The preparation and presentation of the "traditional" Southern spread at home, however, is becoming a ritualistic repast. After describing a full Southern dinner at a family reunion, one visiting observer acknowledged that it was "a ritual banquet, of course, almost as exceptional to them as to me. For half of what was on the table has come from the supermarket, not the garden or the smokehouse or the cellar. No one, least of all Arkansas farm families, eats like this anymore. There aren't hands enough at home to do the cooking or mouths to do the eating, and prices are too high."[39]

Restaurants seldom give as much billing to their vegetables as to their meats. One Memphis catfish establishment covers the subject by saying it serves "All You Can Eat With All The Trimmins," but the Rib Rack in Chattanooga is more specific disclosing that their "plates include cracklin corn bread, homemade beans, cole slaw, and a green onion."[40] Biskits in

Orlando advertises a pint of "Georgia Ham Beans" and a pint of rice and gravy to go with its main fare of "chicken and biskits."[41] The vegetable market, however, appears to be just as vulnerable to franchises as are catfish and fried chicken. The Blackeyed Pea chain, spreading across the Southland like kudzu, claims that "ceiling fans and quilts on the wall combine to make you feel right at home. Incredible chicken-fried steak, fresh vegetables, fried catfish ... are excellent samples of downhome cooking."[42]

While the lowly grit (or is it grits?) has been one of the most popular symbols in the national media and has even been the subject of a feature film, at least one Southerner has confessed that "even when laced generously with redeyed gravy, grits ain't fit to eat."[43] Grits has proven to be a popular breakfast item for Yankee tourists, but many of them have been seen treating it with sugar, an act of sacrilege which immediately identifies them as participants in a Gray Line Tour of Dixie.

Cousin cornbread, however, is an ever prominent symbol of the South—as long as it is made with white corn meal and without sugar or flour. Such a symbol helps solidify an emerging egalitarian vision of Southern distinctiveness, for as one Southerner noted, "humblest of the triad of Southern hot breads, cornbread in all its transmogrifications is outranked according to culinary protocol by bisquits and yeast rolls .... In general, the corn breads are hearty reminders and properly the accompaniment of fare to suit the appetites of farmers and sportsmen, the Southern equivalent of the peasant breads of Europe."[44] Unlike light bread which has utility only for sopping excess barbeque sauce, the versatility of cornmeal lends itself to brim and catfish batter, hushpuppies, corn fritters, hoecake, corn pone, corn squeezin's, corn muffins, corn doggers, spoon bread, corn cakes, batterbread and "corn 'n' clabber," a traditional delight which one Southerner labeled a "hillbilly smoothie" and another proclaimed as "the best combination since rednecks discovered the delicious combination of a Moon Pie and R C Cola."[45]

Beaten biscuits, especially for breakfast with ham and red-eye or sawmill gravy, are also important symbols of downhome Southern culture, but recently even the biscuit has become a mass-produced icon of rural life. Ever since Lively Willoughby invented the canned biscuit in 1931, biscuit-making has been a declining if not dying art. Max Brantley, an expert on good Southern cooking, observed, "Time was, only a few holdout cafes, mostly in the Deep South, bothered to turn out a morning biscuit. Now, just about everyone from Minute Man to McDonald's is in the biscuit business." Brantley credits Jack Z. Fulk of Charlotte, North Carolina, with the rebirth of the commercial biscuit at fast food outlets, beginning as a Hardee's franchisee about ten years ago then opening his own 150-outlet Bojangle's chicken and biscuit chain in 1977. Trading on the downhome myth, Good Old Days Foods in Little Rock now turns out a quarter-million frozen biscuits a week for sale to restaurants.[46]

The Southern fascination with regional foods as badges of cultural distinction has persisted since antebellum times, and it has permeated both the language and the mythology of the region. Historically, the symbiotic relationship between communication and comestibles seemed to emerge simultaneously with frontier democracy. Large crowds were assured at political rallies by featuring barbeque, burgo or Brunswick stew, and the attendant stump speaking at these events cultivated the myth of Southern oratory. The tradition continues today as poll-wise politicians still avail themselves of barbeques and fish fries for fellowshippin' with the corn "crackers" to supplement their slick thirty-second spots. In Congress, Southerners employed the art of storytelling as political argument; they were called "hams," and their stories were labeled "corny." Despite such derision by the high-collar Yankee crowd, they perfected the art of "pork barrel" politics, "brought home the bacon" to their constituents, and "lived high on the hog" themselves.

Of more cultural significance for the contemporary South, however, is the symbolic representation of an emerging vision of a more egalitarian society. Although the Plantation Inn in Raleigh is "surrounded by 26 acres of relaxation," Juleps in Natchez promises "a relaxing experience," The Old South Tea Room in Vicksburg has waitresses dressed as mammies, and the Southern Kitchen chain claims that its colonial furnishings reflect "the grace and hospitality of the old Southern plantations," the South is no longer captivated by its own images of the Cavalier's hunt breakfast or the Planter's mint julep.[47] The vision of culinary distinctiveness is now become one which can be shared by all. When the "Georgie mafia" came to Washington in 1976, one Carter aide was overheard asking, "Where can you buy catfish here? Does anyplace sell Fatback?" Those questions prompted a Southern newspaper correspondent to complain, "When grits are available they are instant. The nearest edible barbeque shack straddles the North Carolina line, 200 miles away. A diligent four-year search by a homesick Southerner has turned up only one country jukebox within city limits. Grocery store clerks routinely throw away the greens and save the turnips."[48] Such observations, though intended to be humorous, served to reinforce the role of regional foods, even for the power elite, in establishing the mythic distinctiveness of the South.

Scholars and students concerned with communication, myth, and ritual in understanding contemporary culture, in the South or in any other region, should be aware of the role of foodways in constructing, changing and reinforcing cultural self-definition. The support role of foodways in the changing cultural myths of the contemporary South has been rather dramatic, and the mythical Old South patrician would be as anachronistic and uncomfortable with the image of contemporary comestibles as he would be listening to country music, driving a stock car, or attending a professional "rasslin' " match. The social relations legitimized by the mythology of the contemporary South, exemplified by its popular diet dialogue, represent a marked change from the rigid caste system of the past. The contemporary comestible communication has contributed to a more egalitarian society in the region, providing a rhetoric which can be readily adopted and rituals in which a greater number of Southerners can participate. As Jody Powell said, "Everybody, black and white, now recognizes you don't have to be ashamed of turnip greens."[49]

Notes

[1] Former Arkansas Congressman Brooks Hays frequently used this quote in his public

speeches, and he admitted borrowing it from Walter Hines Page. "The Raconteur," *Carolina Country*, May 1971, p. 7.

[2]Roland Barthes, "Toward a Psychosociology of Contemporary Food Consumption," in *Food and Drink in History*, ed. by Robert Forster and Orest Ranum (Baltimore: Johns Hopkins Univ. Press, 1979), p. 167.

[3]Peter Farb and George Armelagos, *Consuming Passions: The Anthropology of Eating* (Boston: Houghton Mifflin, 1980), p. 4; Forster and Ranum, p. vii. The leading article on the subject in communication journals is Barry Brummett, "Gastronomic Reference, Synecdoche, and Political Images," *Quarterly Journal of Speech*, 61 (1982), pp. 138-145.

[4]Jack Solomon and Olivia Solomon, *Cracklin Bread and Asfidity* (University: Univ. of Alabama Press, 1979), p. 3.

[5]"Adding Regional Flavor," *Advertising Age*, 2 May 1983, p. M22.

[6]Sam Bowers Hilliard, *Hog Meat and Hoecake: Food Supply in the Old South, 1840-1860* (Carbondale: Southern Illinois Univ. Press, 1972), p. 37.

[7]Hilliard, p. 156.

[8]Rupert P. Vance, *Human Geography of the South* (Chapel Hill: Univ. of North Carolina Press, 1935), pp. 418, 427; Joe Gray Taylor, *Eating, Drinking, and Visiting the South: An Informal History* (Baton Rouge: Louisiana State Univ. Press, 1982), p. 110.

[9]Hilliard, p. 94.

[10]*Atlanta Yellow Pages* (Atlanta: Southern Bell, 1982), pp. 1678. 1683-1684; *Boston Area Yellow Pages* (Boston: New England Telephone, 1983); *Manhattan Consumer Yellow Pages* (New York: New York Telephone, 1980-81).

[11]*Atlanta Yellow Pages*, p. 1662.

[12]*Chattanooga Area* (Birmingham: South Central Bell, 1982), p. 496.

[13]Harnett T. Kane, *The Southern Christmas Book: The Full Story from the Earliest Times to the Present: People, Customs, Conviviality, Carols, Cooking* (New York: D. McKay, 1958), p. 241; Taylor, p. 8.

[14]Redding S. Sugg, Jr., "A Treatise Upon Cornbread," *Southern Voices*, October-November, 1974, p. 41.

[15]Michael Hicks, *The South Made Simple* (Austin: Texas Monthly Press, 1982), n.p.

[16]Stuart Berg Flexner, *Listening to America: An Illustrated History of Words and Phrases from Our Lively and Splendid Past* (New York: Simon and Schuster, 1982), p. 142.

[17]"Another Piece of Fried Chicken, Please," *Southern Living*, July 1982, p. 72.

[18]"Dixie House," *Guestinformant: Dallas/Fort Worth* (New York: LIN Broadcasting, 1983), p. 89.

[19]Hilliard, pp. 46-47; Taylor, p. 114.

[20]"Fast Food Chains Help Transform Chicken Industry," *Northwest Arkansas Times*, 28 August 1983, p. 7C; Margaret G. Maples, "Clinton Frank Cooks With Popeyes," *Adweek*, 12 Sept. 1983, pp. 3-4.

[21]Bill Terry, "Arkansas' Great Moveable Feast: A Catfish Journal," *Arkansas Times*, May 1982, p. 14.

[22]Terry, p. 14.

[23]Rob Morse, "Home Cooking," *The Orlando Sentinel*, 8 April 1983, pp. E1, E10.

[24]Raymond Sokolov, "Fish, Fresh from the Farm," *Natural History*, July 1982, pp. 76, 78.

[25]Sokolov, p. 78.

[26]Sokolov, p. 79.

[27]Paul Greenberg, "Of Medeas, Medusas, and the Media," *Arkansas Times*, August 1981, pp. 23-24.

[28]Hicks, n.p.

[29]Kathleen Zobel, "Hog Heaven: Barbecue in the South," *Southern Exposure*, 5, No. 2 & 3 (1977), p. 58.

[30]Zobel, p. 58.

[31] *Greater Columbia* (Atlanta: Southern Bell, 1983), p. 563; *Lexington* (General Telephone and Electric, 1982), p. 396; *Montgomery* (Birmingham: South Central Bell, 1982), p. 604; *Atlanta Yellow Pages* (Atlanta: Southern Bell, 1982), pp. 1661-1662; *Greensboro* (Atlanta: Southern Bell, 1983); *Orlando* (Atlanta: Southern Bell, 1982), p. 949.

[32]*Orlando*, p. 956; *Montgomery* (Birmingham: South Central Bell, 1982), p. 405.

[33]*Greater Memphis area* (Birmingham: South Central Bell, 1982), p. 847; Advertisement, *The Orlando Sentinel* 8 April 1983, p. E5.

[34]Gary D. Ford, "The South Burns for Barbeque," *Southern Living*, May 1982, pp. 121, 125.

[35]Hicks, n.p.

[36]Nancy Lee, "It's All So Corny, Really!" *Miami Magazine*, July 1976, pp. 88-90; Hilliard, pp. 39-40, 51, 151; Taylor, p. 37.

[37]Larry L. King, "We Ain't Trash No More! How Jimmy Carter Led the Rednecks from the Wilderness," *Esquire*, Nov. 1976, pp. 88, 90.

[38]Mescal Johnston, "Southerners Eat Much More Okra," *Northwest Arkansas Times*, 31 August 1983, p. 11. See also Richard Allin, "How to Get a Northerner To Try Okra," *Arkansas Gazette*, 25 Jan. 1983, p. 1B.

[39]Shirley Abbott, *Womenfolks: Growing Up Down South* (New Haven: Ticknor and Fields, 1983), p. 23.

[40]*Greater Memphis Area*, p. 849; *Chattanooga Area*, p. 496.

[41]Advertisement, *The Orlando Sentinel*, 8 April 1983, p. E5.

[42]"The Black-Eyed Pea," *Guestinformant: Dallas/Fort Worth*, p. 86.

[43]Gorham Kindem, "Southern Exposure: *Kudzu* and *It's Grits*," *Southern Quarterly*, 19 (1981), pp. 199-206; Ernie Deane, "Grits and Blackeyed Peas," *Springdale News*, 28 Nov. 1976, p. 1C; Richard Allin, "Grits Grip Northerners in Bafflement," *Arkansas Gazette*, 14 August 1983, p. 1C.

[44]Sugg, p. 39.

[45]Hicks, n.p.; Bill Au Coin, *Redneck* (Matteson, IL: Greatlakes Living Press, 1977), p. 60.

[46]Max Brantley, "Tasty, From-Scratch Biscuits Cookin' All Over Town," *Arkansas Gazette*, 12 June 1983, pp. 1C-2C.

[47]*Raleigh* (Atlanta: Southern Bell, 1982); *Natchez* (Birmingham: South Central Bell, 1982), p. 175; "Southern Kitchen," *Travelhost: Dallas* 15 May 1983, p. 24. See also Ethel Farmer Hunter, *Secrets of Southern Cooking* (Chicago: Ziff-Davis, 1948), p. vii; and Susan Payne, "Sample the Flavor of Southern Tradition," *Southern Living*, Sept. 1982, p. 169. The economic utility of selling the plantation mystique is discussed in Stephen A. Smith, "The Old South Myth as a Contemporary Southern Commodity," *Journal of Popular Culture*, 16, No. 3 (1982), pp. 22-29.

[48]Roy Bode, "Georgians May Restore Southern Ethos to Capitol," *Arkansas Gazette*, 28 Nov. 1976, p. 22A.

[49]Tom Mathews, "The Southern Mistique" *Newsweek*, 19 July 1976, p. 30.

Women and the Material Universe:
A Bibliographic Essay

Mary Johnson

Artifacts are evidence for historical research which historians ignore at their peril. The man-made environment, like the larger natural environment, affects human perceptions of and responses to events. Thus, the material universe sets limits on human behavior, proscribing certain options and prescribing others. In the fields of transportation, communications and technology, for example, the physical environment has changed our concepts of space, time and work. Historians who work with written documents can enrich their understanding of past events and personalities by taking into account the material conditions and levels of technology contemporaneous with the society in question. Social historians, interested in groups of people who have left few or no written records, cannot afford to neglect nonverbal remains. Fragments of old dishes, pipe stems, old bottles, gravestones and vernacular architecture are the most tangible evidence we have of the activities and values of the ordinary people of previous generations. As James Deetz has argued in his essay *In Small Things Forgotten: The Archeology of Early American Life* (Garden City, N.Y., 1977):

> Material culture may be the most objective source of information we have concerning America's past. It certainly is the most immediate. When an archaeologist carefully removes the earth from the jumbled artifacts at the bottom of a trash pit, he or she is the first person to confront those objects since they were placed there centuries before. When we stand in the chamber of a seventeenth-century house that has not been restored, we are placing ourselves in the same architectural environment occupied by those who lived there in the past. The arrangement of gravestones in a cemetery and the designs on their tops create a *Gestalt* not of our making but of the community whose dead lie beneath the ground. If we bring to this world, so reflective of the past a sensitivity to the meaning of the patterns we see in it, the artifact becomes a primary source of great objectivity and subtlety.

This is particularly true when we consider the historical experience of women. Public documents and the private correspondence of the educated elites rarely allude to the secrets of housewifery, which consumed so much of the time, energy and creativity of women in past centuries. However, the identification and interpretation of common household utensils, furnishings and interior ornamentation can begin to answer a series of questions concerning women's private lives: What were the tasks of housewives? How did they adapt to changing economic patterns? What was their response to technological innovations? How did more functional divisions of rooms affect women's relations with others in the family? What impact did household chores have on women's self-perceptions? A few years ago Ruth Schwartz Cowan outlined an agenda for exploring the interplay between women's attitudes and changing technology in two seminal articles: "The 'Industrial Revolution' in the Home: Household Technology and Social Change in the 20th Century," *Technology and Culture* 17 (1976); 1-23, and "Women and Technology in American Life," in *Technology at the Turning Point,* edited by William B. Prickett (San Francisco, 1977). The recent anthology *Dynamos and Virgins Revisited: Women and Technological Change in History,*edited by Martha Moore Trescott (Metuchen, N.J., 1979), attests to the worthwhile scholarship that can emerge from this line of enquiry. Yet the other questions pertinent to women's relationship with the material universe require that scholars in women's history bring their perspective to the whole range of studies connected with material culture.

Unlike scholars in sister disciplines, historians have disregarded the potential value of artifacts in their research and teaching. Anthropologists, archaeologists, and art historians have traditionally incorporated the study of three-dimensional objects in their work, and over the last three decades they have refined increasingly sophisticated methods for relating objects to their more general social and cultural context. Conversely, professional historians have continued to rely on written documents. Graduate programs in history rarely introduce students to the study of material culture, and the great majority of practicing historians are unaware of the possible insights to be derived from artifacts or the growing body of scholarship dealing with the nonverbal vestiges of past societies. Even the minority of historians who include films and photographs in their teaching and research use such physical evidence mainly to supplement and illustrate their literary sources.

Three major obstacles have tended to discourage historians from using artifacts more extensively. The first and most apparent is inherent in the literature of material culture. The majority of monographs and articles appear in specialized museum and art history publications. They concentrate on the descriptive aspects of the object—its identifying traits, its construction and design, its craftmanship and its outstanding stylistic features. Such an approach characterizes articles in *Antiques,* the most prestigious American journal for the presentation of decorative arts of high culture, as well as the scores of collectors' manuals, museum acquisition reports, museum exhibit catalogues and folk art studies which deal with the commonplace tools and household utensils of previous generations. Kenneth Ames of the Winterthur Museum has rightly observed in his essay *Beyond Necessity: Art in the Folk Tradition* (Winterthur, 1977) that too many of the studies of artifacts are centripetal: they narrowly confine themselves to the description of the objects studied, failing to analyze the social and cultural significance of the objects in question. What is needed, Ames asserts, is a greater number of artifact studies that take a centrifugal approach, elucidating how the artifact informs the observer about broader social and cultural issues.

The second obstacle pertains to the class bias found in many of the objects deemed worthy of preservation and subsequent study by museum personnel. Although this might be expected with art museums, it is also typical of the majority of the two thousand history museums in the United States, containing either period rooms or open door exhibits. Ivor Noel Hume of Williamsburg has himself lamented in "Creamware to Pearlware: A Williamsburg Perspective," *Ceramics in America,* edited by Ian Quimby (Charlottesville, 1972) that some seventy percent of the everyday ceramics of historic Williamsburg have been forever lost since early excavation groups did not believe such objects sufficiently interesting or well-made to merit preservation. I became particularly sensitive to this problem last year while I was preparing the exhibit "Mourning Glory: An Exhibition on Nineteenth Century Customs and Attitudes Toward Death and Dying" for the Eleutherian Mills Historical Library (Wilmington, Delaware). Museum collections and extant trade catalogues provided a plethora of details about the mourning paraphernalia and funeral equipment of the upper and upper-middle classes, but the evidence of the type of dress and mementoes used among the poorer classes was so scarce that I was forced to depend most heavily on the artifactual evidence of the well-to-do classes in my interpretation.

The class bias in object studies cannot be attributed exclusively to the decisions of museum personnel and their principal contributors. The inferior quality and composition intrinsic to objects belonging to the lower classes has often meant that their artifacts have not endured as long as the higher quality objects associated with the upper classes. As Robert Howard at the Hagley Museum has explained, it is far easier to locate the uniform of a Civil War officer than the uniform of a common soldier. Families of the officers often saved the uniforms as heirlooms while families of the rank-and-file soldiers usually converted the uniforms for civilian use as soon as the war ended. Similarly, common caps worn by women in the eighteenth and nineteenth centuries rarely survive. What has remained intact is the special ceremonial caps that in all likelihood were never worn but stored away as keepsakes by their owners. Even the quality of historical photographs reflects differences in class. Many more of the professional photos done for upper-class families have stayed clearer and more visible than those done by the amateurs of the working-class and lower-middle-class families. It might well be that our current assumptions about domesticity in late Victorian America are distorted in that the extant family albums of the upper classes have been critical sources for our interpretations of that period.

A third obstacle lies in the need for extensive sources for identifying the object in question and evaluating it in relation to similar objects of its period. Highly specialized manuals on such subjects as furniture making, joinery, house-building, hardware, plastering, varnishing and wall paper are necessary to identify pieces properly, and literally scores of design books, catalogues and style manuals are required from all parts of the world to isolate unique aspects of the object studied and to compare it to other contemporary objects. Philip D. Zimmerman's "A Methodological Study in the Identification of Some Important Philadelphia Chippendale Furniture," *Winterthur Portfolio* 13 (1979): 193-208, reveals how complex these operations are in modern museum practices. Although historians do not necessarily have to go to the same degree of technical proficiency to deal with the topics they are pursuing, the museum collections are arranged from the point of view of the artifacts. This complicates research for the historian, who often cannot take full advantage of a collection because he or she is unfamiliar with and inexperienced in using the system of indexing.

Four works which summarize the difficulties historians have commonly encountered in trying to work with material culture are:

Ellsworth, Lucius F. and Maureen A. O'Brien, eds. *Material Culture: Historical Agencies and the Historian.* Philadelphia, 1969.

This anthology includes contributions from historians and practitioners of material culture and examines the theories, methods and practical applications of material culture in the United States during the 1960s. Each of the articles considers reasons that academic historians have been reluctant to rely on physical evidence and points out common misconceptions that have separated the historians from specialists in material culture.

Hesseltine, William B. "The Challenge of the Artifact," in *The Present World of History.* Madison, Wisconsin, 1959.

This was the opening address for the 1957 annual meeting of the American Association for State and Local History in which Hesseltine argued that physical evidence could not satisfactorily deal with historians' questions of causality and motivation. While Hesseltine's definition of legitimate questions in history is dated, his point of view about the inadequacy of physical evidence continues to influence a large sector in the profession.

Kouwenhoven, John A. "American Studies: Words or Things?" in *American Studies in Transition.* Edited by Marshall Fishwick. Philadelphia, 1964.

This points out the dangers of relying exclusively on verbal symbols and argues that "direct sensory awareness" of objects in American culture will provide certain kinds of knowledge not found in written evidence.

Lyle, Charles. "The Artifact and American History: An Examination of the Use of the Artifact for Historical Evidence." M.A. Thesis, University of Delaware, 1971.
This studies the evidentiary problems involved in using physical objects with an excellent bibliography of the key works in museum studies and material culture in the twentieth century. It also offers a response to Hesseltine's challenge and makes a strong case for the benefits of physical evidence as tools of historical research.

Current historians will find these obstacles far less formidable than their predecessors did. In recent years practitioners of material culture have borrowed from theories and methods in structural anthropology, kinesics, proxemics, demography, communications, ethnography, geography and archaeology to develop modes of analysis that shed light on the social and cultural significance of artifacts. Claude Levi Strauss' 'structuralism' and Noam Chomsky's concept of generative linguistics have become the point of departure for Henry Glassie's *Folk Housing in Middle Virginia: A Structural Analysis of Historic Artifacts* (Knoxville, Tenn., 1975). Kenneth Ames' perceptive analysis of the Victorian parlor organ as an instrument of social control in his "Material Culture as Non

Verbal Communication: A Historical Case Study," (this volume) draws upon literature in communications, psychology, sociology, history, women's studies and economics. Synthesizing concepts and techniques of industrial archaeology, cultural anthropology, sociology, historical photography and urban geography, Thomas Schlereth has formulated a method for studying "above ground archaeology," which enables one to conduct an in-depth study of the topographical, social, cultural and economic patterns in local communities. His monograph entitled *The University of Notre Dame: A Portrait of Its History and Campus* (Notre Dame, Indiana, 1976), serves as ample testimony to the efficacy of this approach. Equally interesting are the interdisciplinary efforts in the analysis and interpretation of historical photographs. Marshall Peters and Bernard Mergen provide a comprehensive survey of this work with excellent bibliographical suggestions in " 'Doing the Rest': The Uses of Photographs in American Studies,' *American Quarterly* 29, no. 3 (1977): 280-303.

These new approaches to material culture are eroding the elitism and the antiquarianism once so prominent in museum publications and exhibitions. Although there are still a great number of books and journals designed for the audience of connoisseurs, there is a growing body of literature that reflects the broader interpretations of material culture. In the vanguard of this effort is the *Winterthur Portfolio;* a number of recent articles appearing in the *American Quarterly,* the *Journal of American Culture,* the *Journal of Popular Culture, The Journal of Interdisciplinary History, The Journal of Social History, Museum News, History News and Curator* also exemplify the interdisciplinary work in material culture. Outside the world of academe, the more recent concerns are seen in several of the latest living history museums. The guides to these institutions not only study the society and culture of their particular community, but they take part in building and maintaining the historic community. At the Colonial Pennsylvania Plantation, a farm museum in Ridley State Park (Chester County, Pennsylvania), for example, the hostesses, dressed in the appropriate garb of eighteenth-century farmwives, cook meals on an open hearth, spin flax, make cheese and discipline their children. Meanwhile, visitors wandering through the rooms, are permitted to touch pots, pans and furniture and invited to sit in the chairs for a chat with the hostesses.

Four works will give an overview of the most recent trends in the scholarship and practical application of material culture:

"Cultural Artifacts," in the first edition of *Experiments in History Teaching*. Edited by Stephen Botein, et al. Cambridge, Mass., 1978.
Deetz, James. "A New Sense of Another World: History Museums and Cultural Change." *Museum News* 58, no. 5 (May/June 1980): 40-45.
Quimby, Ian, ed. *Material Culture and the Study of American Life*. New York, 1978.
Schlereth, Thomas. *Artifacts and the American Past*. Nashville, 1980.

E. McClung Fleming's model for reading artifacts of the American decorative arts as social documents provides the best introduction for historians interested in "doing history with the dirt on it," as Ivor Noel Hume has referred to the study of material culture. Fleming has outlined his ideas in "Artifact Study: A Proposed Model," *Winterthur Portfolio* 9 (1974): 153-173, accompanied by a case study of the seventeenth-century court covert. Social historians who specialize in women's studies will find this model particularly appropriate in that the decorative arts were so closely associated with the objects women worked with and cared for in their daily routine. Moreover, it can be easily adapted to analyzing artifacts in the practical household arts such as cooking, cleaning and washing.

There are two principal stages in Fleming's plan. The first entails preparing a complete inventory of the physical properties of the artifact in question, determining its provenance, construction, design style and function. The second stage consists in performing a sequence of four operations on the five properties: identification, evaluation, cultural analysis and interpretation. An indispensable guide in reading Fleming's article is Edward Alexander's *Museums in Motion* (Nashville, 1979), which defines the key terms associated with the various operations in artifact study and recommends further reading for each of the operations. Other useful references are: Fred Schroeder's AASLH Technical Leaflet 91, *Designing Your Exhibits: Seven Ways to Look at an Artifact* (Nashville, 1977); Thomas Schlereth, AASLH Technical Leaflet 105, *Historic Houses as Learning Laboratories: Seven Teaching Strategies* (Nashville, 1978); *Teaching Family History,* Papers from Old Sturbridge Village (Old Sturbridge Village, 1981); David E. Kyvig and Myron A. Marty, *Your Family History: A Handbook for Research and Writing* (Arlington Heights, Illinois, 1978); and David Weitzman, *Underfoot: An Everyday Guide to Exploring the American Past* (New York, 1976).

Identification, the first operation, involves classifying, authenticating and describing the object. In the last thirty years this has become an increasingly technical process since curators have begun employing scientific procedures such as wood analysis and optical spectoscopy to detect attributes that cannot be ascertained through visual inspection. The data derived from identification have been and continue to be principal concerns for connoisseurs and museum curators and are recorded in the collectors' manuals and museum acquisitions reports.

Although the great majority of these technical publications do not refer to women or suggest the relevance of the object to women's experiences, the facts themselves can contribute valuable insights for women historians. The description of any common household utensil or ornament yields facts on its history, weight, size, color, intended use, distribution and maker. A.H. Glissman's *The Evolution of the Sad-Iron* (Carlsbad, California, 1970) is a case in point. Tracing the history of the sad, or solid iron, from its origins in the Orient and Scandinavia to its modern form in Western Europe and the United States, Glissman documents how the shape, size, mode of manufacture and functions of the iron have changed between the eighth and twentieth centures. For women historians, two factors immediately stand out in studying Glissman's visual and statistical information: the weight and awkward shapes of the instrument. Not only do these physical characteristics help one understand why eighteenth and nineteenth century housewives considered ironing their most detestable chore, but they suggest how much energy a woman had to expend in executing just one of her everyday chores. Another striking feature of Glissman's documentary is the proliferation of special irons for ruffles and fancy laces that appear in the early and middle decades of the nineteenth century. Was this indicative of the popularity of "The Cult of True Womanhood" found in the prescriptive literature of the period or was it the result of greatly expanded facilities for the manufacture and distribution of ironware? One also wonders if women felt liberated by such gadgets, or if they resented the added burdens implied by the possession of such paraphernalia. Significant as well is Glissman's inclusion of advertisements for Mrs. Potts' patented iron with detachable handle, which first appeared in 1871. This represented the first major innovation in iron design since the sixteenth century and greatly facilitated the use of irons after they had been heated. Although the ads do not indicate who Mrs. Potts was or her motivations, they raise a series of provacative questions about how much women were responsible for the evolution of household technology. The information about the patent contained in the advertisement provides a valuable clue for the next stage of research on this item in the Government Patent Office. Deborah Warner's "Women at the Centennial," in *Dynamos and Virgins Revisited* calls attention to how valuable patent records are for women historians.

Another important facet of identification is studying the manufacturing process. Was the object handmade or machine made? What skills were needed by the craftsman? How long did its manufacture take and what were the precise steps in the process? Some collectors and connoisseurs have developed highly sophisticated methods for recreating historic manufacturing processes. Ellen J. Gehret, for example, has worked with several museum collections of costumes and textiles in Southeastern Pennsylvania in conjunction with the information gleaned from local wills, probate records and census returns to determine how rural clothing in Pennsylvania was made and worn in the late eighteenth century. Her *Rural Pennsylvania Clothing* (York, PA, 1976) is one of the finest collectors' guides on American costume, replete with descriptions of the garments, reproductions of historic patterns and detailed instructions on the exact needles, stitches and materials to be used in replicating the historic dress. Similar excellence in research and attention to detail characterize Lenice Ingram Bacon's *American Patchwork Quilts* (New York, 1973), Marianna Merritt Hornor's *The Study of Samplers* (Philadelphia, 1. /1), Martha Gennug Stearns' *Homespun and Blue—A Study of American Crewel Embroidery* (New York, 1963) and Susan Swan's *A Winterthur Guide to American Needlework* (New York, 1976).

There are also a great many local and regional studies of American needlework in local journals and folklore studies such as *Pennsylvania Folklife* and *Pioneer America*. While these rarely match the quality of the above-mentioned works, they are useful ways to examine regional and ethnic differences among American women, and in some cases needlework leaves visual evidence of buildings and streets of eighteenth and early nineteenth-century America that is totally lacking in verbal sources and other available pictorial artifacts.

Connoisseurship of American foodways has produced a literature as prolific and diverse as American needlework. A particularly outstanding example of this genre is Evan Jones' *American Food: The Gastronomic Story* (New York, 1975). From artifacts of cooking and dining found in museums throughout the United States, as well as old cookbooks, household economy manuals and travelers' accounts, Jones has reconstructed the main components of eighteenth- and nineteenth-century American diets. His favorite recipes, printed in *American Food,* document the immense regional and ethnic variety of American eating habits prior to the age of processed foods and national food chains. Jones' observation that the rise of modern food processing industries has revolutionized American tastes and eating habits suggests a whole area of interesting topics for scholars in women's history exploring the changing patterns of housekeeping in response to the emergence of improved food preservation methods, retail food chains, and food processing industries. Were women freed from household burdens with these advances, or did hours in consumption replace hours once spent in household production of food?

In addition to the information on historic manufacturing from collectors' guides, museums of science and technology often hold exhibits demonstrating manufacturing techniques in the practical and decorative arts. Many of these are organized around an historical theme, which chronicles the evolution of manufacturing from the preindustrial period to the present. Such exhibits can shed light on women's economic roles, especially those concerned with industries that have traditionally employed female labor. The catalogue for an exhibit on woolen textiles at the Merrimack Valley Textile Museum entitled *Homespun to Factory Made: Woolen Textiles in America, 1776-1876* (North Andover, MA, 1977), illustrates this point. The opening section includes engravings of the preindustrial process with women depicted in unskilled jobs and men at the looms and other more complex operations. By contrast, the lithographs and stereopticans of woolmaking in the 1860s and 1870s reveal women at the power loom. The catalogue and labels do not explicitly discuss the ramifications of factory production on women's roles, but the visual documents of the changing modes of production and their impact on women's place in the production process call immediate attention to the phenomenon of modern industry whereby operations become feminized once they require little skill or physical energy. "Direct sensory awareness" of such processes or vernacular objects, as John Kouwenhoven has observed in "American Studies: Words or Things?" "provides an important kind of knowledge about American culture. Perhaps, indeed, the most necessary kind if we are searching for a community of experienced particulars that embodies the dynamic energies of an emergent American culture."

The research methods used in preparing these exhibits are also helpful for historians of women. Rather than rely on secondary accounts of how a thing was constructed, museum specialists insist on learning how to do it themselves and recreating the historic manufacturing techniques by consulting contemporary manuals or interviewing living persons who remember or still practice a craft done in the late nineteenth or early twentieth century. Frank McKelvey of the Hagley Museum, for example, has adapted field methods of visual anthropology as described in John Collier's *Visual Anthropology:* to reconstruct the crafts associated with the production of gunpowder a century ago. His primary sources are individuals who remember how a process was done and are willing to demonstrate it before an observer. Once such individuals are located, McKelvey photographs the craftsperson in all phases of manufacture. When the photos have been processed and made into slides, McKelvey views the slides with the craftsperson in the craftsperson's own home. This informal situation enables McKelvey to elicit information missing in the photographic record and allows the craftsperson to interject anecdotes or additional comments on the craft as he or she looks at the slides. Such a technique could prove invaluable for studying historical household arts such as breadmaking, cheesemaking and quilt making, which are still being done in the more rural regions of the United States. If historians of women had more precise data on how much time, energy, skill were necessary in historical housewifery, we might have insights into why so many nineteenth-century women abstained from active involvement in the public sector. Did they have enough time to reflect on how their position was oppressive? Did they have time to attend to duties outside the home and church? Or, did they have the stamina after housework to attend meetings?

Some additional references on the operation of identification that can be useful in studying women's historic experience are:

Anon. *The Country Kitchen 1850.* Scotia, New York, 1965.
    This is a collection of typical advertisements and excerpts from contemporary household manuals. There is no analysis or bibliography, but it is helpful in developing a listing of typical items in a Victorian kichen.

Buehr, Walter, *Home Sweet Home in the Nineteenth Century,* New York, 1965.
    This is written for a popular audience, but the principal objects found in Victorian homes are identified and described. The careful minutia of detail about gadgets may provide a basis for further study of the part women played in the consumption and invention of gadgets.

Cahn, William. *Lawrence 1912: The Bread and Roses Strike.* New York, 1977.

This is a photo essay of the strike with a useful introduction indicating the highlights of the strike and suggesting themes that could be investigated further in other sources.

Carson, Cary. "From the Bottom Up." *History News* 35, no. 1 (Jan. 1980): 7-9.
This is a brief but informative report on the latest research effort at collaborating methods of the New History with methods of Material Culture Studies at St. Mary's City, Maryland.

Collins, James H. *The Story of Canned Foods.* New York, 1924.
Although this is an early work on the history of food processing, it provides an introduction to the basic historical evolution and the key events in the history of the industry. There is no bibliography, but there are helpful photographs of the industry incorporated in the text.

Cooper, Grace Rogers. *The Sewing Machine: Its Invention and Development.* Washington, Smithsonian Institution Press.
This provides an excellent cornerstone for further more analytical work of the social and economic impact of the sewing machine both inside the household and in the marketplace.

Cotter, John L. "Above Ground Archaeology." *American Quarterly* 26, no. 3 (August 1974): 266-279.
This is not as well refined as Schlereth's methodology, but it does summarize the current ways in which museums employ such techniques and lists useful projects for history classes, using local resources. Accompanying the article is a helpful listing of the museums and landmarks in the National Park Service which have facilities for conducting research in above ground archaeology.

Cunnington, Phillis. *Costume of Household Servants from the Middle Ages to 1900.* London, 1974.
Using excerpts from contemporary journals, letters, diaries, inventories and newspapers, the author shows the evolution of male and female servants' costumes in England. Although she suggests that the clothing reflects social status and servants often aspired to emulate their social superiors, she does not develop this theme in a systematic fasion. No comparable work has been done on American servants, but a study of American servants' dress habits might well prove useful in studying attitudes toward class and diffusion patterns.

Elder, Betty Doak. "Workers of Lynn." *History News* 34, no. 8 (August 1980).
This describes a recent exhibit on the shoemaking industry at Lynn. The selection and organization of artifacts clearly manifest the sexual division of labor that characterized the nineteenth-century industry as well as the changing patterns of family life as the shoemaking industry underwent increasing mechanization and specialization of labor.

Fearn, Jacqueline. *Domestic Bygones.* London, 1977.
This deals with English society during the eighteenth and nineteenth centuries. It singles out the key articles found in the middle and upper middle-class homes. The well-documented discussion of lighting devices is suggestive for comparable research

on the evolution of lighting technology in America and its impact on women's domestic roles and household routines.

Filene, Peter "Integrating Women's History and Regular History." *The History Teacher* 13, no. 4 (August 1980): 483-492.

Filene offers excellent suggestions for including material from portraits and photographs in lectures dealing with family life and domesticity, and he makes clear how such materials can shed light on the private life of men as well as women. "These images," writes Filene, "make the past literally more imaginable. And I find that my students respond with gratifying interest and skill as we read these visual texts in class. From an explicit portrait of a family sitting in front of their Victorian mansion, for example, students make ingenious references about sex roles, attitudes toward children, attitudes toward family, notions of privacy and the function of photographs and the camera."

Gershman, Elizabeth. "Women at Work: How Stamford's Exhibit Traces the Professional Development of Women." *History News* 35, no. 8 (August 1980).

Like Ms. Elder (mentioned above) Ms. Gershamn discusses how practitioners of material culture are currently using the latest scholarship in women's history in preparing museum exhibits.

Gillespie, Charles. *A Pictorial Diderot Encyclopedia.* 2 vols. New York, 1957.

This deals with the crafts and industries of eighteenth-century France, drawing materials from the illustrated volumes of Diderot's *Encyclopedia*. The Illustrations showing the various stages of manufacture clearly indicate the sexual division of labor present in the eighteenth-century industries. Although Diderot only documented industry in eighteenth-century France, his method of interviewing the workers and masters engaged in the various industries and crafts of visiting the workplaces himself led to very detailed accounts of the historic manufacturing processes and the sexual division of labor, which can be compared with sources pertaining to the division of labor among American workers.

Goldschmidt, Walter and Robert B. Edgerton. "A Picture Technique for the Study of Values." *American Anthropologist* 63, no. 1 (1961): 26-47.

This supplements John Collier's description of methodology in his *Visual Anthropology*.

Groves, Sylvia. *The History of Needlework Tools and Accessories.* Great Britain, 1968.

This is the standard reference used by persons working on historic needlework.

Hodgkinson, Ralph. American Association for State and Local History, Technical Leaflet 84, *Learning About Crafts on the Wool Wheel.* Nashville, 1975.

This is representative of a number of leaflets prepared by the American Association for State and Local History to describe the processes of historic arts and crafts. Careful attention is given to both the necessary skills of the craftspersons as well as the available levels of technology. For a complete listing of these leaflets write: Catalog Order Department, AASLH, 708 Berry Road, Nashville, TN. 37204.

Howard, Robert A. and E. Alvin Gerhardt, Jr. *Mary Patton Powder Maker of the Revolution.* Rocky Mount, TN. 1980

This exemplifies the methods of treating historic crafts at the Hagley Museum. Although Howard and Gerhardt do not indicate how common it was to find women involved in the powder industry, women historians might look for additional evidence about how typical or unusual it was during the Revolution for women to be involved in management of industries.

Jendricks, Barbara Whitton. *Paper Dolls and Paper Toys by Raphael Tuck & Sons.* n.d., 1970.
    This is an introduction to a much-neglected topic. As with dolls and doll houses, paper toys need more analytical scholarship on how various toys contributed to socialization and sex-role stereotypes. Equally important are considerations of how the paper toys were related to the developments in paper technology, and what role paper toys played in democratizing leisure activities for children.

Jewell, Brian. *Smoothing Irons: A History and Collector's Guide.* Tundbridge Wells, Kent, 1977.
_____ *Veteran Talking Machines.* Tundbridge Wells, Kent, 1977.

These works follow the format of A. Glissman's *Evolution of the Sad Iron.* However, Jewell adds more precise information on the current collections and includes chronological charts and directories of inventors and makers, which are invaluable for identification purposes.

Kidwell, Claudia B. *Women's Bathing and Swimming Costumes in the United States.* Paper 64, Bulletin 250 from the Museum of History and Technology. Washington, 1964.
    This provides an excellent model for tracing the evolution of various garments and fashion over the last two centuries. The data gathered in this report can be integrated into social history on the changing patterns of leisure as well as women's history concerning changing values and self-perception of women.

King, Eileen Constance. *Antique Toys and Dolls.* New York, 1979.

_____ *The Collectors' History of Dolls.* New York, 1977.

Lifshey, Earl. *The Housewares Story, A History of American Housewares Industry.* Chicago, 1973.
    This offers a comprehensive narrative of the growth of the housewares industry over the last century with attention to technological developments that encouraged innovations in the industry and to changing business practices that altered the mode of manufacture and distribution. This is fully illustrated with a number of full color prints.

Lowenstein, Eleanor. *Bibliography of American Cookery Books, 1742-1860.* New York, 1972.
    This lists 835 cookbooks, deliberately omitting those household economy manuals that have no specific references to food preparation or recipes. Studies on the evolution of the cookbook and the recipes themselves are crucial to our understanding of historic housewifery. Frequently these old cookbooks include moral

lessons and hints on etiquette and medicine which go beyond their ostensible function of giving instructions on cooking.

Matelic, Candace Tangorra. *"Living History Farms." Museum News* 58, no. 4 (March/April 1980): 36-45.

This surveys the current exhibits and research on living history farms. Quite explicitly, Ms. Matelic says that the exhibits are intended to display the arts and crafts of both men and women in rural America. Her listing of further more specialized reading on the subject can provide the basis for scholars interested in women's history to determine where and what research is currently taking place on the history of the household arts.

Miller, Lewis. *Lewis Miller, Sketches and Chronicles.* York, PA, 1966.

These are contemporary sketches of early nineteenth century life in York, Pennsylvania. They are useful documents for getting details on historic costumes and domestic interiors.

Peirce, Josephine R. *Fire on the Hearth: The Evolution and Romance of the Heating-Stove.* Springfield, Mass., 1950.

This is a well-illustrated history of heating stoves from the colonial period until the early twentieth century. Although it lacks analysis, material on the changing modes of manufacture and advertising as well as anecdotes from contemporary letters and diaries about the hearth enable one to get an idea of how important it was for previous generations to have sources of heat and how it was a topic constantly on their minds due to the inadequate sources and technology for heating domestic and public places before the early twentieth century.

Pike, Martha and Janice Gray Armstrong. *A Time to Mourn: Expressions of Grief in Nineteenth Century America.* Stony Brook, 1980.

This was the catalogue which accompanied the Stony Brook exhibit on death. The catalogue treats the visual representations of death and dying in addition to the memorabilia and mourning costumes associated with the Victorian rituals and etiquette for death and dying.

Reid, Joe and John Peck. *Stove Book.* New York, 1977.

This is primarily a picture book of nineteenth and early twentieth century cooking stoves. More analytical studies are necessary on the evolution of stove technology and the significance of the stove in the housewives' lives.

Ring, Betty, ed. *Needlework: An Historical Survey.* New York, 1975.

This is a collection of the best articles in *Antiques* on eighteenth and nineteenth-century American needlework. It is an excellent introduction to the topic, and bibliographical suggestions are included for each facet of needlework.

Schiffer, Margaret. *Historical Needlework of Pennsylvania.* New York, 1968.

This exemplifies the kind of work that can be done in regional history from the study of artifacts.

Sharrer, G. Terry. *1001 References for the History of American Food and Technology.* Davis, CA, 1978.

This is a publication of the U.S. Department of Agriculture, which updates an earlier bibliography. Any one of the topics—refrigeration, meat processing, dairying, canning, etc.—is potentially useful for persons working in women's history.

Strasser, Susan. "Never Done: The Technology and Ideology of Household Work, 1850-1930." Ph.D. dissertation, University of New York at Stony Brook, 1977.
This includes one of the most comprehensive discussions to date of the evolution of household technology, covering the history of every conceivable gadget and appliance and their impact on the nature of household work. Also included is an important discussion of how household technology was often dependent on available public utilities and ample water supplies.

Thomas, Alan. *Time in a Frame: Photography and the Nineteenth-Century Mind.* New York, 1977.
The central theme is that the nineteenth century had the first visual generations to use photography, and this changed their perceptions of their world. To demonstrate this theme Thomas analyzes specific photos of Victorian society and also elaborates ways to interpret visual imagery. His recommendations for comparing photographs of women in their public and private endeavors are of particular interest to scholars in women's history.

Tyron, Rolla Milton. *Household Manufacturers in the United States, 1640-1860.* New York, 1917.
This is a standard reference on the processes of domestic manufactures and their transition to shop and factory manufactures in the course of the nineteenth century. Ms. Tyron collected data from both statistical reports on volume of sales and distribution of manufactures and a number of literary sources, including letters, diaries and observations by travelers.

Warner, Deborah. *Perfect in Her Place: Women at Work in Industrial America.* Washington, 1981.
This is the catalogue accompanying an exhibit at the Smithsonian Museum of American History from the fall of 1981 until the late spring of 1982. It is a thoroughly researched exhibit which reflects the more recent interpretations in the scholarship of women's work. The artifacts vividly portray how women in a wide variety of industries have been confined to the least skilled and the least remunerative positions. On the effectiveness of his exhibit and its catalogue see Joyce Pendery's report in the *CCWHP Newsletter* (March 1982), pp. 7-8.

Wilckens, Leonie von. *Mansions in Miniature: Four Centuries of Dolls' Houses.* New York, 1980.
This is one of the best researched works on the topic.

Worrell, Estekke Absley. *Early American Costume.* Harrisburg, PA, 1975.
This is a well researched work in costume history which demonstrates how the study of dress can enrich our understanding of ethnic history and cultures.

Wright, Lawrence. *Clean and Decent: The Fascinating History of the Bathroom & the Water Closet.* New York, 1960.
This provides a chronology for the appearance of indoor plumbing and various

bathroom fixtures. It should be used in conjunction with Ms. Strasser's dissertation (mentioned above), which examines when the new technology and equipment for indoor plumbing actually entered the average household.

The second operation, evaluation, involves making judgments about the aesthetic qualities of an artifact and comparing its attributes with similar objects of its period in its own geographical locale as well as other regions throughout the world. Significant considerations are: How unique was the object? Where was it traded, and what were the patterns of distribution? What was its relative value in comparison to other possessions in the household? What skills and levels of technology were available to the craftsperson? What was the owner's social status, and which economic classes were most likely to possess the item?

The whole area of taste as "read" in artifacts has tremendous potential for scholarship in women's history. Two early works by Russell Lynes, *The Tastemakers* (New York, 1949), and *The Domesticated Americans* (New York, 1954) pointed out how middle and upper-middle-class housewives in the Victorian era became the arbiters of taste in interior decor and clothing fashion.

Advances in household technology freed these well-to-do women from domestic chores to devote their time to fashion.

More recently William Seale in *The Tasteful Interlude: American Interiors Through the Camera's Eye, 1860-1917* (Second edition revised and enlarged. Nashville, 1981, based on the 1975 edition for Praeger Publishers) has traced the emergence of Victorian taste in interior decoration, using surviving photographs of Victorian homes. Not only has Seale reconfirmed Lynes' earlier observations, but he notes that it was principally women who had their rooms photographed, or who took the time to join photography clubs where they acquired the requisite skills for preserving the image of their homes. Just as Ann Douglas has shown in *The Feminization of American Culture* (New York, 1977) that women's literary tastes came to prevail over American literature in the Victorian era, Seale has documented the feminization of American decorative arts: women's values dominated in determining spatial arrangements of furnishing, the placement and quantity of ornaments, the amount of lighting and heating in a room, as well as the contours, shapes and upholstery for the chairs and sofas. A similar theme appears in George Talbot's *At Home: Domestic Life in the Post-Centennial Era 1876-1920* (Madison, WI, 1976), an exhibit-catalog for photographs of American domestic life. Convincing as these photographic galleries are of late Victorian familial values, one must bear in mind that Seale and Talbot are primarily working with artifacts of upper and middle-class homes. Were these representative of the tastes among the more numerous working-and lower-middle-class families?

There are a number of ways to compare high culture and popular culture in post-bellum America. The catalogues for mail-order houses are an excellent source: comparing items in the catalogues with those advertised in furniture trade catalogues and expensive upper-class magazines and journals, one can detect what influence the high culture had on the appearance and design of the cheaper, mass-produced goods offered in the mail-order catalogues. Thomas Schlereth's discussion of mail-order catalogues in *Artifacts and the American Past* is particularly beneficial for interpreting the information gleaned from the American "wishbooks." One can also consult the histories of the large wholesale and retail chains of the late nineteenth and early twentieth centuries. For example, Lloyd Wendt's and Herman Kogan's *Give the Lady What She Wants! The Story of Marshall Field & Company* (Chicago, 1952) elaborates on the merchandising techniques used to cater to all classes of female consumers. Studies of the 1876 and 1893 world fairs offer additional insights into the diffusion and dissemination of tastes in late Victorian America. Reactions to the exhibitions were analogous to modern public opinion polls in that virtually all social, economic and ethnic groups were represented in the audiences. Other ways for comparing the tastes between the elites and the masses are to study the inventories, wills and probate records of working-class and lower-middle-class families. What similarities are found with items listed in the records of the more well-to-do families? Important too are the oral interviews of persons living in the late nineteenth century. Transcriptions of interviews conducted by the WPA Federal Writers Projects in the 1930s might disclose evidence about common household possessions and attitudes toward the acquisition of household goods. Supplementing such audial evidence from the 1930s are the photographs collected by the Farm Security Administration during the depression which document the types of agricultural work going on in all parts of the country along with intimate views of farm families inside their homes and on their porches.

It is much more difficult to discern patterns of taste prior to the nineteenth century. The manuals on domestic economy and the mail-order trade catalogues so ubiquitous in the nineteenth century were much rarer in the seventeenth and eighteenth centuries. Moreover, there are few extant visual representations of domestic interiors. Pieces of colonial furniture and household ornamentaion that survive were possessions of the upper classes, and in the era before mass production of the lower classes had greater difficulty procuring less expensive imitations of high culture than their descendants in the late Victorian era. Nevertheless, Ivor Noel Hume's *A Guide to Artifacts of Colonial America* (New York, 1970) and James Deetz's *Invitation to Archeology* (New York, 1967) suggest a variety of ways that the archeologist and the historian can collaborate in determining what objects were available and common to the average colonial householder. The effectiveness of their methods are seen in the Colonial Williamsburg Archaeologist Series. Audrey Hume's *Food* (Williamsburg, Virginia, 1978) will especially interest scholars in women's history on account of its rich details of colonial household production and the processing of meats, fruits and vegetables. Another worthwhile source is Abott Lowell Cummings' *Rural Household Inventories Establishing the Names, Uses and Furnishings of Rooms in the Colonial New England Home 1675-1775* (Boston, 1964). Although his inventories typify those of the wealthy families, his introductory essay is an excellent discussion of how to interpret inventories and can be applied to similar documents for lower and middle-class households. Also, John T. Kirk's *Early American Furniture* (New York, 1979), contains valuable suggestions for studying country furniture done by provincial cabinetmakers in order to get a sense of the types of furnishings and styles that would have been available to the less affluent householders.

Connoisseurs and curators at the Winterthur Museum have taken the forefront in research of upper-class tastes in the decorative arts for the seventeenth and eighteenth centuries. Their monographs on colonial and federal furniture, glassware, prints, silver, textiles and ceramics, along with reports of their annual conferences in the Winterthur Conference Series, are standard references in the fields of material culture and are recognized for their excellence in scholarship. These publications serve two important functions for scholars in women's history: first, they provide a basis of comparison with the more middle-class tastes that evolved in the nineteenth century; and secondly, they emphasize the interaction of things and ideas between Europe and colonial America, heightening our awareness of how much European states influenced both men and women in the prerevolutionary era. Future scholarship on upper-class women of colonial America might examine the implications of the continuous intercourse with European society and culture. Equally worthwhile would be a study of how upper-class female tastes changed in the Republic. Do artifacts of the early national period reflect the same efforts of American women to define their roles as Nancy Cott has found in their social behavior and described in her *Bonds of Womanhood* (New Haven, 1977)?

Additional references on the operation of evaluation that can prove useful in women's history include:

Booth, Sally Smith. *Hung, Strung and Potted.* New York, 1971.
    This is an excellent source on eighteenth-century methods of food processing.

Byington, Margaret F. *Homestead: The Households of a Milltown.* Introduced by Samuel P. Hays. Pittsburgh, reprint, 1974, original 1910.
    Using budgets, surviving furniture and old photographs, Ms. Byington creates a picture of the material conditions and family life for the workers of the turn-of-the century company town. Although this monograph was originally done in 1910 and was intended to serve the interests of progressive reformers, it remains an excellent source on the material circumstances of working-class life and a prototype for current studies of blue-collar communities. What makes it so relevant to women's studies is the fact that Ms. Byington tried to look at the material conditions from the point of view of the working-class wife and mother.

Craven, Wayne. *Sculpture in America.* New York, 1968.
    This is the standard reference for the history of sculpture in America from the colonial era until the 1960s.

Cummings, Richard Osborn. *The American and His Food: A History of Food Habits in the United States.* Chicago: revised edition, 1970, original 1940.
_____. *The American Ice Harvest: A Historical Study in Technology, 1800-1918.* Berkeley, CA, 1949.
    These remain classic studies on the history of the ice industry and the evolution of refrigeration in American food preservation. Although Cummings made a great number of suggestions for further study of the social impact of refrigeration in his 1940 study, he did not follow through on these topics in his later works on the history of technology; it is only recently that social historians have begun to explore themes originally proposed by Cummings forty years ago.

Drescher, Nuala McGann. "The Irish in Industrial Wilmington, 1800-1945." M.A. thesis, University of Delaware, 1960.
    Studying artifactual evidence from the homes and former workplaces of the first generations of Irish workers in the Brandywine Valley, Ms. Drescher makes fascinating speculations as to how the Irish managed to retain certain cultural values in the new world despite their apparent assimilation to the dominant values of the Protestant majority of the area.

Federal Writers Project. *These Are Our Lives*. New York, reprint, 1975.

This includes a collection of interviews of people from North Carolina, Georgia and Tennessee conducted by members of the Federal Writers Project, with useful suggestions for organizing the material into life histories. Some of the interviews were never published and remain in typescript in archival collections. To locate those reports you are interested in, consult the Federal Writers Project *Catalog: American Guide Series* (Washington, 1938).

Forman, Benno. "The Seventeenth Century Case Furniture of Essex County and Its Makers." M.A. Thesis, University of Delaware, 1968.

This spells out current methodology for furniture study, which calls for an analysis of the objects as well as their craftspersons and their relation to the larger cultural environment. Forman's mastery of these methods is demonstrated in several of his articles in the *Winterthur Portfolio, Furniture History,* and other more technical journals on material culture.

Hancock, Harold. "The Industrial Worker Along the Brandywine." 3 Vols. Greenville, Delaware, typewritten reports for the Hagley Museum, 1956-1958.

Using inventories of workers killed or maimed in explosions at the du Pont powder mills, records of food and other household goods purchased at the company stores, and records of production from the gardens and fields of the company and workers' homes, Hancock creates as rich and as thorough a report of the material circumstances for Brandywine workers as Ms. Byington did for the Homestead workers. Hancock's reports were never published. Yet they remain indispensable sources for social historians of the mid-Atlantic Region. Ms. Drescher, mentioned above, drew heavily from Hancock's methodology to recreate the experience of nineteenth-century Irish immigrants in the Delaware Valley.

Hummel, Charles. *With Hammer in Hand: The Dominy Craftsmen of East Hampton, New York*. Charlottesville, VA, 1968.

This is an in-depth study of a family of nineteenth-century craftsmen including an inventory of the furniture they made, a listing of their customers, and complete descriptions of their tools and workshop. For women historians, it is somewhat disappointing that Hummel has not been able to find out more about the Dominy women, especially in light of the fact that East Hampton was the original home of Catharine Beecher. On the other hand, Hummel's monograph serves as an outstanding model for recreating historic crafts and can be easily adapted to a study of household arts.

Jackson, John Brinckerhoff. *American Space: The Centennial Years 1865-1876*. New York, 1972.

This is an indispensable work for studying the interaction between material culture and social values in the post-bellum era. The insights on space are particularly important for current interests in women's history concerning women's historic attitudes toward space.

Jones, Michael Owen. *The Hand-Made Object and Its Maker*. Berkeley, CA, 1975.

Using a series of intensive interviews of a southeastern Kentucky chairmaker in conjunction with examinations of the craftsman's chairs, Jones has been able to draw a psychological and social profile of his subject. In contrast to Hummel, Jones was able to gather more material about women in the chairmaker's family and was able to speculate on how much women influenced men's lives in the traditional households of Kentucky. Jones' interviewing technique could be especially useful in interviewing women who still perform traditional household arts as is true in pockets of contemporary Appalachia and in several areas of the Southwest.

Kegley, Mary B. "Pioneer Possessions: A Study of Wills and Appraisals in Southwest Virginia, 1745-1786." M.A. Thesis, Radford College, Radford, VA 1975.
This is one of the few studies based on wills and probate records of the Appalachian area. The data on households provides interesting contrasts with possessions listed for households in other regions for the late eighteenth century.

Kenney, Alice. "Women, History, and the Museum." *The History Teacher* 8 (1974):511-523.
This sets out a number of useful questions for interpreting wills and other information on domestic interiors between the colonial era and the late nineteenth century. Particularly helpful are the questions that will help us determine whether women had any control of their physical environment and whether women acquired increasing responsibilities for the domestic realm as the society became more settled and as capitalism matured.

Kirk, John T. *American Chairs: Queen Anne and Chippendale.* New York, 1972.
This is an excellent introduction to the high culture furniture styles of the eighteenth century.

Madden, Robert R. *Walker Sisters' Home: Historic Structure Report, Part II and Furnishing Study.* Great Smoky Mountains National Park, 1969.
Based on an intensive investigation of the Walker Sisters' farm and outbuildings which are still standing, Madden has been able to reconstruct what the typical routine and chores were for farm families in the Appalachian area. He has made a special effort to record what common household artifacts the sisters used and to note whether the sisters used these artifacts throughout their lives. Photographs of the extant buildings and furnishings embellish the aural evidence. Hopefully, this will serve as a model for additional studies of housewifery in Appalachia while there are still women who remember or continue to practice the "secrets of housewifery."

Michael, Jack. " 'In a Manner and Fashion Suitable to Their Degree': A Preliminary Investigation of Material Culture in Rural Pennsylvania." *Working Papers for the Regional Economic History Research Center* 5 (1981).
This is a sophisticated local study which concentrates on changes in interior space, furnishings and construction materials, and their relationship to the social status of the household owner. Michel also makes a conscientious effort to point out how physical changes influence women's roles and domestic status.

Montgomery, Charles F. *American Furniture—The Federal Period.* New York, 1966.
This is a comprehensive survey of federal styles for high culture furniture with consideration given to both the nature of craftmanship and the economics involved in the furniture industry.

Quimby, Ian, ed. *Arts of the Anglo-American Community in the Seventeenth Century.* Charlottesville, VA, 1973.

_____ *Ceramics in America.* Charlottesville, VA 1973.

_____ and Polly Anne Earle. *Technological Innovation and the Decorative Arts.* Charlottesville, VA, 1973.

These are all part of the Winterthur Conference Series. The contributions not only represent excellent work in the evaluation of material culture, but they also suggest how the research in evaluation might serve as a point of departure for interpreting the objects as social documents.

Quimby, Ian, ed. *American Furniture and Its Makers.* Chicago, 1979.

This includes articles discussing the latest methods used for identifying and evaluating furniture. Particularly worthwhile is Robert Blair St. George's contribution "Style and Structure in the Joinery of Dedham and Medfield, Massachusetts, 1635-1685."

Peterson, Harold L. *Americans at Home, from the Colonists to the Late Victorians.* New York, 1971.

Using paintings and photos of domestic interiors, Peterson documents changing patterns and physical circumstances of homelife between the seventeenth and late-nineteenth centuries. His discussions of each of the paintings and photos serve as excellent guides for learning how to "read" visual texts. Also, this serves as a supplement to the works of Talbot and Seale mentioned above in the text.

Porter, Glenn. *The Workers' World at Hagley.* Eleutherian Mills Hagley Foundation, 1981.

This is the exhibit-catalogue for a current exhibit at the Hagley Museum which depicts the work and homelife of powdermen and their families during the late nineteenth and early twentieth centuries. Centering both the catalogue and the exhibit around a collection of old photos taken and preserved by a company manager, Porter is able to make a vivid display about how inextricably linked the home and the workplace were in the closeknit powdermill community in the Brandywine Valley right into the first decades of the twentieth century. The photo of a housewife, standing outside her home in an apron and watching the powdermill explosion of 1893, is perhaps the most graphic illustration of this.

Rutman, Darrett B. *Husbandmen of Plymouth; Farms and Villages in the Old Colony, 1620-1692.* Boston, 1967.

This studies seventeenth-century farmlife in Plymouth, using evidence culled from inventories and other surviving artifacts.

Schiffer, Margaret Berwind. *Survey of Chester County, Pennsylvania Architecture, Seventeenth, Eighteenth and Nineteenth Centuries.* Exton, Pennsylvania, 1976.

This is an essential reference work for persons interested in the material culture of the mid-Atlantic Region. It lists the work of all the cabinetmakers and the contents of their wills from Southeastern Pennsylvania; a useful introduction indicates how the information was gathered and organized. Before consulting this source, however, one should look at the works of Ivor Noel Hume and James Deetz concerning the interpretation of inventories and will.

Seale, William. *Recreating the Historic House Interior.* Nashville, 1979.

This is invaluable for the layperson who is interested in historic preservation. It clearly elaborates the methodology currently employed in preservation and the key concerns of museum specialists in designing period rooms. For scholars in women's history this calls attention to the atmosphere of the Victorian home in which women spent so much of their time. There is also an important discussion of changing technology in lighting and heating and their respective effects on furniture placement and domestic comfort. Equally interesting is the section dealing with floor covers and mats in which Seale points out the current misconceptions about the use of mats and stresses how linoleum revolutionized Victorian housekeeping.

"Teaching Community History Guides to Readings in Colonial Studies, Family History, Multimedia & Oral History." *The Newberry Papers in Family and Community History.* Chicago, 1977.
    This contains extensive bibliographical suggestions for conducting oral interviews and gathering data for family and community history.

Cultural analysis, the third operation, consists in making relationships between the physical object and its contemporary culture. There are three main approaches employed by scholars looking for the intersections between material culture and modes of human behavior, ideas and social values. The first is to determine the functional aspects of the object in its culture. Was the object utilitarian or ornamental? What were the intended and unintended uses of the object? Did the object convey social status on its owner? What symbolic significance did the object hold in its society? Secondly, how did the culture leave its imprint on the object? Are there visual representations of political, religious or social attitudes? What were the available levels of technology? How did social, intellectual and religious views influence the construction, design and shape of the object? Finally, how does the content of the physical object reflect on its culture? Can one "read" about the social values from an examination of the physical object? What can the object "tell" the observer about the prejudices, fears, loves and spiritual concerns of a culture?

Cultural analysis offers the most exciting prospects for historical research. Not only do the intersections allow for maximum use of audio-visual techniques and the quantitative methods developed by the New Historians of the Annale school, but they bring novel insights and raise provocative questions that cannot be answered if scholars remain locked in their separate disciplines. In his essay "Doing History with Material Culture," in *Material Culture and the Study of Everyday Life,* Cary Carson, a social historian currently working with a team of archaeologists and anthropologists to restore a seventeenth-century site at St. Mary's City, Maryland, expresses the sentiments of a number of historians who have profited from using physical evidence in conjunction with the more traditional tools of the historian:

The New Historians are raising questions that bring the man-made world inside the circle of ideas that interest them most. For the first time real, live, degree-holding, card-carrying historians are interested in things not as mere illustrations, not just as props for teachers.... All these still leave artifacts on the sidelines. What I find encouraging is signs that at last some historians are beginning to look at artifacts as sources of ideas about a whole range of topics that are just now coming into prominence. So far, these scholars are still nibbling round the edges, but they need not stop there. These small beginnings may be part of some larger subject that may ultimately prove to be as full of insights as the new fields of demographic history and the history of the family.

Three examples of the scholarship in cultural analysis will suffice to show why Cary Carson has evinced such enthusiasm. The first comes from Catherine Lynn's recent historical survey of *Wallpaper in America* (New York, 1980). Contained in this carefully researched monograph is a fascinating discussion of the nineteenth-century bandbox. The function of these pasteboard boxes was for ladies to carry small items of clothing or hats on their travels. Before 1840 when the more sturdy leather traveling boxes were marketed, bandboxes were ubiquitous. Wallpaper manufacturers took advantage of the situation and covered these boxes with samples of their stock. Wherever the bandboxes traveled, Lynn explains, the latest fashions in wallpapers were disseminated. Before the emergence of mail order catalogues that brought mass-produced goods within easy reach of farm families, the bandboxes were shaping American tastes. What makes the bandbox all the more important is the fact that Victorian domestic economy books instructed their readers to select wallpaper that would encourage proper moral behavior among children and men of the family. Thus, the utilitarian box also helped to shape the morality and aesthetics of Victorian America.

A second example of cultural analysis is Claudia Kidwell's and Margaret C. Christman's exhibit catalogue *Suiting Everyone: The Democratization of Clothing in America* (Washington, 1974). While Ms. Lynn focused on how the object functioned in its culture, the authors of this clothing exhibit have explored how the democratic ideals impinged on the physical universe. Their two principal themes are 1) the transformation from homemade clothing to ready wear clothing and 2) the transformation in wearing customs from dress according to class to democratic dress whereby everyone strives to dress alike. Unlike so many museum exhibits, this one does specifically address social issues. The oppressive nature of the sweated industries is juxtaposed to the benefits of cheaper more available clothing for everyone. Interesting also is their treatment of the possible tensions between the ideals of equality and individuality. While consumers pressured manufacturers for equal opportunities to dress in a similar manner, there was a simultaneous pressure for manufacturers to respect customers' individuality with a wide selection of sizes and colors to suit the particular physiques and color preferences of the buying public. The historian Daniel Boorstin paid high tribute to the skillful way the exhibit revealed the multiplicity of material and ideological factors that contributed to the emergence and popularity of ready-to-wear in American society.

A final example is drawn from Anthony Garvan's "The New England Porringer: A Customary Artifact," in *The Present World of History* (Madison, WI 1959). This is a classic study of how the physical properties of the artifact "tell" the observer about its culture. Although it has been commonly assumed that the porringer has always been an appliance for weaning infants, there exists no written evidence attesting to its use in colonial times. In studying hundreds of these pieces from Puritan New England, Garvan questioned the long-held assumption, pointing out that the iconography was associated to, and symbolic of, the celebration of fertility between a man and wife. Garvan's ability to "read" the artifact is vividly manifest in his discussion of the tulip or lily motif:

Their presence on the porringer, as upon household articles, suggests Christian love or even ecstasy of divine revelation, a doctrine strongly emphasized by the Puritan concept of election. This correlation of physical love and the vision of divinity seemed, of course, a reasonable one and was borne out by the use of the tulip or lily on New England marriage chests. Moreover, this link is closely forged in the decorative motifs of Pennsylvania, where the symbolism is made doubly apparent in poetic imagery.

Thus Garvan's object-study not only led to a reconsideration of the utilitarian aspects of the porringer, but raised significant questions about Puritan attitudes toward marriage and love, which subsequent scholars have pursued in examining the court and church records.

Garvan's work and the other examples mentioned above attest to how cultural analysis of physical objects can lead to fruitful explorations of women's historical experience. Additional works that might prove equally valuable either for their content or as models for future scholarship in women's history are:

Ames, Kenneth. "The Meaning of Artifacts: Hall Furnishings in Victorian America," *Journal of Interdisciplinary History* 9, no. 1 (Summer, 1978).

This examines the utilitarian and social funtions of Victorian furnishings with keen observations about how the appearance and spacing of objects conveyed class attitudes and values. It also serves as a model for future analyses of household furnishings.

Andrews, Deborah C. and William D. Andrews. "Technology and the Housewife in Nineteenth Century America," *Women Studies* 2, no. 3 (1974): 309-328.
   This is an effort to study the household objects within the larger cultural context, placing special emphasis on the relationship between the prescriptive literature in household economy books and the domestic environment of Victorian homes. In contrast to Ruth Schwartz Cowan, the Andrews make more use of literary sources rather than rely so heavily on the technological changes.

Andrews, Edward Deming and Faith Andrews. *Religion in Wood, Book of Shaker Furniture.* Bloomington, IN 1966.

_____. *Shaker Furniture. The Craftsmanship of an American Communal Sect.* New York, 1950.
   These works study the relationship between the design and craftsmanship and the religious and social values of the sect. The Shaker crafts are best understood, explain the authors, when they are viewed from the perspective of their total cultural milieu.

Aries, Philippe. *Western Attitudes Toward Death from the Middle Ages to the Present.* Trans. by Patricia Ranum. Baltimore, 1974.
   This essay traces changing attitudes toward death and their corresponding impact on all aspects of culture. The analysis of unique customs in Victorian America singles out the important roles women played in defining the rituals and etiquette during the nineteenth-century.

Atwan, Robert; McQuade, Donald and Wright, John W. *Edsels, Luckies and Frigidaires: Advertising the American Way.* New York, 1979.
   This shows the close relationship between advertising and the material conditions of American society. Attitudes toward sex roles, family life, housing, etc. can thus be "read" in advertisements which both reflect and reinforce American values.

Boorstin, Daniel. *The Americans: The Colonial Experience.* New York, 1958.

_____. *The Americans: The National Experience.* New York, 1965.

_____. *The Americans: The Democratic Experience. New York, 1974.*

_____. *Portraits from the Americans: The Democratic Experience.* A Catalogue for an exhibition at the National Portrait Gallery. New York, 1975.
   This trilogy represents one of the few efforts to integrate material culture into American college textbooks, calling attention throughout to the importance of the anonymous masses in determining the course of American civilization. The exhibit catalogue uses portraits of relatively unknown male and female inventors and entrepreneurs to remind us of the persons rarely recognized for their contributions to

American life. While Boorstin himself is not particularly sensitive to the issues concerning women's history, his bibliographical suggestions are immensely useful for introducing historians to the vast literature on material culture.

Braudel, Fernand. *Capitalism and Material Life, 1400-1800.* Trans. by Miriam Kochan. New York, 1975.
Using the methods of structural anthropology, Braudel examines lifestyles throughout the world before the Industrial Revolution. His approach has inspired many monographs on narrower topics, including Aries' study on death.

Browne, Ray B. and Marshall Fishwick, eds. *Icons of America,* Bowling Green, OH, 1978.
This collection of essays concentrating on symbolism in modern American culture contains two essays which are directly related to symbols pertinent to women and the women's movement: Edith Mayo's "Ladies and Liberation..." and Valerie Carnes' "Icons of Popular Fashion."

Chapman, Anne. "Placing Women in the High School European History Survey." *The History Teacher* 12, no. 3 (May 1979): 337-347.
Although this is primarily designed for high school courses, Ms. Chapman's suggestions are equally useful for college level women's history courses. Particularly interesting is her suggestion for studying houseplans in order to determine the increasing privatization of life in the nineteenth and twentieth centuries.

Cohn, David L. *The Good Old Days: A History of American Morals and Manners as seen Through the Sears Roebuck Catalogs.* New York, reprint, 1976, original 1940.
This fascinating study shows how the Sears catalogues mirror American habits and mores in both their advertising and in their merchandise. Letters from Sears customers in the appendix are revealing evidence about how much the mail-order catalogue has influenced American life. One entire section is devoted to merchandise specially designed for female customers.

Constantine, Stephen. "Amateur Gardening and Popular Recreation in the 19th and 20th Centuries." *Journal of Social History* 14, no. 3 (Spring 1981): 382-406.
Studying the changes in workers' housing and the incorporation of gardens for workers in their twentieth-century homes, Constantine argues convincingly that the gardens altered the workers' patterns of leisure, morality and family life. Moreover, he shows how the gardening craze among the lower classes mollified social tensions in twentieth-century England.

Coolidge, John. "Hingham Builds a Meeting House." *New England Quarterly* 34 (Dec. 1961): 435-461.
This studies a public building in a Puritan community as an expression of life in early New England. Although subsequent scholars have questioned the interpretation, the methodology serves as a model for looking at both public and domestic architecture.

Davis, Dorothy. *A History of Shipping: Middle Ages to Retaining Revolution.* London, 1-66.
This traces six centuries of shopping in England from the consumers' point of

view, considering shoppers' attitudes toward fairs, artisans' shops, and markets. Particularly well done is the discussion of the affects of the industrial revolution on the marketing of perishable foods and on the shopping habits of both the wealthy and poorer classes. Although this is centered on English society, it serves as a useful model for studying the sociology of American consumerism.

Deetz, James. *In Small Things Forgotten: The Archaeology of Early American Life.* New York, 1977.
Deetz examines the relations between social and religious attitudes and foodways in colonial New England, as expressed in the shift from using wooden trenchers to individual sets of china allowing each member of the family to have separate dishes. Both the content and the methodology can prove valuable for studying colonial housewifery.

Deetz, James and Edwin S. Dethlefsen. "Death's Head, Cherub, Urn and Willow." *Natural History* 76, no. 3 (March 1967): 28-37.
This studies the relations between attitudes toward death and gravestone markings. Like Aries, Deetz has found a correlation between changing ideas on death and changing iconography on New England gravestones.

Demos, John. *A Little Commonwealth: Family Life in Plymouth Colony.* New York, 1970.
Demos examines how the physical environment of Plymouth reflected the psychological makeup of Puritans. Particularly useful are his remarks about how spatial arrangements of the seventeenth-century household affected familial values and attitudes toward childbearing.

Drachman, Virginia. "Gynecological Instruments and Surgical Decisions at a Hospital in Late Nineteenth-Century America." *Journal of American Culture* 3, no. 4 (Winter 1980): 66-72.
This is an interesting discussion of how the care of women patients was principally determined by the ideas and attitudes of the doctors rather than the availability of improved instruments for surgery.

Dublin, Thomas. *Women at Work: The Transformation of Work and Community in Lowell, Massachusetts, 1826-1860.* New York, 1979.
This includes a particularly useful discussion of the machinery in the nineteenth-century textile industry and the levels of skill needed to operate the various machines. Also helpful is his detailed examination of the boarding houses in which he attempts to ascertain how much privacy and how much social interaction the residents would have had in such living arrangements.

Farb, Peter and George Armelagos. *Consuming Passions: The Anthropology of Eating.* Boston, 1980.
This is a fascinating examination of the connections between eating habits and human behavior in societies throughout the world with examples drawn from both primitive and sophisticated cultures.

Fitch, James Marston. *Architecture and the Esthetics of Plenty.* New York, 1961.

_____. "When Modern Housekeeping Became a Science." *American Heritage* 12 (August 1961): 34-37.

Fitch's book contains an entire chapter on Catherine Beecher's architectural ideas for domestic housing. Although her ideas did not have immediate impact, explains Fitch, they did serve later generations of architects as an inspiration for designing more efficient and easy-to-maintain private residences. His article goes into more detail about the repercussions of Beecher's campaign for simpler, more efficient homes like the model she includes in her *American Woman's Home*. Fitch also points out how Beecher's ideas on space changed rather dramatically between her works in the 1840s and her final works in the 1870s.

French, Stanley. "The Cemetery as a Cultural Institution: The Establishment of Mount Auburn and the 'Rural Cemetery' Movement in *Death in America,* edited by David E. Stannard. Philadelphia, 1974.

Using the cemetery and artifacts associated with early nineteenth-century mourning, French discloses how the Victorian preoccupations with death symbolized many of their attitudes toward life and the material world. In fact, he points out a number of features in rural cemeteries that resemble the living cities of the period.

Giedion, Siegfried. *Mechanization Takes Command: A Contribution to Anonymous History.* New York, 1948.

This anticipates the more recent social history with an effort to show the impact of the industrial revolution on everyday life of ordinary citizens. Several of his themes are relevant to concerns in women's history: the mechanization of the bath, the mechanization of breadmaking, patent furniture, mechanization as it encounters the household, and mechanical comforts in the household. While Giedion himself does not pursue the full implications of these phenomena, he has laid the groundwork for future scholarship.

Glassie, Henry. *Patterns in the Material Folk Culture of the Eastern United States.* Philadelphia, 1968.

This is a pilot study which suggests a series of relations between folk culture and patterns of communication. The attempt to discern regional patterns could serve as a tool for examining the relationship between regional cultures and female patterns of communication.

Goffman, Erving. *Gender Advertisements.* New York, 1976.

_____. *The Presentation of Self in Everyday Life.* New York, 1967.

Goffman's theories of human behavior have provided a number of social historians and specialists in material culture interpretation a framework with which to analyze the relationship between objects and human behavior. See for example, Kenneth Ames' "The Meaning of Artifacts...." His study of advertisements has particularly interesting observations on how advertisers seek to appeal to male and female audiences.

Gowans, Alan. *Images of American Living: Four Centuries of Architecture and Furniture Expression.* Philadelphia, 1964.

This is an examination of the styles of architecture, furniture and interior design as cultural expressions of the broad patterns of evolving ideas and attitudes in

American civilization. A central theme is that what man makes is a tangible expression of what man thinks. Although Gowans confines his study to objects of high culture, it is a model for probing the links between artifacts and ideas. His classification of main trends in the arts in the colonial and federal period is a useful tool for one planning to read further in the material culture of these periods.

"Hands All Around: Social Aspects of Quilting." Slide-tape presentation for the Archives of Appalachia Outreach Program at East Tennessee State University. Johnson City, TN, 1971.
   This is an excellent illustration of the type of work that can well be done in the Appalachian Region where a large number of women remember or still perform the traditional household arts and chores. The slide presentation skillfully blends information on the process of quiltmaking and the necessary equipment with the social interaction that takes place when women come together to sew the quilt together.

Hudson, Kenneth. *Food, Clothes and Shelter: Twentieth Century Industrial Archaeology.* London, 1978.
   This is indispensable for scholars who are interested in the evolution of domestic life in the twentieth century. Although it focuses on British society, Hudson's treatment of such themes as consumerism and food processing is helpful as a guide for investigating similar phenomena in the United States.

Jones, Howard Mumford. *O Strange New World: American Culture: The Formative Years.* New York, 1964.

_____. *The Age of Energy: Varieties of American Experience, 1865-1915.* New York, 1971.
   Using aspects of material culture such as art and technology, Jones discusses the evolution of American character and experience. He is unusually sensitive to the impact of European culture on the formation of American character and artistic expression.

Klapthor, Margaret Brown. "Benjamin Latrobe and Dolley Madison Decorate the White House, 1809-1811." *United States National Museum Bulletin, 241.* Washington, 1965.
   This studies the relationship between ideas and their expression in interior decoration. Although it is a brief study, it is suggestive of what might be done in looking for the feminine contributions to the evolution of American taste in interior decoration during the early national period.

Kleinberg, Susan L. "Death and the Working Class." *Journal of Popular Culture* 11, no. 1 (Summer 1977): 193-209.
   This is one of the few studies on the attitudes and rituals for death and mourning among the lower classes, and it provides a basis of comparison with the better-known mourning rituals and attitudes among the middle and upper classes of the nineteenth-century.

Kouwenhoven, John A. *The Arts in Modern American Civilization.* New York, 1948.
   This emphasizes that there has always been a strong correlation between the

American arts and American ideals. While subsequent scholars have questioned the stress on the uniqueness of American culture, the work represents an interesting attempt to synthesize art and ideas. Moreover, it has historiographical significance. Written immediately after World War II, it reflects the prevailing mood of optimism about the promise of technology. Reading Kouwenhoven thus offers insights into the post-war society, which might help in explaining why so many women of the era eagerly sought to return to their homes from wartime employment.

Laumann, Edward O. and James S. House. "Living Room Styles and Social Attributes: The Patterning of Material Artifacts in a Modern Urban Community." *Sociology & Social Research* 64 (1970): 32-342.
   This is one example of how one can "read" attitudes about space by studying artifacts in the domestic interior. In conjunction with such analysis, Edward Hall's *The Hidden Dimension* (Garden City, 1966) is invaluable. In fact, Hall suggests that men and women actually perceive space differently and thus have different spatial needs.

Lowenthal, David. "Past Time, Present Place: Landscape and Memory." *The Geographical Review* 65 (January 1975): 1-36.
   This is a fascinating discussion of how people think about the past in looking at certain landscapes and landmarks. According to this analysis it would be impossible for any two people to see an object in the same light: each brings his or her impressions based on a whole cluster of experiences and associations.

Loyd, Bonnie. "Women's Place, Man's Place." *Landscape* 20 (Oct. 1975): 10-13.
   Like Laumann and Hall, Ms. Loyd takes up the question of whether women have different concepts of space and spatial needs than men. She also challenges Erik Erikson's thesis that women by nature are more comfortable in dealing with interior spaces while men by nature are able to handle the public spaces and feel more confident about manipulating their environment.

Mayo, Edith. "Campaign Appeals to Women." *Journal of American Culture* 3, no. 4 (Winter 1980): 722-742. (reprinted in this volume)
   Studying campaign gimmicks for the last 150 years, Ms. Mayo shows how the national parties have failed to make the best use of their female support. In addition, her artifactual evidence becomes the basis of an analysis of the relationship between activities of the women's movements in the nineteenth and twentieth centuries and the national political parties. Some of her observations with regard to this topic merit further investigation in other sources. It may well be that Ms. Mayo's article has suggested a valuable means for deepening our understanding of women's political behavior.

Meining, D.W. *The Interpretation of Ordinary Landscapes: Geographical Essays.* New York, 1977.
   This is an anthology of essays, each showing how the landscape can be "read" as symbols of American culture. Several of the essays stress that Americans' associations with landscapes are so often mixed with emotions that one cannot omit considering the psychological impact of the environment on human perceptions and behavior.

Mercer, Henry C. *The Bible in Iron; or, The Pictured Stoves and Stove Plates of the Pennsylvania Germans.* Doylestown, 1961.

This is a study of a common household item as an expression of religious and social attitudes. Since the Germans were early to use stoves in America, there is considerable literature on which Mercer can draw, and his method may prove useful as a model for other examinations of historic stoves.

Nye, Russel Blain. *The Cultural Life of the New Nation: 1776-1830.* New York, 1960.

––––– *Society and Culture in the American Colonies, 1830-1860.* New York, 1974.
These are studies of intellectual history and its relation to the decorative arts of high culture. Little in these is directly pertinent to women's history, but the bibliographical essays accompanying each volume are helpful guides to further reading in the decorative arts and literature of their respective eras.

Orlovsky, Patsy and Myron Orlovsky. *Quilts in America.* New York, 1974.
This historical survey of quilts in the United States is one of the few of this genre to go beyond the evaluation of analysis in order to treat the quilts in relation to their cultural context.

Quimby, Maureen. *Eleutherian Mills.* Greenville, Dealaware, 1973.
This is an interesting effort to study the dynamics of the household of a wealthy manufacturing family through surviving sketches done by the female inhabitants. The artifacts not only tell us about the contemporary domestic life, but they are also valuable sources for recreating the architecture and interior decoration of the original home.

Parr, Albert. "Heating, Lighting, Plumbing & Human Relations." In *Technological Innovation and the Decorative Arts,* edited by Iam Quimby and Polly Earl. Charlottesville, 1973.
Parr makes a number of imaginative suggestions on how better and cleaner lighting and heating as well as indoor plumbing contributed to privacy in the household and promoted different uses of interior spaces. These changes, in turn, led to differences in familial attitudes and modes of communication.

Root, Waverly and Richard de Rochemont. *Eating in America. A History.* New York, 1976.
This is an interesting study of the evolution of American eating habits and their relation to American ideals. Careful consideration is given to the impact of food processing and modern kitchen technology. Also, the chapter on historic cookbooks offers helpful suggestions for interpreting these books as artifacts and provides a useful bibliography for scholars interested in examining the intersection of verbal culture and foodways.

Shumway, George, et al. *Conestoga Wagon, 1750-1850.* Williamsburg, Virginia, 1964.
This represents one of the finest attempts to place an artifact of transportation within its larger cultural and social framework.

Smith, Merrit Roe. *The Harper's Ferry Armory and the New Technology: The Challenge of Change.* Ithaca, 1977.
This is a brilliant study of how social conditions relate to technological change.

Unlike the conventional interpretation that holds that technological innovations affect social change, Smith has discovered at Harper's Ferry that the traditional social values and the existing social organization militated against technological progress despite the facilities at the armory to make advances in gun technology. Smith's whole approach might prove useful in women's history, especially in exploring women's reactions to the influx of household appliances, etc. in the early twentieth century.

Steindfeldt, Cecilia and Donald Lewis Stover. *Early Texas Furniture and Decorative Arts.* San Antonio, Texas, 1973.
    This is an excellent regional study, showing the relationship between the physical culture and the social and geographical features of East Texas. The special section dealing with women's crafts in textiles and how these reflect their local culture could easily be applied to other regions.

Swan, Susan. *Plain and Fancy: American Women and their Needlework, 1799-1850.* New York, 1977.
    Like the Orlovskys' study of quilts, this represents an unusually fine analysis of needlework in relation to women's culture. Ms. Swan explicitly addresses issues prominent in feminist scholarship and offers insights into the ways that needlework both reflected and encouraged socialization patterns and sex-role stereotypes in eighteenth and nineteenth-century America. Valuable also is her discussion of the integral relationship between female education and needlework, examining the curricula of several dozen leading female seminaries and extant products of their students.

Sweeney, John A.H. *Grandeur on the Appoquinimink; The House of William Corbit at Odessa.* Newark, Delaware, 1959.
    This exemplifies the use of a house as an artifact to decipher the social intellectual and cultural life of its inhabitants. Through the construction of the house and its artifacts, Sweeney discloses important patterns of cultural transmission between urban Philadelphia and its hinterland as well as the social aspirations of an upwardly mobile manufacturing family in the tanning industry.

Szuberla, Guy. "Three Chicago Settlements: Their Architectural Form and Social Meaning." *Journal of Illinois State Historical Society* 70 (May 1977): 114-129.

Tate, Thad W. and David L. Ammerman. *The Chesapeake in the Seventeenth Century: Essays on Anglo-American Society.* Chapel-Hill, 1979.
    These essays by the researchers at the St. Mary's City, Maryland site employ methods of the New History in conjunction with examinations of material culture. They have brought new insights into the demographic patterns, diseases, housing familylife arrangements of the region.

Tolles, Frederick B. "Of the Best Sort but Plain: The Quaker Esthetic." *American Quarterly* 2 (Winter 1959): 484-502.
    This is a classic study of how the physical world mirrors the values of a society. Using artifacts of wealthy and prominent Quaker merchants, Tolles elucidates how they compromised between their religious values and their increasing involvement in secular affairs. Similar work might be done in studying the tensions of women

between their private and public obligations as Alan Thomas has suggested in *Time in a Frame.*

Torre, Susana, ed. *Women in American Architecture: A Contemporary and Historic Perspective,* New York, 1977.

This includes examples of all the different projects now going on among scholars and practitioners in feminist architecture and urban planning. Not only do the contributions explore how space has become male dominated, but they offer suggestions for altering existing patriarchal spaces to accommodate women's needs and aspirations in domestic houses and urban communities. Several essays report on the progress of experimental feminist communes in the United States, and one essay deals with the success of a women's building in Los Angeles. Short essays by Gwendolyn Wright and Dolores Hayden, to be discussed later in the essay, are included in this collection.

Trachtenberg, Alan. *Brooklyn Bridge: Fact and Symbol.* New York, 1965.

This represents a study of the utilitarian and symbolic functions of an artifact. In deciphering the meaning of the bridge, Trachtenberg not only traces the practical considerations of its construction and design but also relates its impact on the events and cultural expression of the surrounding communities.

Wallace, Anthony F.C *Rockdale: The Growth of an American Village in the Early Industrial Revolution.* New York, 1978.

Using the methods of an anthropologist and a social historian, Wallace examines how the appearance of machines in a small community transformed perceptions and attitudes and encouraged new cultural patterns as well as new patterns of communication. His section on the female relatives of manufacturers of the area is suggestive for further study on the impact of the early Industrial Revolution on women of the mid-Atlantic Region.

Walsh, Margaret. "The Emergence of the Women's Dress Pattern Industry." *Journal of American History* 66 (Sept. 1979): 288-315.

This discusses both how the dress pattern industry affected women's fashions, but also how the industry itself opened up opportunities for advancement to women with imagination and business skills.

Warner, Deborah. "Fashion, Emancipation, Reform and the Rational Undergarment." *Dress* 14, no. 4 (1978): 24-29.

This is an excellent illustration of how clothing can be studied as symbolic of changing attitudes and interests. Similar developments have been seen with our contemporary women's movement, and Ms. Warner's article should encourage others to examine how modern dress styles mirror changing attitudes and aspirations of women.

Wertenbaker, Thomas. *The Founding of American Civilization, The Middle Colonies.* New York, 1949.

This older work can still be read with profit. It is an excellent attempt to demonstrate how material culture reflects the attitudes of the early settlers in New York toward their homeland. Although Mr. Wertenbaker does not address issues directly relevant to women, persons interested in women's history might use Alice Kenney's suggestions for studying past household organization and contents in conjunction with the wealth of details Wertenbaker has gathered on colonial domesticity in New York.

Wright, Gwendolyn. "Sweet and Clean: The Domestic Landscape in the Progressive Era." *Landscape* 20, no. 1 (Oct. 1975): 38-43.
  This explores how the progressive concerns with purity and efficiency were translated into the design of interior spaces, in particular kitchens and bathrooms.

The final operation in Fleming's proposed model is interpretation. Among specialists in material culture this is regarded as the ultimate objective. In essence, it refers to the question of what does the object mean to the present generation? The answer to these questions vary in accordance with the perspective of the observer. For those interested in economic history the significance may lie in value of the object and the classes who possessed it. For those concerned with the evolution of cultural tastes the object may be significant as an indication of the unique and beautiful features of its craftmanship and design. For those concerned with social issues the object may be studied as a tool for class oppression, or may be interpreted as symbolic of individuals seeking to emulate the elites. For those interested in the formation of American character the object may be viewed as an expression of national aspirations or a symbol of American achievements in science and technology. Freeman Tilden's *Interpreting Our Heritage* (Chapel Hill, revised edition, 1967), William T. Alderson's and Shirley Payne Low's *Interpretation of Historic Sites* (Nashville, 1976) and Craig Gilborn's "Pop Pedagogy: Looking at the Coke Bottle," *Museum News* 47, no. 4 (Dec. 1968): 12-18, set forth the criteria used for interpretations in the present museum exhibitions and scholarship.

In the great variety of interpretations resulting from object-study, however, there are only rare instances in which the object has been interpreted for its importance to women's history. The central purpose of this bibliographical essay has been to point out certain directions that scholars in women's history may go in order to deepen our understanding of women's relation to their material universe.

Just in the last few years there have appeared three works indicating that the feminist perspective in material culture is not only possible but highly desirable: Joan Jensen's "Churns and Buttermaking in the mid-Atlantic Farm Economy 1750-1850," in the *Working Papers of the Regional Economic History Research Center*

(Greenville, Delaware); Gwendolyn Wright's *Moralism and the Model Home: Domestic Architecture and Cultural Conflict in Chicago, 1873-1913* (Chicago, 1980); and Dolores Hayden's *The 'Grand Domestic Revolution': A History of Feminist Designs for American Homes, Neighborhoods and Cities* (Cambridge, Mass., 1981).

Ms. Jensen concentrates on the roles of agricultural women in commercial enterprises by analyzing churns in the context of women's production of butter in Pennsylvania and Northern Delaware. Buttermaking, she argues, was the principal cottage industry after the mid-eighteenth century, and it replaced the earlier domestic industry of clothmaking. The equipment, production, storage and distribution of butter came primarily under women's auspices until 1850 when the mechanization of the industry contributed to its masculinization. In developing her thesis Ms. Jensen follows the very operations recommended by Fleming. In her final interpretation, she concludes that the churn and the process of buttermaking were vital links "by which rural women extend the old concept of productive farm economy into the new industrial era." Thus the object-study of the churn has produced a new paradigm for the study of women's adaptation to early industrialization.

While Ms. Jensen has focused on the artifacts pertinent to women's productive labor and contributions to the marketplace economy, Gwendolyn Wright and Dolores Hayden have centered their research on domestic architecture as artifactual evidence of attitudes toward domesticity, sex roles and space. Ms. Wright has traced the various factors that converged in the early twentieth century to make the model of single family home the most popular form of domestic living for Americans. So appealing was this model, she continues, that it passed down to future generations which in turn have so enshrined the concept of the nuclear family residence that Americans find it difficult to conceive of alternative forms of domestic architecture and family life. By contrast, Ms. Hayden has explored the history of the little known movement of material feminism: a protest movement to the nuclear family home and domesticity. To improve women's status and position in American society material feminists promoted and designed communal living arrangements, more efficient modes of food preparation, cooperative dining and cleaning establishments, and child care centers. The movement ultimately succumbed to the consumerist revolution of the 1920s because of its incompatibility with the fundamental American ideals of democracy and capitalism.

Nevertheless, the blueprints, prospecters of cooperative residences and model towns, and the photographs of model kitchenless homes survive. Through these, Ms. Hayden has not only recreated the history of the long forgotten movement in the heritage of American womanhood, but she has also shed new light on women's contributions to American architectural history and urban planning.

With works such as these the decade of the 1980s promises to be a time when the perspectives of women enter material culture studies, bringing fresh insights, provocative questions, and novel methods. In this way scholars in women's history may begin to uncover the "secrets of housewifery," using household artifacts to decode the social, intellectual, economic, psychological realities of American domesticity.

Please remember that this is a library book,
and that it belongs only temporarily to each
person who uses it. Be considerate. Do
not write in this, or any, library book.

DATE DUE

10/1/01			
GAYLORD			PRINTED IN U.S.A.